Strategy for the West

Strategy
for the West
American-Allied Relations in Transition

EDITORS:
Richard B. Foster
André Beaufre
Wynfred Joshua

Macdonald and Jane's

38951

Strategy for the West

First published in Great Britain in 1974 by
Macdonald and Jane's (Macdonald and Company (Publishers) Ltd.)
St. Giles House, 49/50 Poland Street, London, W1A 2LG

Copyright © 1974 Stanford Research Institute

ISBN 356 08132 X

Printed in the United States of America

STANFORD RESEARCH INSTITUTE is an independent nonprofit organization providing specialized research services under contract to business, industry, the U.S. government, and some foreign governments, particularly those in the developing nations. Since its foundation in 1946 in Menlo Park, California, the Institute's basic aims have been to enhance economic, political, and social development and to contribute through objective research to the peace and prosperity of mankind.

The Strategic Studies Center of SRI was organized in 1954 by Richard B. Foster, Director. Based in Washington, D.C., the Center conducts multi-disciplinary research on the crucial issues of foreign, defense, and international economic policy. With a client structure consisting of the key U.S. government agencies charged with responsibility in these areas, the Strategic Studies Center has long contributed to the ongoing dialogue in both the policymaking and research communities on the critical choices facing the United States, particularly in the field of national security.

To make the timely findings of the Center's research available to a broader public, the Strategic Studies Center is publishing a series of books and monographs. *Strategy for the West,* the inaugural volume in this series, examines security problems of the Atlantic Alliance.

Contents

Contributors

GENERAL ANDRE BEAUFRE, *Retired*
Founder and Director of the Institut Français d'Etudes Stratégiques, Paris.

DR. N. R. DANIELIAN
President of the International Economic Policy Association, Washington, D.C.

GENERAL DUILIO SERGIO FANALI, *Retired*
Former Chief of Staff of the Italian Air Force and Honorary President of the Institute for Defense and Strategic Studies, Rome.

MR. RICHARD B. FOSTER
Founder and Director of the Strategic Studies Center, Stanford Research Institute, Arlington, Virginia.

MR. WALTER F. HAHN
Associate Director for Research at the Foreign Policy Research Institute, Philadelphia, Pennsylvania.

DR. JOHAN J. HOLST
Director of Research at the Norwegian Institute of International Affairs, Oslo.

DR. WYNFRED JOSHUA
Assistant Director and Senior Political Scientist at the Strategic Studies Center, Stanford Research Institute, Arlington, Virginia.

GENERAL J. A. GRAF KIELMANSEGG, *Retired*
Chairman of the Council of the Research Institute for Defense and International Affairs, Munich.

PROFESSOR LEOPOLD LABEDZ
Editor of *Survey*.

MR. WALTER LAQUEUR
Director of the Institute of Contemporary History and Wiener Library, London.

AIR VICE-MARSHAL S. W. B. MENAUL, *Retired*
Director-General of the Royal United Services Institute for Defence Studies, London.

DR. RICHARD PIPES
Director of the Russian Research Center, Harvard University.

MR. SHELDON T. RABIN
Research Analyst at the Strategic Studies Center, Stanford Research Institute, Arlington, Virginia.

Preface

T̲HE establishment of strategic nuclear parity
between the superpowers and the changing environment of American-
European relations underscore the need for orchestrating common
Western objectives and for reforging a long-term U.S.-West European
partnership. The current negotiations of the West with the Soviet Union,
notably SALT II, the force reduction talks, and the Conference on Security
and Cooperation in Europe highlight the necessity for overcoming the
political, military and economic strains that undergird the sense of malaise
in the Western Alliance.

In an effort to evolve strategic concepts more responsive to the
requirements of the seventies, the Strategic Studies Center of Stanford
Research Institute brought together representatives of leading West European and American research institutes and other distinguished Europeans
who had long concentrated on examining new strategies for Western
security. A colloquium was held in Juan-les-Pins, France, from 3-6 May
1973. In addition to the thirty-six participants, fourteen government
observers from Britain, France, Italy, Spain, West Germany, and the
United States listened to the discussions of which concepts best fit a true
and more meaningful partnership.

Beyond serving as a forum for an exchange of ideas among Europeans and Americans, the colloquium met a second major purpose: it
was the prologue for the establishment of a European Defense Research
Institute. The Juan-les-Pins meeting made several specific recommendations for the creation of such an institute. These recommendations are
included in an appendix to this book. As a result of the Juan-les-Pins
decisions, representatives of the European research institutes met in
October 1973 in Paris, where the basic concepts of the new organization
were formulated and, as a first step, a committee of directors of European
research institutes was formed to explore ways of forming such an organization. As a temporary measure, the Institut Français d'Etudes Stratégiques agreed to act as a temporary secretariat.

This book makes available to a larger audience the twelve papers
discussed at the Juan-les-Pins sessions. The papers present the opinions of
the individual authors; they do not reflect the view of their institutions or
their governments. An introductory essay seeks to convey the main themes
and conclusions of the conference and the flavor of the actual dialogue.

All those who were associated with the colloquium gratefully acknowledge the support of the Advanced Research Projects Agency of the Department of Defense which made the meeting possible. We also express our gratitude to Stanford Research Institute which supported the publication of this volume. It is a pleasure to thank Mr. Sheldon T. Rabin of the Strategic Studies Center who played an indispensable role as colloquium coordinator. He was ably assisted by Mrs. Ilse Muller and Mrs. Alla Pietsch, both of the Center.

Finally, the editors thank the authors whose papers are included in this volume. Their efforts and the discussions of the distinguished participants accounted for the success of the Juan-les-Pins meeting. We hope that the results of the conference as reflected in this volume will contribute to the transatlantic dialogue on developing a new security consensus among the United States and its West European partners.

Richard B. Foster   André Beaufre
Wynfred Joshua   Paris, France
Washington, D.C.

American-Allied Relations in Transition: A Synthesis of the Conference Discussions

Wynfred Joshua and Sheldon T. Rabin

The Nixon Doctrine explicitly recognizes the changing strategic environment of American-European relations and the need to evolve a strategy that can endure beyond the challenge of the seventies. The bilateral and multilateral negotiations of the Western allies with the Soviet Union further underscore the urgency for developing a set of common goals in order to strengthen Western cohesion. Yet the domestic pressures in the United States to reduce defense expenditures and the military presence abroad, as well as the codification of strategic parity in SALT I have deeply affected the European perceptions of the U.S. commitment to West European security and defense. The crisis of confidence in the transatlantic alliance—given the immediacy of negotiations with the Soviet Union, notably SALT II, the force reduction talks, and the Conference on Security and Cooperation in Europe—highlights the need for reforging a long-term U.S.-allied partnership and for or-

1

chestrating common Western objectives and a common coherent strategy.

In reshaping the Western security and defense posture, the role of Western Europe needs to be identified. There appears to be a divergence, however, in the perceptions of the United States and its allies of the part Western Europe should play in the global or even the Atlantic context. The issue of France's role, moreover, continues to bedevil the Western allies. If not an integrated ally, France's determination to defend the West must nevertheless be harnessed to a Western strategy. Against this background the crucial concerns that dominated the dialogue at the conference of the Strategic Studies Center of Stanford Research Institute in May 1973 at Juan-les-Pins, France, were: (1) American and European concepts of Europe's role in the Alliance, (2) the evolvement of a grand strategy that marshals all resources of the Western allies, and (3) France's role in the Alliance. The conference brought together distinguished strategists and researchers from the United States and Western Europe who had long concentrated on developing new security concepts. It was a testimony to the importance of France's place in the ranks of the Western allies that the meeting was held on French soil.

I. THE SOVIET CHALLENGE

There appeared to be a widespread belief among American and European participants alike that the threat of direct Soviet armed aggression against Western Europe had markedly, declined. At the same time, however, they were acutely aware of the progressively improving Soviet military capabilities vis-à-vis the West. The European participants in particular stressed the stark superiority of Soviet conventional forces in the European theater. In addition, the European members warned that while the weight of the military balance in the center of Europe was clearly in favor of Moscow, Soviet capabilities had grown at an even faster rate at the flanks of NATO.

The utility of Soviet military force, however, was largely seen in an indirect fashion as the instrument to back up Soviet political initiatives. The détente climate notwithstanding, Soviet goals in Europe had changed little. The Finlandization of Western Europe remained a fundamental Soviet objective. Realizing, however, that a détente climate served Soviet ambitions more effectively than a cold war environment, the Soviet Union would be unlikely to embark on an aggressive course and risk galvanizing the West Europeans into a concerted defense buildup.

Several European participants stressed that the Sovet Union pursued a grand strategy which was derived from Russian tradition, and which orchestrated political, diplomatic, military, and economic courses of action, and coordinated all instruments of power toward its more enduring goals in which the control of Europe featured prominently.

Conducive to the Soviet objective of Finlandization of Western Europe was the political malaise in the European nations. Despite European prosperity, the individual European nations were beset with profound domestic crises. The gradual paralysis of political will in the West European nations appeared to many participants the most ominous development. Some felt that particularly Scandinavia, where the will to cooperate in Western defense was least developed, constituted Western Europe's weakest link.

Few saw any real progress toward the harmonization of European political and military policies. Prospects of European unity that transcended the economic dimension appeared even more remote to most European participants. So did, therefore, the possibility that Western Europe would be able to assert political influence commensurate with its population, size, or economic strength. Yet a concerted effort in the political and military realm was clearly seen as a prerequisite for coping with a Soviet campaign of political coercion and blandishment. In light of the parochial focus of many of the younger generation and their neutralist bias, the future offered little optimism about the prospects of Western cohesion and European solidarity. Several participants pointed to the radicalization of the universities, notably in West Germany. Still, a few discussants expressed a different view and argued that the European Community offered the potential for promoting political and military collaboration among its members. On the whole, however, most speakers felt that the political inertia of the West European nations and the limited prospects for European unification combined to create an environment in which the Soviet objective of Finlandization could come within Moscow's reach.

II. THE NEED FOR A GRAND STRATEGY

If there was clearly a consensus on the nature of the Soviet challenge and the political dimension of the Soviet military threat, there was a similar expression on the need to evolve a broad overall strategy. Such a strategy should go beyond purely military considerations and harness the military as well as the political, economic, and technological resources of the West. But beyond the general acceptance of the urgency to develop such a strategy, there was no agreement on the prescription. Participants differed on some of the key political ingredients and on the military and economic components of such a strategy. This divergence derived partly from the different national perspectives of the conference participants, partly from their different concepts of the roles of the United States and Western Europe in the Western Alliance.

An American participant warned that the inability of the West to identify acceptable terms for the new transatlantic relationship portended dangers for the East-West negotiations on security and economic questions. There was an incongruence, from his vantage point, between European desires to see the United States continue shouldering the major burden in the military arena, and European readiness to compete unfairly with their Atlantic partner in the economic realm.

A second American participant explained that the very essence of the Nixon Doctrine was the need to establish strategic stability in order to prevent nuclear war. In the current U.S. concept political and military stability in Europe was to be the cornerstone of the emerging global order. But this implied that the interests of the European nations, both East and West, and the interests of the United States and the Soviet Union would have to be accommodated in some type of a negotiated solution. At the same time, this led to a fundamental contradiction in U.S. policy: On the one hand, Washington sought to negotiate with Moscow to reduce the chances of nuclear war; on the other hand, the United States would have to retain a strong alliance and continue to extend its nuclear umbrella over Western Europe in a partnership arrangement.

Contrary to their American counterparts, the European speakers harbored doubts over the U.S. commitment to the security and defense of Western Europe. Their major ally, in their view, apparently sought to limit its European ties. The American retreat was partly reflected in the portents of U.S. troop withdrawals either in a unilateral fashion or through a negotiated formula at the force reduction talks. Other signs of U.S. disengagement could be seen in the dwindling credibility of the U.S. nuclear guarantee to the defense of Western Europe. While most participants underscored the need for the continued coupling of the U.S. strategic nuclear forces to the defense of the European continent, few European spokesmen believed that this linkage had remained unimpaired. The arrival of strategic nuclear parity, the May 1972 SALT accords, and Vietnam war fatigue were the key developments that had eroded the credibility of the U.S. nuclear pledge. The discussion clearly indicated that the United States needed to clarify its perception of the role of its strategic nuclear forces in the Western defense posture.

One participant took issue with the requirement to retain the coupling of Western Europe's security to that of the United States. He argued for a two-pillar concept of the Alliance in which Western Europe would assume full responsibility for its own defense, including its nuclear protection. Others suggested that Western Europe be divided into three regional defense groupings: a northern sector of Scandinavian countries which would be reluctant to join in a new cooperative defense effort anyway; a central region of Britain, France, West Germany, the Benelux, and possibly Italy with a new European-based defense structure; and a southern Mediterranean flank where unique politico-military problems and strategic location argued for establishing an entity separate from the center. The creation of a southern group, depending heavily on naval forces for its defense, might facilitate extending the shadow of Western power to protect Western interests in the Middle East, Persian Gulf, and Indian Ocean regions. Several of the European conferees sharply disagreed and warned against the disruptive effects which the formation of different groupings would have on the Alliance.

III. THE MILITARY DIMENSION OF GRAND STRATEGY

Without necessarily accepting the removal of U.S. nuclear protection of the European continent, the European participants stressed the need for devising a new Atlantic partnership in which their countries would have a greater voice in alliance councils and would take on a greater share of the defense burden. The various formulas that were proposed clearly reflected different national biases. Without necessarily decoupling the United States from Europe's defense, the majority of the Europeans called for strengthening the British and French nuclear forces—either separately or in a joint arrangement—as the core around which the defense of Europe could be organized. The European strategic deterrent forces, several participants maintained, would have greater credibility for Europe than the more powerful nuclear panoply of the United States. This was true even in their role for extended deterrence, for neither France nor Britain could seriously contemplate abandoning West Germany or Italy to the Soviet Union.

Various participants, Americans as well as Europeans, urged that London and Paris should begin collaborating in the nuclear field. This would not necessarily require, according to most arguments, surrender of national control or a supranational decision-making organ. One European conferee reminded his audience that the United States remained a major obstacle to an Anglo-French nuclear entente. The British were prevented from any nuclear data-sharing by their agreements with the Americans. As long as the United States continued its restrictive interpretation of the Mac-Mahon Law, Britain remained tied to its obligations to the United States. Moreover, unless opinions in Washington changed, the prospects for American assistance to the French nuclear program remained equally remote.

Several European participants advocated that the Europeans take the initiative in strengthening the Western defense arrangements. As a first step, one of the speakers suggested the formation, possibly within the framework of the Western European Union or perhaps the Eurogroup, of a European standing group which would examine procurement problems, new weapons development and deployment, training, doctrine, and a whole range of other issues that could pave the way for the creation of a European defense command. Once this command would be established, presumably within the midterm period, the major responsibility for the defense of Western Europe could be shifted from NATO. Such a structure would permit a more efficient and rational division of labor in defense responsibilities within Western Europe.

Meanwhile, France should be accorded a greater role in the policy-making process of the Western Alliance on defense matters. One discussant made an eloquent plea for lifting the present quarantine from France in the military realm, without, however, insisting that it surrender its independence or freedom of maneuver. As several of his colleagues had advocated, he endorsed nuclear collaboration between France and Britain and subsequent coordination with the United States. The proponents of enhancing British and French strategic capabilities also emphasized the need for London and Paris to develop a tactical nuclear weapons arsenal. Several participants insisted that the entire range of weapons, from the bullet to the thermonuclear weapon, be available to the European allies.

A minority took sharp issue with these ideas and cautioned that a bilateral or trilateral nuclear club in the Western Alliance would divide the allies more starkly into nuclear and non-nuclear members or equal and less-equal ones. Nuclear planning should remain the domain of all members concerned. Special consideration should be given to the views of countries in which the targets are located and those in which warheads are stored or deployed. It was probably not a coincidence that some of the representatives of the smaller powers and West Germany subscribed to this position.

The deterrent value of tactical nuclear weapons was unanimously affirmed. But when it came to the role of tactical nuclear weapons if deterrence were to fail, a split emerged similar to the one that existed on the role of French and British nuclear forces. Most speakers held that the combination of Soviet superiority in conventional forces and Soviet blitzkrieg tactics made the conventional defense of Western Europe untenable. Several conferees, both American and European, made a case for the early use of tactical nuclear weapons. To restore confidence in the Alliance, the West Europeans should be assured that tactical nuclear weapons would be used against Soviet aggression when the military situation required this. As far as the Soviet perception was concerned, however, there should remain uncertainty as to the timing and circumstances in which the Western allies would resort to the use of tactical nuclear weapons.

Tactical nuclear weapons were clearly seen as a complement to, rather than a substitute for, the conventional fires. Still, not only should the purpose of their employment be to support military operations and halt the enemy's thrust, but their use should also carry the political aim of showing the aggressor allied resolve to defend with all means. For this reason, as one participant held, their first use should be accompanied by a political declaration stressing the risk of escalation to the aggressor.

Some argued that the United States should retain control of the tactical nuclear weapons available to the Alliance. Others, who also endorsed the strengthening of European strategic nuclear forces, advocated that the Europeans, presumably the French and British, acquire as quickly as possible their own tactical nuclear panoply. As one conferee put it, the West could only deter a war that it was prepared and able to fight. Several made the case for deploying more accurate and cleaner tactical nuclear weapons with smaller yields. The technology was in hand and a number of European participants pleaded strongly that the United States, as a minimum, fully inform its allies about characteristics of the new weapons and, if possible, make the technology available to its allies. Particularly the political leaders need to be educated about the capabilities and effects of the various types of smaller nuclear arms and their political significance.

The European conferees displayed a keen interest in the so-called mininukes, which they defined as relatively clean weapons with yields of below 50 tons and a CEP of a few feet. The introduction of controllable mininukes would widen the range of options for the allies. A couple of speakers went so far as to propose that the threshold between the mininukes and conventional arms be eliminated; the former should be treated as part of the conventional arsenal. The present barrier to their use, which was primarily psychological, should therefore be removed. One of the participants sharply disagreed. Without necessarily rejecting the early use of tactical nuclear weapons, he pointed out that his experience had taught him that no political leader would be prepared to surrender control over nuclear weapons. The decision to use a nuclear weapon, mini or maxi, remained fundamentally a political decision.

A few of the participants from the smaller NATO powers were concerned that their companions were advocating a new strategy and warned that the time was not ripe for reopening the debate on the nuclear strategy of the West. According to one conferee, the problems in Western Europe were essentially political and could not be solved by changes in the military strategy of the West. Moreover, in his view, the West Europeans were not interested in the nuclear and military dimensions of the European situation. The political, psychological, and economic fissures in American-European relations needed to be solved first.

Other evidence that not every participant attached the same importance to the tactical nuclear component of the Western defense posture could be seen in the suggestion that the West negotiate a "no-first-use" agreement with the Soviet Union. It was pointed out by others that an accord not to be the first one to use nuclear weapons against a conventional aggression would effectively neutralize the tactical nuclear deterrent and greatly enhance the political utility of Soviet conventional forces. The West Europeans would be left in the shadow of massive Soviet conventional power. It was probably no surprise that some of the West German representatives vigorously took exception to this proposal.

Although opinions differed regarding the relative merits of tactical nuclear weapons, there was a much broader consensus on the role of and need to improve the conventional capabilities. Conventional forces were still required, partly for psychological reasons, partly for purposes of defense to stop an initial attack, or if necessary to be used in conjunction with the nuclear forces. Neither American nor European conferees, however, could contemplate the possibility of a sustained conventional conflict in Europe.

The topic of advanced military technology, including the technology for precision guided munitions or the so-called smart weapons, elicited sharp interest on the part of the European participants. Many felt that the precision guided munitions and other advanced systems, such as remotely piloted vehicles, offered the promise of a reduction in cost and manpower and, at the same time, markedly increased military effectiveness. The American government was repeatedly and strongly urged to make the new technologies available to its European allies.

Some of the participants cautioned not to overestimate the consequences of modern technology. Technology could contribute to solving the strategic and perhaps even the political problems, but it provided by no means the full answer. The Soviets, moreover, were bound to acquire similar technologies and improve their weapons systems and firepower, thereby neutralizing at least part of Western progress. Not all conferees shared this opinion. If the new technological advancements for both tactical nuclear weapons and conventional weapons could be incorporated into the current capabilities, a situation could be created in which neither the Soviet Union nor the Western allies would be able to mount a sustained offensive against one another. From this point of view it did not matter whether the Soviets could develop similar advanced systems, because a stalemate at the local level could ensue just as a standoff existed at the strategic level. If the West could bring this situation about, the participant maintained, the political as well as military advantage which the Soviets now derived from their overwhelming conventional capability would be neutralized.

In short, most participants, Americans as well as Europeans, saw a great deal of merit in the new military technologies and called for the study of their potential impact on the Western defense posture. Although not everyone extended this requirement to cover the tactical nuclear stockpile, there was a general consensus that technological expertise should be harnessed to support the Western cause.

IV. THE ECONOMIC DIMENSION OF GRAND STRATEGY

While the principal focus of the discussions was on the political, military, and technological components of grand strategy, the conference voiced concern that American-allied economic relations today were all too frequently conducted without regard for their political and military implications. Many participants commented that policies in one area were likely to reinforce or obstruct progress made by the Alliance in other fields.

There are several economic problem areas that impact on the cohesion of the Alliance. The most visible area concerns the dispute over restructuring the international trade and monetary arrangements.

Some American participants attributed the trade and monetary disputes to conflicting U.S. and European perceptions of the nature of the European integration effort. The United States saw the European Community as wealthy and moving progressively toward greater economic unity and strength. However, the American participants believed that the European governments rejected this view and insisted on seeing themselves as a group of rather vulnerable middle-sized states seeking to engineer a very fragile integration process. Consequently, progress in overcoming the trade and monetary obstacles was partly a function of changes in European government perceptions of the European Community and its future evolution. These American participants concluded that the West European nations should assume the responsibilities that accompanied increased economic power, and should make the key concessions in the pending negotiations with the United States.

A quite different view on trade and monetary problems was voiced by the European participants.[1] Many of them placed the blame for the collapse of the Bretton Woods system on the U.S.

---

1. The views of many of the European participants were reflected in the response of General André Beaufre (France) to the paper presented by Dr. W. R. Danielian (U.S.). General Beaufre's comments are found in Appendix C, "The Economic Controversy: A European Viewpoint."

refusal to introduce economic austerity measures in the late 1960s. They recalled that France and other European countries had warned the United States that it had to impose economic restraints, and not pass off to Europe the costs of domestic inflation. But Washington had regarded these warnings as unfriendly suggestions.

A number of European participants were particularly critical of the liberal economic measures that President Nixon had proposed to remedy the monetary and trade problems. These measures were designed to reduce tariffs and nontariff barriers, provide freer access for American agricultural goods in foreign markets, and remove gold from any international payments role. These participants suggested that priority should go instead to a new monetary system with an international currency not denominated in dollars. Other European conferees added that the effort to resolve current economic problems should be comprehensive and include the development of common policies on energy and multinational corporations.

In his 1973 State of the World Report, President Nixon highlighted another major economic problem area. He called on the Atlantic Alliance to seek this year a lasting solution to the balance-of-payments difficulties caused by the U.S. military presence in Europe. Statistics presented at the conference showed that the U.S. balance-of-payments deficit on the military account was about $2.2 billion, if allowance was made for devaluations. Existing offset arrangements reduced this figure to $1.6 billion, which constituted the net deficit on the military balance of payments.

Several American participants observed that unless the U.S.-European economic problems were solved and the deficit on the military account remedied, the U.S. Administration, already pressed by Congress, might feel forced to withdraw American troops from Europe. A number of European conferees agreed that the resolution of the balance-of-payments problem was a requisite for persuading the American people that the U.S. military presence needed to remain in Europe.

While there was general agreement that the Europeans should do more to ease the U.S. burden for the Western defense effort, the conferees were divided over the form that this effort should take. One American participant presented his idea for an International Security Fund, a multilateral clearinghouse for deficits on the military account. Several European participants suggested, however, that changes in the trade and monetary systems alone would not be sufficient to offset the economic burden of the U.S. troops in Europe. Moreover, it was wishful thinking to expect Western Europe to restructure its trade and payments arrangements simply to help the United States correct its balance-of-payments deficit. Even if the European governments saw this option as desirable, it was naive to believe that any lasting solution could be achieved in one year's time. The real solution lay elsewhere. The United States should exercise greater self-discipline and fiscal-monetary responsibility.

The present U.S.-European economic discord came at a time of growing Soviet activity in world trading and monetary markets. Increased East-West trade, technology transfers, and freer capital flows were recognized by the conferees as contributing to a relaxation of international tensions. However, there was a solid consensus urging greater Western awareness of the potential political as well as economic dangers involved in expanding East-West economic relations.

It was noted, first, that as a centralized economy the Soviet Union had absolute control over its own market. It could favor certain customers and suppliers over others, thereby obtaining significant bargaining leverage in international economic dealings. If the West failed to reach a common policy on trade and monetary arrangements within the next few years, the Soviet Union could use its bargaining leverage to aggravate further the lack of cohesion among the Western trading partners.

Both American and European participants warned the West to avoid becoming too dependent on the Soviet Union as a market for agricultural products and industrial technology, and as a supplier of energy and raw materials. Such dependence might force the West to make unilateral concessions in economic negotiations, and because of the linkages in the international system, in politico-military negotiations as well. The conference urged that the West reach a consensus on the economic dimension of grand strategy before engaging in more extensive East-West economic activity.

There was considerable discussion on another area that would condition a new grand strategy: How would the European entity evolve, and what would be its international economic role? Oddly enough, one group of participants, mostly Americans, entertained a more optimistic view of Europe's future than most of the European participants had.

Most of the Americans asserted that the European Community

was a strong and vibrant economic unit steadily progressing toward greater economic integration. Progress in the economic realm would, they claimed, eventually be translated into European political and defense collaboration, and would result in a larger global role for Europe. They believed that not only *should* Europe do more—for example in Western defense and in the removal of trade barriers—but that Europe *could* do more in these matters. Having successfully achieved many of the original objectives of the Treaty of Rome, the proverbial Old Testament of Europe, the time had come for a redefinition of the European Community's international status and responsibilities.

A second group of mostly European participants granted that significant economic achievements had been realized, but drew quite different conclusions. One participant referred to Jean Rey's famous statement that "Europe will be made by money or it will not be made at all." He observed, however, that while money (and the expectations of the benefits that integration would bring) helped, it *alone* could not lead the European Community to further integration in economics, and to collaboration in politics and defense. The most important variable was political will; at this point, this ingredient was not present. Without political will and without an overwhelming external threat or challenge to galvanize this will, the European Community would not progress much beyond the Common Market stage of integration.

One European conferee warned that some of the proposed American economic policies could vitiate the attempts of the European Community to achieve economic and monetary union. For example, several European participants resented the American demand that the Common Agricultural Policy and its variable levy be modified to allow for greater access for U.S. agricultural products; yet these were the most concrete achievements of the Community! These conferees added that any U.S. policy that impeded European integration would promote the traditional Soviet objective of preventing a West European union.

V. DEMANDS OF NEGOTIATIONS

Grand strategy finds its implementation not only on the battlefield or in the chambers of the high priests of finance and trade. Perhaps the most critical arena where the players meet is at the East-West negotiations on security and arms control. With SALT I an event of the past, the key negotiations are SALT II, the arms reduction talks in Vienna, and the Helsinki Conference on Security and Cooperation in Europe.

An American participant elaborated on his interpretation of the U.S. approach to the negotiations. Washington appeared to be pursuing a strategy of linkages. Its aim was to build an interlocking structure of agreements in such a way that conflict or obstruction in one area would risk destroying the entire structure. The American government apparently hoped to create a vested interest on both sides in mutual restraint. If the Soviets sought to conclude an agreement on trade or technology, they would have to cooperate in other areas, such as in the security negotiations. The U.S. strategy of linkages implied that (1) the Soviets could be bargained with, and (2) despite the adversary relationship between the superpowers, the two powers could identify selective areas for cooperation.

The participants generally concurred that the present negotiations were fraught with dangers. The inability of the Alliance to define a common strategy with respect to an optimal NATO posture and its failure to arrive at a concerted position left the issues to be solved in the East-West negotiations rather than in a West-West forum. In the East-West negotiations, however, the Soviet Union clearly had the advantage. It did not have the same problem of having to forge a consensus among its allies as the United States had. Consequently, a relatively unified Warsaw Pact faced an uncoordinated Western Alliance and neutral nations.

The Soviet Union would have ample opportunity to exploit the divisions in the Western Alliance. For one thing, in order to split the United States from its allies, the Soviet Union sought to encourage in the perception of the West European nations the notion that the superpowers were forming a condominium. In this bilateral relationship the United States would be prepared to compromise the interests of its allies in its efforts to reach an agreement with the Soviet Union.

The Soviet goal to create the image that the superpowers determined Europe's destiny was evident in Moscow's effort to inject the American forward based systems (FBS) in SALT. The U.S. nuclear capable aircraft deployed in Europe were directly tied to the defense of Western Europe; to discuss these systems in a bilateral context would engender profound concern among the U.S. allies. Even in a multilateral context, at the force reduction talks, for example, the delicate issue of FBS could easily be exploited by the

Soviets to create divisiveness within the Western Alliance, which lacked an agreed position on the FBS. This split was also reflected at the Juan-les-Pins conference itself. One participant pointed out that the nuclear capable aircraft could invite Soviet pre-emption and create instability in the Western posture. A second advanced the argument that the utility of the FBS should be evaluated not only in terms of their capability to reach Soviet territory, but also in their ability to perform interdiction missions in areas east of NATO where Soviet troops could be concentrated. As such the FBS fulfilled the role of "intermediate deterrent" and not just one of escalation. Another conferee agreed and stressed the function of the FBS as a link in the chain of deterrence.

Another explosive issue that the Soviets would undoubtedly try to press at SALT II was an accord to prohibit the transfer of technology for offensive nuclear systems. Again, this would serve to enforce the image of a Soviet-American condominium and deepen the tensions between the United States and its British and French allies. It would also effectively foreclose any American support to a potential Anglo-French nuclear endeavor. The United States, in the opinion of one participant, was at a distinct disadvantage in SALT because it was forced to labor under its commitment under the Non-Proliferation Treaty.

The European participants warned their American counterparts of other Soviet ploys in the negotiations, such as the possibility of proposals for a no-first-use agreement and the creation of a nuclear free zone in central Europe. The majority of the European conferees felt—and their American colleagues agreed—that either possibility would leave Western Europe at the mercy of superior Soviet conventional forces and would decouple the security of Western Europe from that of the United States.

In the conference at Helsinki the Soviets were seen as seeking to win recognition of their World War II gains and to legalize the ideological division of the European continent. The Soviets hoped to promote the disintegration of the NATO Alliance. They would probably propose instead, if not at Helsinki then in another forum, a security pact for Europe which would allow them a senior voice in all decisions affecting European arrangements.

Several participants were of the opinion that the force reduction talks carried with them the most serious risks for Western cohesion. The Vienna meetings were cited as a salient example of Soviet efforts to instill the perception of a superpower entente. Most

European participants expressed skepticism about the force reduction talks. They pointed out that the Soviets had recently introduced some 1200 to 1500 T62 tanks into Eastern Europe without recalling any of the older type tanks. The latter would obviously be used for bargaining purposes at Vienna. Furthermore, the Soviet Union would withdraw its forces for only a few hundred kilometers; this would not diminish Soviet capability for endangering the security of Western Europe or for exerting military pressures all along the line from Finland to Turkey. Geography, as Napoleon reportedly once said, was the destiny of nations.

A few conferees advanced the thesis that the Soviets, beset with fears of a two-front conflict, were genuinely interested in reducing their forces in Europe. One of the participants, however, explained that Soviet dominance over the Eurasian land area remained a fundamental and traditional objective of the government in Moscow. The Soviets might try to solve their two-front problem by trying to become a Far Eastern naval and air power without abandoning their efforts to achieve a position of superiority in Europe, and for that matter, in the Middle East. In this respect several participants underlined the Soviet concept of a grand strategy in which all regions of the globe were interrelated.

One of the conferees expressed concern that the arms reduction talks could lead to a system of arms control that would vitiate or destroy the Western Alliance if restrictions on movement, use, and logistical support of forces were negotiated. If the Western allies at Vienna would accept limitations on the reintroduction of equipment and forces, on the maintenance and allocation of equipment, on deployment of weapons and troops, and on logistical support, the entire internal defense arrangements of the Alliance and its constituent members would become subject to an international agreement, an agreement which the Soviets helped to decide.

These types of discussions served to illuminate why some of the participants repeatedly emphasized the need for the Western allies to articulate their common political objectives and to identify a common strategy that related the military components to the political and other aspects. Indeed, the main theme of the conference was clearly the necessity to orchestrate all elements of strategy and to develop a global perspective. The need to counter somehow the trend away from international concerns and allied collaboration was voiced many times at the conference table. It was recognized that this was largely a matter of reviving national will rather than designing new or stronger military structures. The latter merely reflected a concept of national purpose and shared allied goals. To the extent that the conferees dwelt on the military ingredients of collaboration, the focus was on the political use of military capabilities and on the political implications of military strategy and tactics. In essence, a major lesson of the conference was the message that the United States and its allies not become engrossed in searching for narrow technical and military formulas at the negotiations lest the political implications compromise the cohesion of the Western Alliance.

The Emerging U.S. Global Strategy: Its Implications for the U.S.-European Partnership

Richard B. Foster

I. A NEW REALISM IN INTERNATIONAL AFFAIRS

A. Toward a New International Order

This paper describes the approach of the Nixon Administration to the creation of a new international order based on a multipolar world. The United States and its allies—the West European nations in particular—will assume new global roles in this era of a new realism in world affairs. The approach of the Nixon Doctrine and its implementing strategy toward the strategic interactions among the major world powers differs radically from that of administrations during the cold war. The overriding strategic objective common to all nuclear states—that of preventing nuclear war by cooperating to avoid nuclear confrontations—is in dialectical contradiction to the continuing conflict between the two social systems represented by the United States and the Soviet Union. How this cooperation-conflict dilemma will be resolved in a new international politics that is neither capitalist nor communist is the challenge of the "era of negotiations." Certainly all-out nuclear war between the United States and the Soviet Union is no longer a feasible means of resolving national conflicts of interests, ideology, and politics. The Clausewitz dictum that war is an extension of politics by other means has been fundamentally altered by the strategic nuclear deterrent equation. Mutual deterrence in the age of strategic nuclear parity has resulted in negotiations that led to the Moscow Arms Accords of May 1972 and to the agreements in principle between the United States and the Soviet Union.[1]

The application of these principles to the members of the main U.S. alliance—NATO—must now be clarified. Until these principles are interpreted, perhaps modified, then accepted by the West European partners of the United States, these U.S.-Soviet agreements will remain a barrier to U.S.-European understanding.

B. A General Political Principle for NATO

An alliance is primarily a political agreement and all guarantees are political; the North Atlantic Treaty is a purely defensive alliance whose aims are political. "Politics is the beginning; politics is the end," as the Soviet scholars are fond of repeating. Matters of political will are not subject to easily quantified demonstrations, and mutual confidence does not necessarily flow from cost-effectiveness studies, no matter how skillfully presented. An alliance system depends on many perceptions of mutual political interests, as well as on the political intentions and will of the party viewed as the principal guarantor by the other members of the alliance. Political will, however, is not enough: relative military force capabilities may—indirectly to be sure—become the arbiters of the resolution of a crisis. One of the paramount U.S.-allied objectives—throughout all stages of negotiation with the Soviet Union—is to deny the Soviets a degree of political utility to their offensive military force that they can exploit for political coercion. Some European and U.S. observers are concerned that the SALT I negoti-

---

1. As in the 26 May 1972 Agreement on Principles of Relations Between States.

ations left the Soviets in a militarily advantageous position in Europe. At the same time, no NATO nation is seeking such an offensive military force for NATO.

A general principle that might be used to guide not only the U.S.-Soviet and NATO-Warsaw Pact arms limitation and arms control negotiations, but also U.S. and NATO military planning, might be phrased as follows:

NATO policy should be to provide a valid sense of military security in Western Europe without unduly inhibiting constructive political, economic, and other Western initiatives toward and negotiations with Eastern Europe and the Soviet Union.

C. The Heritage of the 1960s

Even such a limited alliance principle as the above has been difficult to formulate and to reach agreement on. In part, this stems from the United States' preoccupation with military power, particularly nuclear weaponry.

In the decades of the fifties and sixties the U.S. nuclear strategy overemphasized quantitative force-to-force comparisons, and tended to ignore or underemphasize the political or indirect value of military power. During the era of U.S.-Soviet confrontation, the United States also tended to treat both nations as two giant weapons systems locked in some kind of mathematically determinable arms race. This view has been described as an "action-reaction" closed system. This led to the belief that strategic nuclear parity based on mutually assured destruction and, conversely, mutually assured vulnerability, demonstrated by "war outcomes" of population fatalities, was the only way to stop this action-reaction arms race. Both the United States and the Soviet Union were assumed to share the belief that nuclear war, no matter how limited in the beginning, would automatically escalate to mutual suicide. This assumption was the basis for the belief among many U.S. policymakers that once strategic nuclear parity was achieved and the parity was maintained over time, nuclear weapons would no longer be a consideration in international politics. This assumption has not proved to be true.

Now, in the seventies, the foreign policy of President Nixon seeks a more realistic approach to superpower relations. *This new approach springs from the strategic necessity of preventing nuclear*

*war without at the same time either abandoning U.S. allies or
surrendering U.S. global interests in a retreat to a neoisolationist
policy.* The Nixon Doctrine is based on a greater appreciation of the
importance of political, economic, and other nonmilitary considerations in formulating foreign policy goals and in the conduct of
diplomacy. However, even though recognition is given to the overemphasis of the 1960s on highly theoretical quantitative models of
the international strategic interaction process, the Nixon Administration still recognizes the importance of maintaining the capability
to make rigorous cost-effectiveness analyses of alternative weapons
systems and military force structures. Such quantitative analyses are
a necessary complement to integrative, multidisciplinary approaches
to devising and evaluating alternative national and allied strategies.

D. The Contrast Between American and Russian Styles

The United States has tended to emphasize the quantitative aspects
of Mutual Force Reductions (MFR), sometimes losing sight of the
political advantages that the United States enjoys over the Soviet
Union. For example, U.S. troops, aircraft, and nuclear weapons are
in West Germany and other NATO nations by invitation of the
European allies; Soviet troops and aircraft serve as occupation
forces in the East European Warsaw Pact countries.

Yet the Soviets have no intention of resorting to war with the
United States in Europe to achieve any of their political aims. The
Soviets place equal weight on strategic thinking and the physical
elements of military power. The Soviet leaders believe they have a
superior diplomacy based on a superior strategy on a global scale,
and they expect to come out ahead with the combination of an
offensive strategy and diplomatic initiative. Their future strategy
requires a political settlement in Europe which confirms the present
frontiers, and includes an agreement not to use force to change
these frontiers. The Soviets tend to stress the indirect or political
utility of military force as part of a long-range strategy that seeks to
probe and defeat the U.S. and NATO strategy and to exploit the
vulnerabilities and weaknesses of the Western nations' domestic
political systems.

The United States, on its part, cannot consider MFR or the
Conference on Security and Cooperation in Europe (CSCE) without
considering the Mediterranean and the Middle East and the nature
and roles of both the U.S. and Soviet forces in these areas. The

United States must give more weight to political factors in a
qualitative analysis, rather than depend on a primarily quantitative
approach in evaluating alternative courses of action and in analyzing
such complex strategic problems as presented by SALT II, MFR,
and CSCE.

Since partnership requires that the views and approaches of allies
be carefully studied and understood, the United States and its allies
must join together to study and understand Soviet strategy and
objectives if we are ever to concert our negotiations. If, as Sun Tzu
commented several millennia ago, the proper objective of one's own
strategy is the defeat of the enemy's strategy, it is certain that the
failure of the West to make a serious study of Soviet strategy is a
weakness in our negotiating posture. The open approach of the
Nixon Administration to allies in the "partnership principle" offers
a basis for such a joint U.S.-West European examination of Soviet
strategic thought.

E. The Partnership Principle

The positive political goals of the Nixon Doctrine and the Kissinger
diplomacy need more stress. In particular, the aim of creating a
multipolar international system in which U.S. allies play an increasingly important role in global diplomacy provides a positive framework for our discussions in this symposium. The U.S. vision of a
future global order is not one of a static world. Rather, such a
future international system must (1) allow for a considerable degree
of freedom of political choice among allied and neutral states,
(2) set limits on the use of force in the settlement of differences
between national states, and (3) set limits on the expansionist aims
of imperial states, particularly Russia and China. American leaders
are negotiating bilaterally with adversaries—the Soviet Union and
the People's Republic of China—and at the same time trying to
develop a set of new arrangements with our allies under the partnership principle. According to this principle, each ally is free to
develop its own foreign policy and to define its global roles.

At the heart of the Nixon Doctrine's vision of a multipolar world
lies the recognition of the differences between Russia and China;
monolithic global communism is no longer "the threat." At the
same time, care is taken to ensure that our diplomacy does not
contribute to the outbreak of a Sino-Soviet war. The People's
Republic of China needs the political and diplomatic support of the

United States and other Western powers vis-à-vis the main threat to
its independence—the military forces of and ideological differences
with the Soviet Union. In turn, the Soviet Union is seeking a
political settlement in Europe in order to free her hands in dealing
with China.[2] Since the Soviet Union represents the main threat—
military, economic, political, and ideological (including subversion
of Western governments by proxy Communist parties)—to America,
Western Europe, Japan, and China, it is important to understand
the difference between the American and Russian strategic concepts, objectives, and policies toward Europe, and between the
American and Russian visions of the future global order.

II. AMERICAN AND SOVIET PERSPECTIVES OF THE FUTURE: A CONTRAST

A. The Soviet Perspective: Soviet Concepts of Strategic Superiority

As stated earlier, the Soviets believe that strategic superiority depends as much on having a superior strategy as on having superior
military force. Therefore, the Soviet Union stresses professionalism
in its military and civilian strategic and policy planners. The Soviet
Union supports a carefully graduated system of awarding higher
academic degrees, through the doctoral level, in its research institutes, major military academies, and universities.

The United States, on the other hand, has no trained cadre of
professional strategic and policy planners. U.S. higher military
schools and research institutes do not directly award higher academic degrees. As a result of the American overemphasis in the 1960s
on the purely technological and quantitative aspects of the strategic
arms competition with the Soviet Union, Americans have tended to
give too little consideration to the quality of Soviet strategic
thought. Nevertheless, a sophisticated appreciation of Soviet strategic thinking is essential if the United States is to develop an
adequate theory of the dynamics of U.S.-Soviet strategic interactions. In their doctrinal writings, the Soviets stress the strategic
utility and the political value of nuclear weapons, including the
diplomatic utility of a perception of a margin of strategic nuclear
superiority not directly usable in war. The Soviets apparently also

---

2. For example, Chinese leaders fear that mutual force reductions in
Europe between NATO and the Pact nations would free the Soviet Union to
transfer forces to the Sino-Soviet border if Soviet leaders deemed such a troop
movement necessary.

stress the indirect political use of military power in developing criteria for designing their forces. A large share of the Soviet economy is directed toward increasing the power of the state relative to that of the Western nations.

B. Soviet Concepts of Doctrine and Strategy

There are at least two areas in which the Soviets are rather explicit about the political utility of the growing power of their military establishment. First, they see the rise in their strategic nuclear power vis-à-vis the United States and NATO as limiting Western strategic and policy options by arousing fear of the consequences of Soviet military capabilities. The Soviets consider the devolution in Western (NATO) strategy from "massive retaliation" to "flexible response" with a "conventional emphasis" to be the result of this process. Second, the Soviets see their growing military capabilities as providing the umbrella under which they can perform their "international duty" of aiding and abetting "national liberation" and "anticolonial" wars with minimal danger of the conflict escalating and threatening the Soviet homeland itself. In the Soviet view, these indirect attacks on the West will be effective in the long run.

The increased reach and flexibility of Soviet military capabilities have permitted the Soviets to apply their doctrine of "just" wars to both Vietnam and the Near East. In both cases Soviet political, economic, and military aid to the "just" belligerents appears to be neither an accident nor the result of a process of incremental decisions leading to a level of involvement not originally contemplated. Rather, the Soviet leaders were cognizant of the course they had chosen and provided they proceeded cautiously, it served to test international reactions and to evaluate the implications of each succeeding commitment.

The destructiveness of nuclear weapons is such that Lenin's dictum on the inevitability of war between "socialist" and "capitalist" camps was modified by Khrushchev in 1956 when he declared that "world war" (presumably global nuclear war) was not "fatalistically inevitable."[3] This is to say that deterrence of an American

---

3. Although the idea was popularized by Khrushchev in his speech delivered at the 20th Party Congress in 1956, it had been foreshadowed four years earlier at the 19th Party Congress by Stalin, who argued that the contradictions (likely to lead to war) within the capitalist camp were greater than those between the capitalist and the socialist camps. Neither the military nor the civilian leaders have given any indication of wanting to modify this Soviet doctrine even if Khrushchev is no longer given personal credit for it.

nuclear attack on the Soviet Union is possible but can by no means be guaranteed. Hence, the Soviet military establishment must be prepared to fight a nuclear war as a last resort. Soviet military strategy does not envisage a premeditated surprise attack on the United States or on NATO-Europe designed to hasten the historically determined demise of capitalism, because the expected damage to the Soviet Union from the U.S. retaliatory blow would be too great.

This Soviet perception—shared by the United States—that the consequences of a nuclear war outweigh any possible political aims and strategic objectives served by such a war is the basis for the U.S.-Soviet "era of negotiations" in the Nixon Doctrine. But the Nixon Administration has no illusions about the long-term aims of Soviet foreign policy toward Western Europe. The Soviets prefer a détente that retains the bipolarity of the cold war, a world in which the United States and the Soviet Union agree to spheres of influence on a global scale. Ideally, the Soviets would prefer an international system in which their sphere—the Soviet Union itself and Eastern Europe—was closed to Western penetration, while the rest of the world—particularly the United States, Western Europe, the Middle East and Japan—was open to Soviet political and diplomatic initiatives. Détente Soviet-style would become a form of graceful historical capitulation of Western nations to the Soviet (or Russian) imperial will without the risks of war with a united West. The global strategy that underlies the American vision of a peaceful multipolar world is in stark contrast to the Soviet vision of a U.S.-Soviet condominium under which the global power position of the United States would gradually erode and become weaker relative to Soviet power.

The U.S. effort to thwart Soviet attempts to dominate the entire Eurasian World Island in the name of Russian security does not require the demise of either the Russian state or the Soviet system. Rather, Americans, and most Europeans, welcome the opportunity to openly compete with the Soviet social system while at the same time cooperating with Soviet leaders to prevent the outbreak of a devastating nuclear war.

C. The American Perspective: The Nixon Doctrine—
"Strategy for Peace"

A "generation of peace" is the unifying theme in all of President Nixon's foreign policy statements. Many of his critics have dismissed this objective as part of the Nixonian rhetoric designed to enlist U.S. domestic support for the devolution of U.S. involvement in Vietnam. Nevertheless, from the point of view of a strategist, it may be usefully treated as a concrete goal of U.S. foreign policy. At the same time the Nixon Doctrine reflects the acceptance by the United States of realistic limits to U.S. power and influence, and it signals a change in the underlying U.S. philosophy concerning the strategic interaction process between the superpowers. Two elements of the President's strategy for peace—strength and partnership—are presented as making possible the third—meaningful negotiations. The U.S. foreign policy for the seventies outlined in President Nixon's four foreign policy reports to the Congress[4] has as one central focus a sustained U.S. effort to alter the Soviet-American competition in nuclear arms to less dangerous forms of competition through negotiation.

Recent American Presidents—Eisenhower, Kennedy, Johnson, and Nixon—as well as Khrushchev and his successors in the Kremlin, have long been aware that some form of relatively "peaceful competition" between the two opposing social systems must be substituted for nuclear confrontation policies between America and Russia.

The new realism of the Nixon Doctrine, on which the current détente is based, involves a much greater U.S. sensitivity to the dynamics of globally operating factors—sociological, political, economic, technical, and military—than did American diplomacy through the 1960s. The U.S. has reached a different perception of the political stability and economic staying power of both great communist states. Furthermore, there is a growing recognition on the part of the United States of basic conceptual differences between the superpowers—differences in military strategy and doctrine, and differences in perceptions of the political value and strategic utility of nuclear weapons. The Nixon foreign policy recognizes that America and Russia formulate and carry out their national strategies using methodologies appropriate to their histories and their political institutions. It is surprising that the United

---

4. See Richard M. Nixon, *U.S. Strategy for the 1970s: A New Strategy for Peace* (Washington, D.C.: U.S. Government Printing Office, 18 February 1970); *U.S. Strategy for Peace: Building for Peace* (Washington, D.C.: U.S. Government Printing Office, February 1971); *U.S. Strategy for Peace: the Emerging Structure for Peace* (Washington, D.C.: U.S. Government Printing Office, 9 February 1972); and *U.S. Foreign Policy for the 1970s: Shaping a Durable Peace* (Washington, D.C.: U.S. Government Printing Office, 3 May 1973).

States has for so long "mirror-imaged" U.S. strategy and thus imputed U.S. strategic concepts and doctrines to the Soviet Union. Equally surprising is the length of time it has taken for Americans to begin to accept that our European partners also have different views and perspectives of the future from those held by Americans.

D. New Roles for Europe

The Nixon-Kissinger concept of a new international political system is based on a dynamic—not a static—equilibrium among the developed nations and between them and the lesser developed countries whose social, economic, and political systems are still in a state of flux and evolution. This concept of a dynamic equilibrium in international relations among several competing major power centers (five, if Western Europe is treated as one, with the United States, the Soviet Union, China, and Japan as the other four) is not the same as the more static concept of the balance of power among status quo national regimes that grew out of the Concert of Europe at the end of the Napoleonic Wars. The century of peace in Europe which followed was shattered by the first truly global war in 1914, and the international system that was in large part based on an isolationist America, a weak Russia, a European-centered colonial system, and weak Asian countries was profoundly altered by World War II. A nostalgic desire to return to the international system foreshadowed by the Congress of Vienna is unrealistic. Nuclear technology alone has rendered such a status quo concept obsolete. A new international order is emerging, one in which the West European nations—imperfectly organized as they are to play a unified global political role—have already achieved a new independence from American economic support through cooperation in the European Economic Community (EEC), but still need American military (nuclear) guarantees for their security. Yet Western Europe can move toward either a passive form of neutralism, accommodation to the Soviet designs in Europe, or a more creative partnership with the United States and Japan in erecting a new international system. Such a system requires increasing cooperation in the economic, trade, monetary, ecological, raw materials (e.g., oil), and political arenas as well as in military strategy and mutual security. For the achievement of this kind of U.S.-European-Japanese cooperation, the new American realism in international affairs must be understood, and the idea that America is turning inward in a neoisolationist reaction to Vietnam laid to rest.

III. AMERICAN, RUSSIAN, AND EUROPEAN STRATEGIC
     INTERACTIONS AND THE "MASS" CONCEPT

A. The Dialectical Nature of American, European, and Russian
   Strategic Interactions

The new international system will emerge out of the resolution of
the dialectical[5] conflicts in which the United States, Europe, and
the Soviet Union—as three centers of global power—currently find
themselves. For example:

- The United States and the Soviet Union are negotiating in
  SALT II and MFR to limit nuclear arms and their role in the
  global diplomacy of both powers, based on the necessity to
  prevent nuclear war by cooperating to avoid nuclear confrontations.

- The United States and its NATO partners are working hard to
  retain the credibility of the U.S. nuclear guarantee to Europe
  to prevent Soviet diplomatic use of nuclear or conventional
  forces to threaten or coerce the European NATO allies. These
  efforts are in conflict with the U.S.-Soviet negotiations to
  prevent nuclear war by cooperating to avoid nuclear confrontations. The Europeans, therefore, rightly insist that the Soviets must be deterred from attacking or threatening Western
  Europe by the risk of escalation to nuclear war, while the
  American preference is to raise the nuclear threshold. At the
  same time, the United States is retaining nuclear options
  necessary to deter less-than-all-out wars of aggression in Europe and elsewhere.

- The West European nations are making a major effort to
  enlarge and deepen intra-European economic cooperation in
  the EEC, while at the same time negotiating trade agreements
  with the United States, Japan, the Soviet Union, China and
  East European nations, as well as those nations in the Middle

---

5. "Dialectics," as used in this paper, is a logic of the history of interstate
interactions. The dialectical method is the resolution of opposites through
conflict into a higher synthesis. The reverse process may also exist. The use of a
synthesis is either to reconcile or to control the nature of the conflict that
resolves differences. It is a useful method of analyzing the interactions of
strategic decisions of adversary states. For example, an application of dialectical methodology is that which describes the U.S.-Soviet historical relationship
as consisting of both opportunities for cooperation and possibilities for conflict, often with one nullifying the other.

East that provide the oil which is the life-blood of the "economic miracle" of European economic growth. The U.S.-West European-Soviet negotiations in the CSCE, mutual force reductions, as well as the *Ostpolitik* of the Federal Republic of Germany (FRG) all affect and are affected by the bilateral U.S.-Soviet negotiations to prevent nuclear war. The European nuclear states—the United Kingdom and France— hold the view that their nuclear forces may influence the U.S. decision to use its strategic nuclear forces, thus strengthening the solidarity of NATO and adding to the credibility of the nuclear deterrent. Yet in all European states a premature euphoria about détente has emerged, which makes it increasingly difficult for the leaders of these nations to persuade their parliaments to support military forces and thus share the burden of defense more equitably with the United States, so that the West can negotiate from strength.

B. Prevention of Nuclear War as a Common Aim and Dialectical Necessity

One logical development that might lead to the resolution of these conflicts could arise out of the most elemental aim of all states: survival. Because it is in the vital interest of both the United States and the Soviet Union to prevent an all-out global nuclear war, a dialectical necessity exists to cooperate to prevent confrontations that might lead to such a global nuclear conflict. This *strategic* necessity in turn may lead to a higher synthesis: a new international *politics* underpinning a global order. At the same time, the conflict between the two social systems arising out of fundamental differences—a conflict that stops short of all-out nuclear war—tends to prevent convergence of the two systems. A historical cause of war between states will persist with all the dangers of the past. Hence, the pragmatic (or dialectical) necessity of preventing nuclear war operates equally on the United States, the Soviet Union, and the West European nations. The basic shared aim of preventing nuclear war will set limits not only on the use of military force but also on the aims of all national states. As mentioned above, the two most dangerous characteristics of nation states—claims of absolute sovereignty and claims, backed by force, to the territory of others—must be altered in the following ways:

- *Limits on sovereignty.* For example, the historical Russian— now Soviet—insistence on secrecy concerning its military forces has been qualified by the SALT I agreement of May 1972, in which the United States and the Soviet Union agreed to noninterference with national means of inspection. This accord in effect abridges the sovereignty of both states by their mutual agreement to limit secrecy concerning each other's nuclear forces.

- *Limits on expansionist aims.* For example, the Soviet proposals of noninterference in the affairs of other states and the nonuse of force to alter state boundaries would tend to undermine the legitimacy of such military actions as the Soviet invasion of Czechoslovakia in 1968.

C. The Necessity for a Positive Negotiating Aim

Because the nuclear deterrent equation is independent of social systems—nuclear war would mean the probable end of the politics and the societies of both capitalist and communist states—there is no ideological advantage in such a war for one system over another. In an all-out nuclear war the Soviet economic resources, population, and political system would just as surely be destroyed as would those of the United States and Europe. Hence the aim of preventing nuclear war requires that negotiations to achieve that aim be removed from the ideological arena. Equally important is the conversion of an entirely negative and destructive aim—that of assuring the destruction of an aggressor in retaliation to an attack which destroys one's own nation—to a more positive aim.

This can come about through acceptance of the fact that one cannot assure the survival of one's own nation without also assuring the survival of the adversary nation (that is, from destruction in an all-out nuclear war). Nor does the condition of mutual deterrence resulting from the mutuality of assured destruction offer a mutual positive aim for negotiations. Mutual assured destruction as one possible boundary outcome of a nuclear exchange[6] is a historical condition that has emerged between the United States and the Soviet Union in the event of such an all-out nuclear war. However,

---

6. "One possible boundary outcome" is a necessary qualification. For example, the "fatal inevitability of escalation to all-out war" that some strategists assume to follow upon the defensive first use of tactical nuclear weapons in Europe is just that—an assumption. It is at least equally valid to assume that a defensive doctrine for the use of tactical nuclear weapons would terminate the aggression and bring about a negotiated settlement before all is lost. At the same time, the risk of escalation must be kept alive; paradoxically, this instability is the necessary condition for strategic stability.

this historical condition need not commit the two nuclear superpowers to the rigid strategy of military forces designed only for mutual assured destruction. Rather, this historical situation creates a need for a more stable strategy, one that takes into account the necessity for strategic stability on the Central European front, a stability achieved without surrendering either the political independence and freedom of West European states or American interests in Europe.

D. The MASS Concept

One such concept has been advanced by the author in another publication.[7] It can briefly be described as the Mutual Assured Survival and Security, or MASS, concept. MASS is a positive goal of such arms limitation negotiations as SALT and MFR, since no state can negotiate to commit suicide—for example, to perpetuate its own vulnerability and to assure its destruction by an opponent. Nor is the "halting of the arms race" a sufficient goal; it may be that strategic stability—if that is the desideratum of the negotiations—is better achieved by a controlled (or limited) continuation of the arms race.[8] As stated earlier, the MASS concept must be rooted in the most fundamental statement of mutual self-interest: "I can only assure my own survival and security by assuring you, my adversary, of your survival and security." Such a general concept is necessary as a common negotiating aim between the United States, the West European powers, and the Soviet Union. Thus the strategic imperative consequent upon the very destructiveness of nuclear weapons may bring about a new international political order based on a concept of mutual self-interest—mutually assured survival and mutual security.

It is now evident that decisive strategic nuclear superiority of one superpower over the other is no longer an achievable goal if both sides remain in the nuclear arms race. The driving force behind the arms race is technology. SALT I in effect codified the basic problem of the arms race, namely, that it had no specific goal

7. R. B. Foster, "The Nixon Doctrine: An Emerging U.S. Policy," *National Strategy in a Decade of Change* (Boston: Lexington Books, D. C. Heath and Company, September 1973).

8. A somewhat remote analogy is the "war on inflation"; no one wants the consequences of a complete halt to inflation: a recession or a depression. A "controlled inflation" seems to produce a beneficial result: a stable, growing economy.

except to deny the other side strategic superiority arising from a technological breakthrough. Thus both sides have been pursuing essentially a negative or denial strategy, that is, to prevent the other side from achieving unilaterally an exploitation of new technology that might yield either decisive superiority or politically usable marginal superiority. Neither side has a clear idea of how to formulate or how to control the so-called technological arms race. No technological solution to the problems posed to society by technology has yielded itself. There is no alternative to the development of a new international politics to bring under control the technology of the means of mass destruction, to prevent nuclear war, and to avoid confrontations between the major powers that might lead to nuclear war.

IV. THE NIXON DOCTRINE AND GLOBAL STRATEGIC INTERACTIONS[9]

A. An Independent Europe: The Cornerstone of the Global Structure of the Nixon Doctrine

President Nixon has stressed the primacy of Europe[10] and the maintenance of an independent, strong, and stable Western Europe as the foundation of any global order in which U.S. interests are maintained. The United States has maintained the coupling of its strategic nuclear deterrent to Europe in order to provide protection against Soviet coercion either by nuclear arms or by conventional forces. As noted earlier, this "extended deterrent" has been extremely difficult to maintain, with the result that every few years a review of NATO strategy has taken place. The current strategy of flexible response is based on a balanced force concept and includes a conventional response phase as well as a role for tactical nuclear, theater nuclear, and U.S. strategic nuclear force options. However, France disagrees with both the strategy and the organization of NATO.

The credibility of the American nuclear guarantee to the

---

9. This section is adapted from the author's "The Nixon Doctrine: An Emerging U.S. Policy," *National Strategy in a Decade of Change* (Boston: Lexington Books, D. C. Heath and Company, September 1973).

10. Europe is here defined as the West European states that gain their security and maintain their independence under the protection of the American nuclear umbrella, plus Sweden, Switzerland, Austria, and Spain in West Europe, and Yugoslavia in East Europe.

Europeans has gradually eroded, and U.S.-Soviet bilateral negotiations, particularly in SALT I and now in SALT II, have tended to undermine the confidence that the West European nations have in the U.S. nuclear umbrella. Yet there is no foreseeable substitute; the nuclear power of England and France is insufficient to provide a credible deterrent to the Soviet nuclear might poised against Europe. Moreover, both the French and the British lack tactical nuclear weapons that could replace the several thousand such weapons in the American arsenal based in Europe. The United States so far has been unwilling to change its policy concerning technical aid to the French nuclear force. If we are to keep our commitment to NATO-Europe, we cannot deny such aid and at the same time unilaterally reduce our forces in Europe and thus tend to decouple our strategic deterrent. Hence there is an indefinitely continuing requirement for the U.S. strategic umbrella based on the coupled strategic deterrent. Needed is a new strategic concept and a different organization for NATO which will make it easier for the United States to accept new directions in its nuclear policy that would make Europe more independent of U.S. military power and in turn would meet French objections to NATO's strategy and organization halfway.

B. Vietnam, Eastern Europe, and the Middle East

1. Vietnam and Southeast Asia

The U.S. fighting role in South Vietnam has been terminated under the cease-fire agreements of January 1973, and all U.S. forces have been withdrawn. These two developments have removed major impediments to negotiations with the Soviet Union on the one hand, and have made possible the improvement of relations with our West European partners on the other hand. Much has been said about Vietnamization and the Vietnam experience, but two points are worth mentioning:

- While the United States has removed its ground forces from South Vietnam, some capability has been retained for conducting air strikes in Southeast Asia. This is, therefore, still an area of potential conflict in which U.S. forces could be engaged, as in the post-cease-fire bombing of Cambodia. Hence, this area will continue to affect interactions between the United States and the Soviet Union, the United States and the People's Republic of China, and China and the Soviet Union.

- The profound effects of the Vietnamese war on U.S. domestic politics and on the American view of its role in the world are yet to be fully felt. The Vietnam experience led to the implementation of the all-volunteer army and a major reduction of the U.S. armed forces. The U.S. Army in particular has undergone a major reduction in force; this may well affect the stability of the West European strategic deterrent, since the ground forces are perceived by the Europeans and the Soviets as a major link in the chain of deterrence. A strong effort is being made by the Nixon Administration to overcome the tendency toward neoisolation and withdrawal from the world which the American force reduction may suggest. Since the European strategic balance is crucial to the stability of the entire global system envisaged in the Nixon Doctrine, it is imperative that any American reduction in European-based forces take place in a gradual and well-planned fashion, with some corresponding reduction in the Soviet forces as well. Hence the necessity for a concept of mutual force reduction in NATO and the Warsaw Pact.

2. *Eastern Europe*

In the period between World War II and the late 1960s, Eastern Europe was an area of potential East-West conflict. Today, however, Eastern Europe is an area of potential internal conflict, that is, conflict between the Soviet Union and her East European allies. To a very large extent the East European nations in the Warsaw Pact remain "unwilling partners" with the Soviet Union. In the cases of Yugoslavia and Albania—these two communist states have undertaken independent foreign policies—Yugoslavia looks to the West for her main sources of trade and aid, and the Albanians have aligned themselves with the People's Republic of China. Romania, too, has shown in recent years an increasing independence in its foreign policy. It can truly be said that President Nixon's road to Peking led through Bucharest. Romania's independence is further illustrated in its 1972 invitation to Prime Minister Golda Meir of Israel to visit Bucharest.

Some of the neutral West European states, particularly Sweden, Austria, and Switzerland, are in close cooperative relationships with

West European states. It may be that such cooperative "neutral positions" will provide a nonbloc alternative for East European nations who wish to loosen their ties with the Warsaw Pact without joining NATO. The independent communist states thus may have some "place to go." The possibilities of trade and technical cooperation with the West provide a strong incentive for these East European states to seek an accommodation with the West, without necessarily challenging the security of the Soviet Union. However, so long as the Soviet Union sees East Europe as a buffer zone necessary for its security, it may look on Western efforts to expand relations with East Europe as a form of political aggression, as in the Czechoslovak experience of 1968. Nevertheless, the freer political movement of the East European states is an inherent part of the Nixon Doctrine.

3. The Middle East

The Middle East poses two sources of potential superpower conflict:

- The Arab-Israeli conflict might draw the United States and the Soviet Union into confrontation.
- The oil-rich Persian Gulf, with the increasing competition for oil between the United States, Western Europe, and Japan, might become a source of conflict, particularly if the Soviets enter into close relations with other Arab states as they have with Iraq.

Current U.S. support for Israel, as well as our alignment with Iran, have been a source of some concern—even friction—between the United States and certain members of NATO. It will take a major diplomatic effort on the part of the United States and Western Europe to avoid a falling out in this region, particularly over oil policies. Throughout the foreseeable future, the Middle East will also require constant attention and highly skilled negotiations with the Soviet Union to avoid being drawn into a dangerous U.S.-Soviet confrontation.

C. The Far East: The Two Major Powers

1. China

The Chinese are genuinely concerned about the possibility of a Sino-Soviet war, particularly the threat of a Soviet nuclear strike.

Although the Soviet Union denies any such intent, it certainly has the capability today (1973), at least, for a nuclear disarming strike. This is the third area of potential U.S.-Soviet conflict (in addition to the Middle East and Southeast Asia). It is by far the most dangerous because such a conflict would result from a war between two nuclear powers—Russia and China—and such a war might not be limited to these two powers. Hence the People's Republic of China (PRC) must be brought into the great power negotiations and discussions designed to prevent nuclear war and to reduce the possibility of a confrontation between any two or more of the five (current) nuclear powers.

2. Japan

Japan has a partnership relationship with the United States and a U.S. nuclear guarantee against both Russian and Chinese nuclear threats. The Nixon Doctrine recognizes Japan as a major power and part of the multipolar international system now evolving. Japan is in the unique position of gaining its international political strength solely through its economic and trading power, without a large military force and without an independent nuclear deterrent. Japan has signed but not ratified the Non-Proliferation Treaty and is thus keeping open its options for acquiring a nuclear force in the future.

It is interesting to note that by virtue of its non-nuclear status Japan has degrees of freedom of action that it might not otherwise have. One of these degrees of freedom is that Japan can concentrate its resources and attention on economic concerns. Japan is potentially a major source of economic capital for both the Soviet Union and China. In the near future the two great communist powers may find themselves competing with each other and with Japan's current customers, the less-developed countries, for Japanese investment resources.

Japan has one overwhelming vulnerability in its economic system: it is dependent on Middle East oil and long sealines of communication, without any means to protect its tankers. Japan is dependent on the U.S. naval presence to protect from Soviet naval interference its lifeline from the Persian Gulf, through the Indian Ocean, to the Eastern Pacific and to its own shores. This points up an interesting anomaly, namely, that the two great naval powers, the United States and the Soviet Union, are not the major trading nations but Japan and the West European states, which do not have strong navies, are.

D. Pacific Basin States

With the exception of Australia and New Zealand, the Pacific basin states, particularly the two politically volatile yet strategically important island nations of the Philippines and Indonesia, have severe economic and political problems. South Korea has shown a marked ability to sustain a high economic growth, but it has also undergone severe internal political stresses as President Park Chung Hee increases his autocratic control at home.

The internal politics of all these Pacific basin states have been affected by the normalization of U.S. relations with the People's Republic of China, formerly regarded as the "enemy" of these smaller states. As the "threat" began to recede, the internal politics of the Pacific basin states radically changed, as illustrated by the introduction of martial law in the Philippines by President Marcos. America has found, as did Britain in an earlier day, that parliamentary democracy based on constitutional government is a perishable export to Asia.

E. Taiwan: An Example of New Roles for Independent Small States[11]

Taiwan, governed by the Republic of China (ROC) regime, may serve as an example of the latitude of movement that smaller nations are capable of effecting in a multipolar world. Taiwan's potential importance to every balancing power in the region and the relative ease with which realignment can be made, should its government be so disposed, increases its potential options for movement and, implicitly, its value as an ally. The following are two roles that the Republic of China on Taiwan might play in the future:

- As an alternative Chinese government, the ROC remains a potential candidate, useful to those more powerful nations that are interested in having at least a "second China" to serve as (a) detractor of an *already* hostile PRC or (b) a balancing factor should the PRC *become* more hostile or fall under a dangerous Soviet influence. To the Soviet Union, Taiwan's usefulness falls under the first category, aside from the

---

11. R. B. Foster, H. A. Twitchell, and Y. L. Wu, "Taiwan: A State in Transition," SSC-IN-73-47 (Menlo Park, Calif. SRI/Strategic Studies Center, 4 September 1973).

potential military value of Taiwan and the Pescadores to the Soviet navy. To the United States and Japan, Taiwan's usefulness falls under the second category. In the case of the United States and Japan, however, the same purpose can be served if the ROC government does not insist on its claim to be the legitimate government of mainland China as long as an independent Taiwan stays outside the PRC's control.

- One long-range solution to the PRC-ROC dilemma that suggests itself as acceptable to the PRC is the two-state, one-nation concept, in which the PRC would see Taiwan as a "window" to the capitalist world in somewhat the same manner as it views Hong Kong and Macao. Thus the Mao regime (tempered with the *Realpolitik* of Chou's diplomacy) may find it advantageous to have an arms-length politico-economic-trade relationship with the capitalist West so that its domestic politics would not be "corrupted" by too many Western contacts in the Chinese mainland.

F. Multipolarity Extended: The Underdeveloped Continents

1. Africa

The United States has recognized that it cannot unilaterally provide the necessary strategic stability to the underdeveloped continents of the Southern Hemisphere. The burden of Western assistance must be shared with the West Europeans—perhaps through the European Community—and with Japan. The chronic inability of the African states to transform themselves from tribal entities into modern states means that this area will remain a potential source of internal conflict for many decades to come. Aside from the strategic importance to the West of the Horn of Africa and the growing Soviet influence over the North African states on the South Mediterranean littoral, there are no basic problems in terms of conflicts of interest between the superpowers in this region. The chances of a major nuclear confrontation in Africa are remote.

2. Latin America

Similarly, there are no basic conflicts of interest between the superpowers in Latin America. The United States has learned to live with the Cuban communist presence in the Caribbean, and has adopted a hands-off policy with respect to the Marxist regime in

Chile. While the problems of development will continue to plague both Latin America and the African nations, the prospects for significant breakthroughs in national development are certainly greater in Latin America. The growth of the Mexican and Brazilian economies represents a potential source of stability in the continent. If the politics of Argentina can be stabilized, it would be a potential source of great wealth. If capital from both Japan and Western Europe can be attracted in greater quantities to Latin America, the potential for national and regional development can be increased.

3. *The Indian Subcontinent*

In this region there are both cooperative and conflictive relations between China, Russia, and the United States. This area of the globe has plagued the United States with its unresolved civil wars, increasing problems of scarcity of resources, and inadequate food supplies. India, Pakistan, and Bangladesh, for example, with their problems of political instability inherent in all the ex-colonial Asian states, have been a continuous concern for United States policy. By his efforts to prevent India from launching total war against Pakistan during the Bangladesh crisis, President Nixon not only reinforced American relations with China but set certain limits on the expansionist dreams of the Indians, who were emboldened by support from the Soviet Union. But India's nuclear appetite may well grow if it loses confidence in the Soviet or in the American nuclear guarantee against China. Unlike Japan, India has not signed the Non-Proliferation Treaty and probably would not ratify the Treaty even if it signed. Nor has China signed or ratified the Treaty, which is India's excuse for not signing.

The situation in India typifies the domestic instability common to all the countries in this region. The Indians have not been able to establish and maintain a socio-political system capable of coping with widespread domestic poverty in an organized fashion. The problems of underdevelopment and of an uncontrolled growth of population, coupled with the interests in this region of external great powers, virtually ensure that this area will remain a potential source of conflict between the superpowers for years to come. Similar instabilities in Pakistan provide a tempting target for Soviet exploitation.

V. THE SOVIET CHALLENGES IN EUROPE: NAVAL POWER ON THE FLANKS AND NEGOTIATIONS IN THE CENTER

A. The Flanks of NATO and the Soviet Navy

The growth of Soviet naval power and its maritime fleet not only gives Russia a global reach, but more immediately exposes the northern and southern sea flanks of Western Europe. The vulnerability of Norway to Soviet naval forces based in Murmansk and operating in the Norwegian and Barents Seas is painfully obvious, as is the increased vulnerability of North German ports and Denmark to the Soviet fleet based in Kaliningrad and operating in the Baltic Sea. Of more strategic importance, however, is the Soviet naval presence in the Mediterranean, based in the Black Sea but capable of support from ports in the North African littoral. If the Soviet proposal to reopen, under international control, a widened and deepened Suez Canal capable of transitting any Soviet naval vessel (but not necessarily U.S. carriers) were to be carried out, then the Red Sea, the Persian Gulf, and the Indian Ocean might well fall under the strategic influence of the growing (both quantitatively and qualitatively) Soviet naval fleet. Europe's oil supply lifeline, as well as Japan's, would be subject to the good will or, more likely, to the interests of Russia.

The flexibility of Soviet diplomacy is further exemplified by its completely different strategy on the central front, where it is carrying out a strategy from an increasingly strong military position.

B. Soviet Negotiations and Arms Limitations in the Center[12]

A new challenge to U.S. and NATO policy-making and military planning in the central front comes from Soviet diplomatic initiatives based on an orchestrated political strategy for strategic nuclear arms limitations (SALT II), the Conference on Security and Cooperation in Europe (CSCE), Mutual Force Reduction (MFR, formerly MBFR), and bilateral treaties, particularly the Moscow treaty with the FRG. The Soviets are alert to opportunities to

---

12. This section is adapted from the author's article "Negotiations and Arms Control in Europe," *The United States and the Demands of Detente Diplomacy,* Research Monograph Series, No. 14 (Philadelphia: Foreign Policy Research Institute, May 1973), pp. 42-56.

exploit problems within the NATO Alliance that tend to fractionate
the Alliance; they will seek agreements on weapons, forces, research
and development limitations, economic trade agreements, technological transfer, and principles of relations between states that will
take advantage of existing divisive tendencies within each NATO
nation and between the states that constitute the Alliance.

C. Soviet Negotiating Strategy after SALT I

If the United States takes a narrow view of its objectives in SALT II
and does not correlate its objectives for SALT II/CSCE/MFR
negotiations with those of its principal NATO allies, several key
issues will be vulnerable to Soviet negotiating diplomacy in Europe.
The Soviet long-term objective in Western Europe is to bring about
a change in the political relations between the United States and
Western Europe. In pursuing this objective the Soviets seek to
exploit an emerging conception in Western Europe that the correlation of forces is changing as a result of U.S.-Soviet strategic parity.
The Soviets are convinced that in the long run "internal contradictions in the capitalist camp" will occur and that Soviet diplomacy
can use these contradictions to its own advantage. Thus the Soviets
are basing their policy on the premise that they can win without
war through a diplomacy that maximizes the indirect use of military forces in negotiations.

Soviet long-range strategic objectives toward NATO-Europe (and
neutral European states as well) can be summarized as follows:

- to erode U.S. will to "stay in the game" of European security
  and to encourage U.S. tendencies to withdraw forces from
  Europe;

- to erode the confidence of Western Europe in U.S. will and
  competence in all areas, including economic, trade, and
  monetary areas;

- to induce and encourage complacency in Western Europe, with
  a détente policy, leading to unilateral reduction in forces;

- to fragment the NATO Alliance and to inhibit political and
  economic integration of Western Europe, particularly the
  Common Market;

- to erode the will of individual nations to resist Soviet influence
  and to exploit anti-American attitudes (as, for example, in
  Sweden);

- to fractionate individual nations and provoke internal divisiveness (as, for example, in Italy and Yugoslavia);
- to "Finlandize" Western Europe in order eventually to incorporate Western Europe into the Soviet sphere of interest, ideally as part of the "socialist camp" under Soviet dominion.

There are four nuclear weapons issues that represent such potential, exploitable contradictions in East-West negotiations:

- the coupling of the U.S. strategic nuclear deterrent to the defense of Western Europe,
- the "nuclear free zone" issue, affecting both tactical and theater nuclear weapons, and the "no-first-use" issue,
- the forward based system (FBS) issue,
- the British and French independent nuclear deterrent issue.

D. The Decoupling Issue

The Soviets will attempt to exploit the condition of strategic parity codified in SALT I as a condition that leads to the decoupling of the U.S. strategic deterrent from the defense of NATO-Europe. The main issue here is the perception of the European allies concerning the political will of the United States to stand up to the Soviet Union in a crisis that bears on the security of Europe as a whole or on a single NATO member state. This political perception is dependent upon a psychological state of mind—a noncalculable quality—and it has irrational as well as rational elements, one of the latter being demonstrable military capabilities that are links in the chain of the extended U.S. nuclear deterrent. Two of these military capabilities—troop strength and U.S. strategic force options short of assured destruction—are discussed briefly below.

1. Troop Strength

The issue of troop strength has been most forcefully brought up by the West German government. Even the French government has raised the issue of the probable loss in confidence by the Europeans in the U.S. commitment to the defense of Europe if the United States were to withdraw troops from Germany without a reciprocal Soviet concession. This "confidence factor" itself is not a precisely calculable element. A unilateral U.S. reduction in its troop strength in Europe is self-defeating on at least three counts:

- It would lower the threshold of initial use of tactical nuclear weapons.

- It would confirm the worst fears of the Europeans: that the United States was adopting a neoisolationist policy and abandoning Europe to its own devices.

- Finally, it would encourage those Soviet planners who believe that history is going their way, and would confirm their conviction that, if they wait, the West European nations will accommodate to Soviet political hegemony under the weight of preponderant—if not decisively superior—Soviet military strength.

2. Strategic Force Options

The U.S. domestic debate over the consequences of SALT I, in which a large group argues for unilateral U.S. restraint in research and development particularly, is fertile ground for Soviet diplomacy. With no overt action on the part of the Soviet Union, the U.S. Congress has refused to deploy the NCA ABM[13] defense around Washington, D.C. or to allocate funds for accurate MIRVs, yet these actions would have been permitted under the SALT I accords. The United States' failure to take action serves as a unilateral restraint on the U.S. research and development programs for strategic nuclear forces, and this in turn inhibits the development of strategic counterforce options that are designed to couple the U.S. strategic deterrent to the defense of Europe.

E. The "Nuclear Free Zone" and the "No-First-Use" Issues

It is recognized that U.S. and European objectives in mutual force reduction negotiations are concerned with the reduction of Soviet conventional ground forces, particularly their armored divisions. But the least understood—and most difficult—negotiations are those that directly affect the relationship of forces, namely, strategic nuclear, theater nuclear (including allied nuclear), tactical nuclear, and conventional forces—both U.S. and allied and both active and reserve.

In SALT II, in MFR, or possibly in CSCE negotiations, the Soviets may make a proposal for a "nuclear free zone" in Central

---

13. "National Command Authority Anti-Ballistic Missile" defensive system deployment.

Europe, similar to the Rapacki Plan of the 1950s. This Soviet initiative would exploit the lack of a clearly defined policy in the United States for the role and utility of tactical nuclear weapons. It would also be aimed at West German fears that (1) the United States would decouple its strategic deterrent from the defense of West Germany and fight a "tactical nuclear war" (strategic to the Germans) principally on German soil, and (2) any initial use by the United States in NATO of a tactical nuclear weapon in the event of a massive Soviet conventional attack on Germany would automatically escalate to theater nuclear war, thus destroying Germany and Western Europe in the process of trying to defend them. The Soviets have already begun a propaganda campaign to convince the West Europeans (and Americans) of the virtues of their proposals to denuclearize the central front and to accept a treaty calling for a "no-first-use" of tactical nuclear weapons, thus reviving the political utility of superior Soviet conventional forces that they enjoyed in the days of the Korean War.

Yet it is evident to the Germans and other allies that the decoupling of the U.S. strategic deterrent from the defense of NATO-Europe and the removal of U.S. tactical nuclear weapons from Europe would subject Germany to Soviet coercion based on superior Soviet conventional forces.

The Soviet proposals for a "nuclear free zone" and a "no-first-use" agreement exploit existing differences within the United States and between the United States and its European NATO allies over the political value, the strategic role, and the military utility of tactical nuclear weapons. These two Soviet proposals have another built-in Soviet advantage: they discourage any attempt by the United States to make qualitative improvements in its tactical nuclear weapons and delivery systems, such as in the areas of small, controlled yields, improved accuracy, and tailored weapons effects to minimize collateral damage. Parallel Soviet diplomatic initiatives could be taken to increase U.S. domestic pressures for a Comprehensive Test Ban (CTB) treaty, which would bring to a halt all improvements for both strategic and tactical nuclear weapons.

Neither the United States nor its principal NATO allies are prepared to negotiate such critical issues as a "nuclear free zone" and a "no-first-use" treaty with the Soviet Union. Far more study and consultation are required before any unified allied position on these issues can be expected to emerge. These issues require

West-West negotiations first, before East-West negotiations can be conducted in a spirit of partnership.

F. The Forward Based System (FBS) Issue

For over a decade the Soviet Union has consistently raised the forward based system issue. In the Soviet statement of 1 July 1968 concerning "some urgent matters" on arms control, the Soviet government reiterated the importance of forward based systems. On 1 June 1972 a Soviet spokesman announced that SALT II should closely follow SALT I, "in order to maintain the momentum generated by the Summit."[14] The spokesman went on to say that although no agenda had been fixed for the next round, Soviet officials "would like SALT II to deal with long-range strategic bombers, aircraft carriers and forward based systems, meaning American tactical fighter bombers based in Europe."[15] No mention was made of Soviet medium-range missiles aimed at Europe.

During the SALT I negotiations the Soviet Union defined a strategic weapon as one that could reach the homeland of either side. The issue of the definition of strategic forces in Europe has profound implications for reciprocal force reductions. The Soviets do not consider their IRBMs, MRBMs, and medium-range bombers as strategic weapons, since they are not designed to reach the U.S. homeland. Yet U.S. nuclear-armed tactical aircraft based in Europe (mostly in West Germany) are counted by the Soviet Union as U.S. strategic means of delivery.

At this phase the FBS issue should not be discussed in U.S.-Soviet negotiations. Like the issues of the "nuclear free zone" and "no-first-use," the FBS issue involves a problem requiring resolution of contradictory views within the United States and between members of the Alliance.

G. The British and French Nuclear Deterrent Issue

The issue of effective British and French nuclear deterrents is not yet resolved in terms of U.S. policies. We are unclear whether we should encourage British-French nuclear cooperation, whether it is in our interest to involve the British and French in our own strategic force planning, and whether the SALT II negotiations

---

14. See the *Washington Post* article by Marilyn Berger (2 June 1972).
15. *Ibid.*

and/or the CSCE should include discussions of the British and French nuclear forces. The Soviets have insisted that the British and French strategic forces, particularly the nine Polaris-type submarines that are currently scheduled for deployment, be counted as part of the U.S. strategic forces. Again, this should be resolved in discussions between the United States and its allies before it is included in negotiations with the Soviet Union.

VI. NEEDED: A U.S.-ALLIED "GRAND STRATEGY"

A. Dangers of Euphoria

Henry Kissinger recently described the SALT II negotiations as one of the most challenging intellectual problems of our time. It is certain the United States will not soon nor easily "solve" the four interrelated arms control issues described in the previous section. The euphoria already created in the Western democracies by the current détente atmosphere as a result of the SALT I accords—not to mention the FRG-Soviet Moscow Treaty, the agreement to hold a CSCE next spring, and the most recent U.S.-Soviet agreement to discuss MFR at the same time—makes it difficult, however, to retain the strength of the West's bargaining position with the Soviet Union. And no amount of intellectual effort can replace elements of U.S. power that are unilaterally thrown away. The aim of the arms control negotiations is to improve the security of all concerned—the United States, the European nations, and the Soviet Union. The cause of mutual security and peace is not advanced if one side obtains an advantage in the balance of power because the other party forfeits major elements of its power. The confidence of the United States' European allies in U.S. competence and political will is eroded by such U.S. actions which reflect an obsolete view of national sovereignty. We need to husband every element of our power for purposes of bargaining with the Soviets if we are to retain, much less increase, the security that we and the West Europeans now enjoy.

B. Strategic Military Planning and Arms Control

Before any single military force element can be considered as a candidate for East-West arms control negotiations, the United States and its allies need to clarify in West-West negotiations their policies and military doctrines concerning the relationship of these various military forces that make up the links in the chain of deterrence. One thing that should not be considered as negotiable, however, is the legitimacy of the U.S. security interests and presence in Europe.

There is a tendency in the West to postpone planning for military forces and armaments once negotiations on arms limitation and disarmament have begun. Yet the two—arms and arms limitation— are complementary. An effective arms control and arms limitation strategy must be complemented by a corresponding policy for the development of force postures and weaponry. Arms control considerations heavily influence the qualitative characteristics of those forces and weapons. A clearer idea of the political objectives and the military missions of the U.S. and allied forces in the central front is needed. Military force objectives have usually been stated in purely military, or in quantified cost-effectiveness terms, without sufficient attention to political objectives and often diverse military missions. One of the most difficult tasks for U.S. planners associated with future military forces and nuclear weapons based in Europe is the re-examination of the basic mission of those forces in light of future political objectives. For example, one of the primary missions of the U.S. forces in Europe is to enhance the will of the NATO allies to resist Soviet coercion and to give those allies a sense of security that underpins their long-range political and economic planning in intra-European institutions. Another aim is to ensure that the U.S. nuclear guarantee continues to have meaning so that basic U.S. national security policies such as nuclear proliferation will continue to be viable.

C. Prospects for the Future

The 1960s saw the maturation of American power. The limits of U.S. power were learned in Vietnam; Americans learned that there was a limit to the exploitation of natural resources and the pollution of the land and waters of the continent; they learned from the monetary crises and devaluations of the dollar that there were limits to the strength of the U.S. economy in the global arena. But in learning these limits, Americans did not lose their confidence and did not retreat to a nuclear fortress America. Rather, they saw the need to return to an earlier vision of America's role in the world, that of making the world safe for democracies *without* attempting to impose democratic regimes on all nations of the earth.

What is needed in this new international milieu is indeed a new vision of international order. This vision can be energized not only by the fear of the destructiveness of nuclear war, but also by the positive vision of a pluralist, multipolar international system in which each nation pursues its self-interests within the limits imposed on all nations. In the past it had been assumed that the Monroe Doctrine gave the United States the right to exclude any "foreign" social system from the Western Hemisphere. Certainly the acceptance of Castro's Cuban regime by the United States is an indication that the Monroe Doctrine is viewed with a new realism.

At the same time, the pursuit of independent foreign policies in East European states, as in Romania, and even independent economic and social systems, as in Yugoslavia, indicates that Soviet dominion in that region is weakening. The guarantee of security of the Soviet Union can no longer be based on the hegemony of the Soviets over their East European neighbors.

The Conference on Security and Cooperation in Europe gives the United States an opportunity to take the lead in enunciating the great principles that will underlie the new international politics designed to prevent all-out nuclear war. These principles will certainly include at least the principles of the nonuse of force to change national boundaries and the encouragement of trade and technological exchange between all nations, whether members of economic blocs or independent neutral states. The West-West negotiations in preparation for the CSCE should concentrate on reaching agreement on these principles.

It is clear that President Nixon continues to place Europe and NATO at the top of American foreign policy priorities. The thought expressed by Henry Kissinger, long before he became President Nixon's chief foreign policy advisor, continues to be valid for the new milieu: "If Eurasia were to be dominated by a hostile power or a group of powers, we would confront an overwhelming threat, and the key to Eurasia is Western Europe, because its loss would bring with it the loss of the Middle East and the upheaval of Africa."[16]

D. Force Posture Implications of the New International Politics

The Nixon Doctrine defense posture is based upon the concept of the indivisibility of deterrence of attacks on either the United

---

16. Henry Kissinger, *Nuclear Weapons and Foreign Policy* (New York: Harper, 1957), pp. 269-270.

States or its allies. Therefore, a balanced force structure of strategic and theater nuclear weapons and adequate conventional capabilities is required.[17] Strategic, theater, and conventional capabilities must be coupled so that the role of strategic weapons will not be limited to mass destruction. U.S. and allied forces must be linked in an operational sense, and not merely added up on a balance sheet of free world forces. The goal is deterrence of conflict at all levels, and a readiness to act if deterrence fails.

To implement such a defense posture, forces should be designed that can terminate conflict rapidly and enable participants to reach negotiating thresholds where options other than escalation to all-out nuclear conflict exist. This concept is consistent with the necessity described earlier in this paper to supplant the historical condition of mutual assured destruction by a political concept of mutual assured survival and security (MASS). If deterrence were to fail, requirements for war termination call for force options short of massive destruction of cities. Notable among those options are tactical nuclear forces based on the most advanced technology available for precise delivery on military targets and a simultaneous minimization of collateral damage. In Europe as well as in other theaters, the timely, flexible response of U.S. and allied forces to attacks on the Alliance has the objective of deterring (preventing) such attacks or quickly terminating the conflict should deterrence fail.

There are four general principles regarding the NATO force posture that can be drawn from the interpretation of the Nixon Doctrine presented in the preceding pages. These principles for the design of the NATO force may also be applicable in the long run to the design of the Warsaw Pact forces and might eventually be acceptable to the Soviet Union.

- NATO policy should be to provide a valid sense of military security in Western Europe without unduly inhibiting constructive political, economic, and other Western initiatives toward and negotiations with Eastern Europe and the Soviet Union. (This was stated in the first section of this paper.)
- More explicitly, NATO's policy to defend Europe should be based on deterring any war with the Soviet Union in Western

---

17. M. R. Laird, *Defense Department Report FY 1973*, p. 24.

Europe. If deterrence fails, the goal is to terminate war without advantage to either side and without enlarging the scope of the war or prolonging it.

- The NATO force posture should be developed so that it will appear to the Soviet Union to be clearly in line with the defensive nature of the NATO Alliance and not designed for pre-emptive offensive operations.

- The NATO force posture should be designed for endurance over the long haul, and not based on an expectation of fundamental convergence of the two systems. NATO policy should encourage a political settlement between the United States and Western Europe on the one hand, and the Soviet Union and Eastern Europe on the other.

The implications of the Nixon Doctrine for the U.S. force posture in Asia and other areas where the United States has vital interests are conceptually similar to the principles stated above, although in these other regions there would be a greater emphasis on sea and air forces. The Nixon Doctrine stresses initial reliance on an indigenous ground force response to internal or external aggression. U.S. ground units must be ready, however, to respond where U.S. interests and the urgency of the situation require military action. Close coordination is required among U.S. land, sea, and air forces, and in turn close cooperation is required between the American and indigenous forces. The doctrine of rapid conflict termination requires some limited capability for rapid and early response in situations short of general war.

A minimum network of overseas bases remains essential for forward deployment. The trend seems to be toward joint basing rights, both for political purposes and to encourage U.S.-allied cooperation. The principles of partnership and burden-sharing imply that regional security groupings of free world nations should be encouraged to enhance a regional sense of security, responsibility, and capability.

Overall, the military planning implications of the Nixon Doctrine must be interpreted with the understanding that the new American foreign policy was designed to cope with a time of transition as well as with the longer term. Today's security requirements are much more complex than they were in the cold war era. The new requirement, as recognized by President Nixon and Dr. Kissinger, is to orchestrate all the elements of national strength—political, economic, technological, social, psychological, as well as military—into an effective, total political power for peace.

E. Needed: A "Grand Strategy" for the West

The West has many advantages over the Soviet-style communist system. The political appeal, economic productivity, technological inventiveness, and social mobility of the free, open societies of the West are greatly feared by the Soviet leadership. The current repression of Russian intellectuals and dissident political critics is evidence of this fear. If we in the West learn to coordinate these positive elements of our national power—such as our economic, technological, psychological, and political advantages over the Soviet Union—we will be less dependent on raw military power for our security. The era of "peaceful coexistence" in a multipolar world faces the Soviets with a form of containment that has grown from natural historical causes. The dialectical movement of history will favor those nations whose political aims can be achieved without recourse to war and who have earned and will defend their own independence and freedom.

U.S.-European Economic Issues in the East-West Politico-Military Context

N. R. Danielian

I. POLITICAL PERCEPTIONS

A cynic once remarked that "economics and politics are the seamy sides of one another." In this paper I have been asked to address both of them in what we might call the "West-West" context, and to relate them to the East-West dimension generally and with specific reference to defense.

The trouble with such geopolitical (or, as is becoming fashionable in Washington, such geo-economic) terminology as "East-West" is that it is essentially two dimensional. Actually we almost need a third dimension to describe the multilevel, multipolar world power structure that is emerging. For example, the United States finds itself involved in a number of triangular relationships of great importance:

- with Western Europe, on the whole question of defense and détente vis-à-vis the Soviet Union;
- with Russia, and to a lesser extent China, and also with certain European allies, in the responsibility for managing strategic nuclear power;
- with Russia and China, and also Japan, on questions of security in Indochina and the Far East generally;
- with the enlarged West European community and Japan in economic cooperation—and competition.

In addition to these overlapping and sometimes conflicting relationships, the United States also has important bilateral and multilateral ties with the rest of the world—Latin America, Asia, the Middle East, Africa, and Eastern Europe.

America finds itself in a period of transition in a number of these important relationships: from confrontation to conciliation, vis-à-vis the two large communist powers; from unlimited worldwide involvement to the more restricted role implied by the Nixon Doctrine; from a preoccupation with political and military affairs to a newfound concern for economic and financial challenges abroad and social changes at home; and, in its self-image, from omniscience to uncertainty. This flux of change does not make it any easier to talk intelligently about U.S.-European relationships.

Europe, in turn, is going through a period of self-examination and tends to be egocentric with the problems of enlargement and restructuring of its own institutional framework. "Europe," however we define it, has yet to develop a global perspective, although, whether consciously or unconsciously, the European communities are extending their "special relationships" from the North Sea to the Mediterranean, and from the African associates to the Caribbean. Except for worrying about Japanese competition and seeking to get in on the ground floor of Chinese trade, Europe's preoccupations have been mostly with the Soviet Union and Eastern Europe.

Even the increasingly critical reliance on Mideast oil has not led to any kind of a concerted policy toward the Arab OPEC countries. There is not a glimmer of a cohesive European policy toward Latin America, the Indian subcontinent, or the Far East. But the United States still has interests, responsibilities, and commitments in these areas, which is one reason why the costs of our continuing involvement in European defense, and defense of Europe's oil lifeline, are an increasingly controversial issue in and out of Congress.

If, as someone has said, the only certain thing one can say about the future is that it is inevitable, the *kind* of a future we are going to have for our children is by no means predetermined. Much depends on whether a broad international consensus can be reached about the type of future those of us in the developed world want to have. While it may be difficult to get agreement on precise definitions of what we want, it should not be too difficult to agree on what we would like to *avoid*.

For example, virtually no sizable group that I know of anywhere in the Atlantic world would opt for a Soviet-style state socialist system, whether under the dominance of Moscow or local copies thereof. Even the radicals of today find the traditional socialist-communist approach to an economic and political system outmoded. Ideology apart, I would assume that there would be no substantial vote for a system, whatever its nature, which was effectively controlled by or dependent on Soviet Russia—or China, or Japan, or even the United States, for that matter.

For another example, although the mercantilist nation-state concept seems to have a long half-life, I doubt whether very many people would cast an explicit vote for a return to the nineteenth century system of competing national politico-military-economic entities, each pursuing "beggar-thy-neighbor" policies. Economic nationalism, as well as national socialism, has become outmoded, by force of technological development.

One could, of course, go still further back in history to many models built on the concept of empire. If the Roman model is not suitable, what about that of Charlemagne, which, after all, covered what is now the heart of the Common Market? Kaiser Wilhelm and Adolph Hitler tried it too, in my own lifetime, with unhappy results. The imperial system would appear to offer little to us in the late twentieth century.

By default, then, if not by design, we appear to be reaching toward a system of regional federalisms: the one being slowly built here in Europe; that already constructed in North America, with Canada as a not always "silent" partner to the United States; that which may come to exist, in fact as well as theory, in Russia, and to a lesser extent among the COMECON countries of Europe. LAFTA

and the Andean Code countries are also haltingly moving toward
regional integration. By virtue of its enormous economic power and
potential, Japan is becoming almost a "bloc" unto itself, not
unwilling to extend its "Co-prosperity Sphere" by economic
penetration into other parts of Asia.

What are the outlines of a desirable system of relationships
among these various groupings? We presumably want these regional
entities to conduct their economic intercourse on a basis of the
maximum possible freedom of movement of goods, services,
technology, capital, people, and ideas; we want them to collaborate
in improving the lot of the two-thirds of humanity that still lives in
a condition for which underdevelopment is, at best, a euphemism;
and we want them to conduct their mutual relationships without
force or threat of force and with a maximum of collaboration on
the common problems affecting their societies.

Whether such noble objectives can be obtained, even in part,
depends on how Europe and America—and Japan—manage their
mutual relationships and whether their policies toward Russia and
China encourage or inhibit the slow evolution of their leadership
toward a constructive exercise of international responsibility in
economic, as well as political and military, affairs.

II. ECONOMIC FRICTIONS

Against that background of a blueprint for common survival, let us
then look at the current areas of friction in U.S.-West European
economic relations.

In part, we are dealing here with a conflict of concave and
convex mirror images of each other. The American image is that the
United States helped a weak and divided Europe recover from the
ravages of war to maintain its independence against what was then
perceived as a clear and present danger from the East. As President
Nixon once put it, the United States felt that it had survived the
war with all the "chips" and had to pass them around so that others
could play the international economic game. We have been passing
these chips around for almost three decades. From across the
Atlantic, Europe looks wealthy and powerful with an increasingly
united economy. Americans are therefore asking themselves
whether artificial currency values, the lack of reciprocity in certain
trading relations, and a disproportionate sharing of the defense
burden are not being maintained too long. Internal problems and
currency crises have reinforced this feeling of "enough is enough."

Europeans, however, still look at us as reflected in a convex mirror, fat and opulent. From the European perspective, I am sure it is difficult to see how a group of middle-sized countries trying to find their way through a tight maze of internal and regional problems could appear as an economic threat to anyone. They look at themselves in a concave mirror, lean and lonely. There is a feeling of neglect, even of betrayal, in the apparent changes in attitude by the world's wealthiest country, which they had once looked upon as a fairy godmother in economics and a father figure in defense. Americans are in the process of cutting their own image down to size, and this process encourages them to see themselves—and to act—more like other countries in looking after their own interests. It is taking too long, perhaps by ten years, for Europeans and Americans to see themselves as they are, in a flat ordinary mirror.

These conflicting perceptions have led to a number of disputes. The issues discussed below are some of those involved.

A. EEC Enlargement

Europe of the Six may have made sense in political terms, but some of us have always wondered about the economic impact on the United States. Nevertheless, the U.S. Government has long been on record as urging the inclusion of Britain. Thus from Six, or Seven, the Europe of the Nine is now a fact; and it came into being as the U.S. position in the world economy changed for the worse, as reflected in the chronic and growing American balance-of-payments deficits. The Nine has now engaged in a kind of shotgun wedding—or at least arrangements for cohabitation—with most of the other members of EFTA. It is also developing association agreements with a number of key Mediterranean countries: Spain, Greece, and Morocco, for example. And it has allowed the entire eighteen members of the Yaoundé Convention certain preferential treatment in trade. It is offering the same preferences to the twenty-one developing Commonwealth countries. Even if this is responsiveness to the pleas of others, some of them legitimate, rather than aggrandizement for its own sake, the effect on outsiders is the same: trade discrimination. The volume of the trade of these countries may be relatively small, but the Community's existing reciprocal trade preferences with thirty-six countries—some of which call for "reverse preferences," meaning special treatment for the EEC's exports to them—cannot help but be an issue.

The United States is seeking authority in the new trade bill to give the type of generalized preferences to developing countries which the EEC already is giving; this may help remove this particular bone of contention from the list of issues if the European Community gives up its reverse preferences.

B. Agricultural Trade

Probably the single most divisive source of economic friction between the United States and the EEC is the Common Agricultural Policy. The United States seeks a rational development of world agriculture on a basis of comparative advantage, and the advantage of the United States lies strongly in its productive, technologically modernized agricultural sector. The European Community, for varied political and social reasons, created an agricultural program based on high price supports and consequent high consumer food prices, which has caused overproduction of many commodities and has served to exclude or sharply limit imports of many agricultural goods.

The limitation of agricultural imports has been conducted through the so-called variable levy, which effectively removes whatever price advantage exists in the landed cost of agricultural goods subject to it. It negates also any price advantage of dollar devaluation. As a consequence, the value of U.S. shipments to the EEC of six of the goods subject to the variable levy decreased absolutely from 1964 to 1972, from $499 million to $461 million. By contrast, U.S. shipments of agricultural goods *not* subject to the levy grew from $834 million to $1,430 million in the same period, a growth caused primarily by oilseed and oilseed products exports, for which the EEC has a zero duty bound in GATT. Occasionally the EEC threatens even this sector of agricultural trade with enormous internal taxes.

The United States has rights under GATT to seek compensatory adjustments for any trade discrimination or duties incurred as a result of the enlargement of the Community. Extension of the Common Agricultural Policy to the three new member countries will cause major harm to an important U.S. export market. The three are import markets for some ten million tons of grain yearly. (If they had retained their previously bound tariffs, it is thought that they would have grown to fifteen million tons in the next five years.)

With the application of the variable levy, high internal price supports, and consequent increased domestic production, these grain markets will be largely lost to the traditional suppliers, costing them about $800 million annually, over a third of which would be lost by the United States. Nevertheless, the initial position of the Community has been to deny that any harm had been or would be suffered by the United States because the average level of *industrial* tariffs in the Community would be lower than those previously in force in the three new members, and lower than the United States itself imposes.[1]

By and large the Common Agricultural Policy acts against the broader interest of the peoples of the EEC, who pay for it in food prices well over world levels. The Community is trying to reduce the number of marginal farmers through attrition, instead of through competitive pressures. In an era in which the United States is experiencing great difficulties in achieving a balance-of-payments equilibrium, to the detriment of world monetary stability and perhaps even a continued growth of world trade, it seems especially inappropriate for the EEC to obstinately hold to a policy that works against both its own domestic interests and world stability.

Whatever the political difficulties of change, it remains a fact that the system chosen by the Community is "a flagrant violation of both the spirit and the letter of GATT."[2] It should not be beyond the capability of enlightened leadership to phase out this system over a period of years, and meanwhile to help control European inflation by special agricultural access agreements for external supplies and by treating the social problem of marginal farmers through direct adjustment or income maintenance payments. What the European loses as a taxpayer he would more than recover as a consumer!

C. Nontariff Barriers

As tariffs come to have a reduced importance to trade, nontariff trade barriers (NTBs) are correspondingly becoming more significant, and more controversial. The major European Commu-

---

1. This is true, however, only when Europe's low raw materials tariff is used to offset the slightly lower U.S. tariffs on finished manufactures. The overall industrial average in the EEC is lower than in the United States by only a percentage point and could hardly be considered compensatory for the loss of agricultural markets.

2. This is not an American slogan; rather it is a statement from an off-the-record discussion with a senior GATT official who, while equally critical of some American policies, said he was so dedicated to the principles of his organization that he had to "call a spade a spade."

nity examples are the Common Agricultural Policy and the border tax adjustments of the TVA; other European nontariff barriers are generally set by the individual countries and not, as yet, by the EEC as a whole. The border tax problem is especially difficult, rooted as it is in different national tax policies. The United States does not seem likely to adopt a national sales tax at all, let alone in a degree commensurate with the EEC's practice. Consequently, it cannot engage in similar rebates of sales taxes on exports. Nonetheless, despite its program of rebating the TVA for exporters, the EEC has chosen to protest the U.S. DISC program, which defers U.S. income taxes on exports. (The discriminatory effect of border taxes depends on the degree to which direct taxation of industry, as in the United States, is passed on to the consumer, a degree that varies with each industry and is thus hard to deal with in international agreements.)

Other nontariff trade barriers, imposed by the individual countries in the EEC—such as quotas, discriminatory purchasing programs, compulsory import licensing, labeling and health and safety requirements—also pose a difficult problem, because in many cases they have been instituted for reasons other than protectionism, although they often serve protectionist functions as well. The United States is certainly not blameless in this respect, and imposes a number of health or safety inspection requirements on foreign producers. Europeans also often cite the "American Selling Price" system of valuation for certain chemicals as an American NTB. Perhaps the greatest hope for the panoply of small, trade-distorting, nontariff barriers is greater international coordination in setting and applying standards, and a greater spirit of cooperativeness on the part of those countries experiencing trade surpluses yet still maintaining some unnecessary NTBs. GATT has identified some 800 varieties of NTBs, so this subject is obviously too complex to explore in any detail.

D. Japanese Competition

America also feels that the EEC has been unduly restrictive with respect to Japanese exports, particularly consumer goods. And Europe, I suspect, believes that the United States has been seeking to direct the formidable Japanese export penetration toward Europe and away from itself. One justly wonders whether GATT and the principles of unconditional most-favored-nation treatment were written only for the benefit of Europe.

E. The Energy "Crisis"

European, Japanese, and American interests also overlap and perhaps conflict with respect to their mutual growing dependence on petroleum imports, pending the development of nuclear and other alternatives. The European Community imports over $12.6 billion of petroleum supplies, Japan over $3.5 billion, and the United States may go up from $4.9 billion in 1972 to nearly $9 billion worth in 1973 as a result of the liberalized import policy. They may, therefore, compete for supplies and over prices, particularly if OPEC maintains an effective producers' cartel. They are also going to be competing for the foreign exchange with which to buy the oil, both through exports and in attracting the oil sheiks' "petro-dollar" investments to their own areas. Whether forums and topics of fruitful collaboration to mitigate the inherent conflicts can be developed among Europe, Japan, and the United States remains to be seen.

F. International Finance

In addition to these trade issues, there are longer-range problems of investment and of cooperation on international financial and monetary matters. Some observers have warned of the danger that the EEC, in its development of new industrial and technological policies, might discriminate against U.S. investment interests in Europe by limiting government procurement, subsidy, or other "rationalization" programs to "European" firms and excluding firms affiliated with American-based companies. Such a step backward, away from the "national" treatment of foreign investments—which the United States does give, by and large, to all foreign investors—would prove undesirable in the long run for all concerned.

Another problem is the proliferation of exchange and capital controls throughout Europe, controls born of short-term necessity during the onslaughts of speculation in recent years, but controls which also will adversely affect the rational development of economic activity in Europe, by both strictly European and multinational firms alike. The OECD is working on a revised Code of Liberalization of Capital Movements, a subject deserving priority attention and implementation as soon as sufficient monetary stability is restored.

G. Multinational Companies

A word needs to be said about the multinational corporation which is increasingly cast as a "villain" in many parts of the world. The AFL-CIO in the United States terms it "a modern-day dinosaur which eats your jobs"; it is called an instrument of American imperialism in Latin America; Europeans sometimes refer to the "Coca-Colonization" of their continent. In fact, the MNCs' most eager partners at the moment may be the communists!

While I do not support everything that is done by or in the name of the multinational corporations, many of the allegations against them are based on misinformation, some undoubtedly propagated in a search for scapegoats. Study after study has shown that the American multinational corporations are, in the aggregate, helpful to the U.S. balance of payments and employment, and their favorable contribution to the economies of their host countries is also often overlooked. They are, in fact, a vehicle for the efficient use of resources on a global basis, and the notion that they are somehow beyond the control of governments ignores the fact that they are subject to the jurisdiction of towns, states, regions, nations, and international treaties everywhere they operate.

Also, they are all too frequently identified in the public mind as an American phenomenon; in fact, of the world's ten largest chemical companies, to take one example, only three are American and seven are European (three German and one each British, Dutch, French, and Italian).

The role of the MNCs is too complex a subject for extended discussion here, but such problems as may exist need to be examined dispassionately and on the basis of fact, not emotionalism or self-defeating nationalism. Any misunderstanding in Europe that leads to frontal attacks on American investments and multinational enterprises will have incalculable consequences in political, perhaps even military, collaboration.

H. The U.S. Balance of Payments

All these problems have as a common denominator the critical condition of the U.S. balance of payments. Our organization has specialized in this subject, and it is no satisfaction that our gloomy predictions have been proved correct over a period of many years. The facts speaks for themselves.[3]

3. This material draws on IEPA's book, *The United States Balance of Payments: From Crisis to Controversy* (Washington, D.C., 1972; Walker and Company distributors, 720 Fifth Avenue, New York, New York 10019).

- Although the incredible liquidity deficit of nearly $23 billion in 1971 recovered in 1972, the basic balance remained at the intolerable level of nearly $10 billion notwithstanding the currency realignment.

- As U.S. reserve assets declined and liquid liabilities grew, the central bank reserves of West Germany and Japan skyrocketed.

- Until the massive decline in the U.S. trade balance in 1971, the deficits were entirely incurred in the governmental or public sector; all activities in the private sector—including capital outflows and tourism—were in surplus, although not enough to offset the government deficit.

- By 1971, with the single exception of a tiny private sector surplus in miscellaneous services, only the direct investment account was in surplus. Everything else—merchandise trade, tourism, other investment, military, government grants and loans—was in deficit.

- U.S. foreign direct investment outflows have been erroneously blamed as a cause of the U.S. problem; the income from these investments, including royalties and fees, has exceeded the outflow substantially in every year since 1960. Many European officials and economists are completely misinformed on this point. They still blame U.S. direct investments for the payments deficits.

- By geographic area, the United States was in basic balance deficit with virtually the entire world in 1971 and 1972. The surplus which the United States formerly had with Western Europe has turned into a deficit. In 1971 it was second only to that with Japan; the improvement in 1972 was due to capital flows exclusively. As indicated later on, a sizable part of this deficit is on the military account; another major portion is in tourism and, as of 1972, in merchandise trade, where there had been a surplus of $2 billion as recently as 1970! It is surprising that so many presumably well-informed Europeans still talk about their "deficit" with the United States as though this were a fact instead of history!

- Although U.S. agricultural exports have been rising (to nearly a quarter of U.S. total exports) there have been wide fluctuations by commodities. One is struck here by the continuous rise in the one commodity, oilseeds, not covered by Japanese quotas or the European variable levy, and the drop in feedgrains and wheat when the CAP went into effect.

These rough highlights disguise another international payments phenomenon, that of circular flows. Although much U.S. bilateral aid is now tied to U.S. procurement, the increasing funds channeled through multilateral institutions are not, and aid to India, for example, comes from the U.S. public sector and often finds its way back through European or Japanese suppliers to their central banks. The same is true of U.S. military expenses in the Far East.

Accompanying and a very significant part of the steady deterioration in the U.S. balance of payments has been a rapid increase of imports to the U.S. market. In fact, merchandise imports tripled in less than a decade, while U.S. exports only doubled. The "swing" on the merchandise trade account with the EEC of Six plus Britain has amounted to $1 billion just from 1971 to 1972; so it should not be surprising that Americans feel that Europe *is* a part of the problem and that it must either cooperate in helping the United States find the solution or be prepared to live with the consequences.

The consequences are: added inflationary pressures in Europe as the U.S. deficit dollars pour into central banks and are exchanged for local currencies, an enormous and destabilizing overhang of $82 billion in U.S. liquid liabilities, an unavoidable lack of convertibility for the dollars held abroad, and recurrent international currency crises and speculative forays. Another consequence will be a strong economic and political impetus toward American military disengagement from Europe, and toward protectionism.

The meaning of all this is that the U.S. dollar, now unpegged from the Bretton Woods system, is "devaluable" like any other currency. To the extent that this permits greater accommodation of exchange rates to market forces, this may be good; but it means that the United States, like any other country, must now live under the international discipline of the balance-of-payments mechanism.

It is the fond hope of many classical economists, as well as just plain optimists, that the two recent devaluations of the dollar (amounting to 16.5 percent on a weighted basis), plus the prospect of further depreciation of the dollar, if needed, through flexible exchange rates, will rectify the situation. Obviously, these changes will help; but they cannot and will not solve the problem. A careful look at the composition of the U.S. balance of payments reveals, as noted earlier, that the deficits continue to be almost two-thirds in the public sector, and here devaluation hurts rather than helps. For example, the cost of U.S. troops in Europe in balance-of-payments terms has gone up by almost 25 percent in the last two years due to currency adjustments. So has U.S. Government interest payments on its obligations abroad. Also, the cost of the essential raw materials and petroleum, which must be imported from abroad in ever-increasing quantities, has risen sharply.

In other trade commodities, the elasticity or price sensitivity has proved to be far less than commonly supposed, and the well-known "perverse" initial effect of devaluation may continue for quite a long time before quantities are affected sufficiently to offset the added costs. Even in areas where the classical theory may apply, the opportunities for expanded exports may be restricted by various nontariff barriers such as the variable levy in Europe or Japanese quotas. In still others, the United States is, in effect, a sole or residual supplier and cannot sell more because of cheaper prices for foreigners, and a number of other substantial markets have devalued their own currencies along with the dollar.

Finally, to the extent that exchange rates *do* have the desired effect on the U.S. balance, other countries will adopt measures to limit this effect. The French two-tier exchange rate system denies the United States the full advantage of devaluation in improving its exports. The proliferation of capital controls in Europe is another example. Thus the present or any future devaluations cannot be regarded as a panacea. It is doubtful that "equilibrium exchange rates" can be reached via market forces without unacceptable consequences for the United States and other countries as well, especially the holders of our dollars, unless the United States undertakes, with the help of other countries, to restore a basic discipline in its payments structure.

The Vietnamese war was certainly no more popular in Europe than in the United States; as it hopefully draws to a close, however, the Europeans no longer can use the excuse that they do not wish to help the United States finance its ill-advised foreign adventures. Moreover, the very substantial economic aid that the United States has committed itself to supply in Indochina will prevent significant improvement in the balance of payments.

Many of these issues will come to a specific negotiating focus in the next year or two, and the President's proposed trade bill seeks the authority to enable him to negotiate effectively both bilaterally and multilaterally on the wide range of specific problems necessary to restore the U.S. balance of trade and payments. He is also seeking unilateral authority to impose temporary restrictions against products or countries which discriminate unfairly against the United States or where trade deficits prove too intractable. I suspect that the President is going to get much, if not all, of the authority he is requesting, and that its application will not always be a pleasant experience for other countries.

But the alternative is almost certainly worse; for without this approach there is a very good chance that Congress would enact highly protectionist legislation involving mandatory and permanent quotas of the kind proposed, for example, in the so-called Hartke-Burke bill. This would have the effect of limiting U.S. imports by at least $12 billion, and other countries might retaliate, initiating an economic escalation that could end in a worldwide recession—if not, indeed, another depression.

The European view often expressed by Common Market officials is that, in effect, the status quo is satisfactory to them, but that if the United States wishes to negotiate they will do so on a "reciprocal and balanced" basis as long as there are symmetrical results. The problem with this attitude is that the magnitude of the U.S. difficulties requires an asymmetrical result, at least in the short term, if equilibrium is to be restored. One can only hope that the European political leaders will take a farsighted and strategic view of this problem. For the status quo is simply not tenable in the long run for anyone.

III. THE COMMON DEFENSE

The common defense of the Atlantic Community is now deeply involved in these problems of economics, because the U.S. commitment to NATO costs money, therefore affecting its budget and rate of inflation, and because it generates foreign exchange expenditures, and hence is a substantial factor in its balance-of-payments deficits. Of course, there have always been issues about the optimum strategy for NATO in the light of its resources, on the quality as well as the quantity of the contribution from various countries—including the United States during the Vietnam drain—and over matters of nuclear control. Many of them are covered in detail in other papers for this conference; in any case, it would not be appropriate for me to address this knowledgeable audience on this subject.

It is often said that NATO is a victim of its own success in having turned Russia away from confrontation and toward negotiation—on strategic arms limitation, on "European security," on balanced and mutual force reductions, and on a variety of economic matters. Even among the experts attending this conference there are probably differences of view about the so-called threat from the East. The pessimists undoubtedly feel that as long as the Soviet Union maintains formidable military capabilities which could be employed or credibly threatened against Western Europe, NATO must keep its military deterrent and defenses, and its political confidence in them. Others would argue that the military ingredient is still important in an international balance of power, and that the maintenance of a stalemate which makes the employment of military force counterproductive is an important influence on future Soviet intentions. Still others would add that détente is by no means an irreversible process and that, in a relatively totalitarian system, leadership and policies can change overnight.

My own view is that while there is undoubtedly some truth in the foregoing, ever since the Soviet Union has achieved a sufficient deterrent of its own to make a Hitler-like thrust to its security improbable, the real nature of Soviet ambitions has been economic and political rather than military, at least in Western Europe.

The Soviet leadership offers two basic promises to its own citizenry as well as those of its satellites: security against external (German and Chinese) invasion, and economic advancement—better production and distribution of wealth.

It has, in fact, delivered on the first promise. With its nuclear deterrence—some would say preponderance—it is unthinkable that there can ever be a 1914 or 1941 type of invasion of Soviet territory.

The Soviet system, though it has improved the lot of its people measurably since Tsarist times, has not yet been able to elevate its productive plant, technology, and production and distribution to levels comparable to the West. This, then, is their second, and most immediate, objective, witness the worldwide campaign and unabashed concessions they are willing to make to obtain credits, technology, and most-favored-nation treatment. It is ironic that communist systems from Peking to Moscow depend on help from the hated capitalist systems for their success. What makes this game dangerous is the certainty that they are not averse to using military (overt or subversive) pressures to achieve their economic aims. Economics has supplanted ideology for the time being as the operative impulse, but it has not rendered military technology completely obsolescent as an international factor. Let us then discuss the ways in which the Soviet Union can utilize the existing conflicts in the Western world to its advantage.

The absolute control which a centralized state trading economy has over its own market, and its ability to give specially favorable terms to customers or suppliers, gives it significant bargaining leverage, particularly in dealings with competing nations and enterprises. We have seen this happen in continually liberalized terms of credit, export of technology, and flagrantly favored treatment of "old" friends. You can not really blame them, but the old adage applies: "Buyer beware"!

The COMECON countries can and have offered to serve as an assembly line for Western Europe in some industrial components, pointing out quite frankly that what they have to offer is "cheap labor." You can imagine the future political turmoil that will ensue when European and American labor starts complaining of being displaced by "slave labor."

The Common Market has found it extremely difficult to meet the agreed timetable for a common commercial policy toward Eastern Europe and the Soviet Union; and in a growing sense, Western Europe, the United States, and Japan are all rivals for increasing their share of East-West trade. The balance-of-trade and balance-of-payments deficits of the United States are the most influential arguments advanced in favor of approval of liberalized credits, technology exports, and most-favored treatment of Soviet exports. Moscow and Peking have become veritable oriental bazaars, Babylons of babbling Western bargain hunters, hawkers, and bicycle salesmen alike.

Trade and travel have done more to spread civilization and cement friendships than armies and invasion, and should be encouraged. But there are some strategic considerations here, too. While it makes sense for Western Europe and the United States to buy energy and raw materials from Russia and to sell it wheat and industrial technology, there are some dangers in too great a dependence for either resources or markets on a system in which this leverage can be used for further political and economic concessions.

Financial problems also need to be kept in perspective. One can imagine a Russian grand strategist boasting of the success he has achieved by frightening the West in general, and the United States in particular, into spending itself into figurative, if not literal, bankruptcy. A logical mind could easily envisage that the rousing of expectations among the masses and of fears among the military have certainly one thing in common: they both lead governments into overspending. The strains on the West's monetary and financial system are all too obvious.

In the case of the United States they express themselves in balance-of-payments and budgetary deficits of monumental proportions, with the resulting inflation causing serious internal social strains and the imbalance of trade resulting in corrosive effects upon European-American relations.

Still another pressure point is the Russian influence on the Arab oil producers; her own relative self-sufficiency gives her a considerable potential for mischief in the relations of Western Europe, Japan, and the United States.

If Western expectations of détente are allowed to outrun reality, the Soviet Union has many lines with which to fish in the troubled waters of the Atlantic world.

If, therefore, some continuing political solidarity and common defense capability remains important to the kind of world we hope to achieve, Western statesmen must come to grips with the internal economic issues, not only in the areas enumerated above but also in the defense field itself.

Americans feel that the basic sharing of the defense burden is inequitable, considering that the United States must maintain a multidimensional deterrent while Europe is primarily concerned only with defending its eastern frontier; and there is some support for this view in the statistics. The United States, even after Vietnam, is spending 6.5 percent of its GNP on defense compared with an average figure of 4 percent for NATO Europe. It is paying the high costs of a volunteer army, while the Europeans are letting their own military service obligations dwindle, and the ratio of military manpower to population continues to be lower there than in the United States.

The subject can be and has been debated ad nauseam, and I do not propose to discuss it here. But even assuming that both America and Europe are equally concerned with maintaining a viable defense posture in Europe during a period of détente, and that their relative efforts are acceptably if not fully proportional to the respective stakes and capabilities, there is one dimension in which this is clearly not the case.

This is the balance-of-payments consequences of the fact that the United States maintains a significant portion of its general-purpose forces in Europe, where they add to the balance-of-payments problem I have already discussed. Unless this is resolved, it is going to be difficult indeed for the American public to tolerate for long continual devaluation of the purchasing power of their currency, and perhaps even import and other controls to ration foreign exchange earnings, in order to help defend an affluent Western Europe. In 1971, gross U.S. military outflows worldwide were $4.8 billion, with a net deficit, after the deduction of military sales, of $2.9 billion, of which over one-third was with Western Europe. In 1972, after the first dollar devaluation the figures were $4.7 billion gross, and $3.5 billion net worldwide, with $1.6 billion in the EEC countries alone.

The Germans like to argue that their so-called offset agreements, mostly in military purchases and U.S. Government promissory notes (with interest!), have neutralized a substantial amount of the U.S. deficit. The facts are that for 1968 through 1973, only about $2 billion of the $6.3 billion U.S. gross deficit on military account with Germany was neutralized by the transfer of real resources, i.e., military procurement. More than half of the $5 billion which was theoretically "covered" by offset agreements was in the form of financial measures, i.e., interest-bearing loans by Germany to the United States.

Since 1950 the cumulative foreign exchange costs of U.S. common defense programs in Europe, including troop deployments, amounted to $26 billion. This is *net* after the deduction of all military sales, and of course the budgetary costs to the United States, including grants of military equipment, were far higher, at least twice as much. This $26 billion of foreign exchange represents a sizable part of the $50 billion of accumulated U.S. current liabilities owed to Europe as of April 1973!

The implications are clear: Either the U.S. presence is going to have to be thinned down to a level where the balance-of-payments costs can be neutralized by present "offset"-type arrangements, or some new solution to the problem will have to be found. Some defense experts believe that the Nixon Doctrine can and should be applied to Europe. The Europeans would then take over responsibility for European defense, with a much smaller American force— say three divisions and supporting air power (and a cadre to maintain the equipment for a second corps) plus nuclear custody detachments—put at the disposal of a European SACEUR. If such a "solution" is satisfactory to Europe, then the balance-of-payments neutralization should be far easier. But if Europe is serious about wanting the United States to maintain approximately the present size and quality of its ground and air forces in Europe, then European leaders have an opportunity and an obligation to come forward with a solution which will neutralize the foreign exchange costs. It will be difficult enough to defend the budgetary costs, but neither U.S. external finances nor the world monetary system can afford the continued drain of well over a billion dollars a year for U.S. military presence in Europe.

The argument that the United States is affluent, therefore "you can afford it," does not apply. True, we can print paper dollars, and give them to Europe. But we have heard too many lectures from central bankers and finance ministers about cheap, surplus, unconvertible dollars being forced on them to give much credibility to this argument. Here is one place where they can put their money where their mouth is, and help the United States strengthen the dollar. With an economy producing nearly $700 billion gross national product, the 250 million people of the EEC countries can certainly afford, and find the means, to contribute an additional billion or more to the common defense.

To avoid adding the political and military disruption which a withdrawal of sizable U.S. forces from Europe would add to the economic strains on the Atlantic world, we have proposed an "International Security Fund," a multilateral clearinghouse for deficits on military account. Net deficits, after various procurement and other bilateral offsets involving transfer of real resources, would be cleared via a transfer of foreign exchange resources through the Fund from countries in surplus to those in deficit on military account, principally the United States. Britain would both contribute to and draw from the Fund. The multilateral feature would ensure some contribution from all the NATO countries which benefit from the U.S. forces stationed in Germany but do not help with their balance-of-payments consequences. That might make it easier for Germany to meet the extra costs she would have to bear.

Whether the optimum solution is multilateral or bilateral, some solution is a *sine qua non* of continued Atlantic defense collaboration. If a solution is not found, and soon, there is a real prospect that the Congress will force withdrawal of U.S. forces. And that would be such a handsome payoff to the Russian economic strategy that they could pursue their politico-economic objectives in Europe against a backdrop of an overwhelming military preponderance. What the resulting lack of confidence in Europe could do to Europe's own hopes and to Atlantic cooperation can only be speculated.

IV. CONCLUSIONS: ON DETERMINATION AND COMMON SENSE

Taken out of the total context, each of the economic and defense issues I have touched upon can be thorny. To a citrus grower in California or a farmer in Normandy, loss of an agricultural market can be serious. No political leader can ignore his problem any more than he can ignore the factory worker who loses his job or the defense contractor who loses business. But there are ways of handling these problems other than distorting the international economic system by passing on the adjustment costs to foreigners.

I have talked about a $1 billion-plus military balance-of-payments problem and a series of trade issues which could involve that much again. Investment and tax issues are generally fewer and more difficult to assign values to but even though $2 billion is a lot of money for any of us, let us look at the total stakes: Two-way trade between the European Community and the United States is on the order of $30 billion, and the United States has $31 billion in direct and portfolio investments in Europe. Europeans have just as much invested in the United States ($32 billion), although a greater proportion is in portfolio investments. The U.S. Government spends over $250 billion a year; the European Community governments spend well over $100 billion. Counting only the U.S. forces directly related to European defense, NATO's annual expenditure on defense exceeds $35 billion.

Europe and the United States produce and consume more than half of the world's gross national product, although together they have only one-eighth of the population. They share many common heritages and ideals. Somehow it seems incredible that a $2 billion problem looms so large in relation to a combined GNP of $1.5 trillion, annual trade of $30 billion, and a mutual investment stake of $60 billion.

If the United States can regain its international solvency—and thus maintain relatively open access to its market, by rectifying its basic balance by that much with Europe, somewhat more with Japan, and a lesser amount with Canada—it seems logical that everyone should have a stake in helping. Even a shift of European resources amounting to, say, $10 billion over five years until the balance-of-payments emergency is over and during the most delicate phase of transition in East-West relations, looks small in comparison with the $50 billion of military and economic aid transferred by the United States to Europe since World War II.

It is not too much to ask, then, that Europe pay more for its defense, and buy more agricultural products[4] from the United States, both to its own advantage, so that the principles of freedom and of liberal trade, as well as the common defense, can be assured.

The foregoing inventory of problems does not disclose any which should not be susceptible to a solution with good will and a determination to manage the issues intelligently on both sides. Perhaps I am reflecting the bias of the American side of the Atlantic; but I nevertheless feel that, in their own interest, Europeans can and must do more to upgrade their own perceptions of the problem so as to recognize that America does have some *real*, as opposed to imaginary, economic headaches, and to adopt the posture of a statesman who will help, within the limit of his capabilities, rather than that of a hard-bargaining technician. If this kind of speech were made by a *European* leader in Europe it would make global headlines, for the response in America would be enormous and there would be a rush to meet Europe more than halfway in solving problems rather than lecturing about them. But I suppose it would be naive to hope for a European "General Marshall" to come forward so soon after General de Gaulle!

As a minimum, we should adopt as a motto, not "we will if we can," but rather the more determined formulation: "We can over-

---

4. Massive Soviet purchases of U.S. grain in 1972 have foreclosed temporarily this option by causing skyrocketing U.S. grain prices and shortages of supply.

come our current problems *because* we so will!" And if we do so, as I believe we must, there is still a challenging agenda ahead.

As noted earlier, America and Europe share with Japan a serious shortage of energy. Instead of competing for scarce and ever more costly supplies (and in earning the foreign exchange to pay for them), is there not room for collaborative research on a massive scale to develop nuclear power and other alternatives to petroleum dependence? Should there not be some joint contingency planning to assure continued access to oil resources on an equitable basis?

Are there joint ventures between U.S. and European firms which could be undertaken in making modern technology available to the developing world?

What about an effort to rationalize agricultural policies and production on a global basis to increase the quality as well as the quantity of world nutrition?

Can we, in concert, develop a prosperous and conflict-free international economic system, encompassing investment and finance as well as trade?

Can we strive, jointly, toward universal acceptance of the venerable principles of national, reciprocal, and most-favored-nation treatment to trade, travel, and investments?

Efforts to reform the world monetary system are now going forward; but as in the other complex areas of fruitful collaboration, tomorrow's prospects will depend on our ability to handle the issues I have described. Monetary reform deals with a mechanism. It cannot succeed alone unless the underlying problems are brought under control.

Finally, to close on the East-West theme, there is still much to be done before Russia and her East European allies can become full and constructive participants in the international system, no matter what differences remain in ideologies and social systems. If West-West frictions and burden-sharing issues flare into real divisiveness and economic conflicts, the incentives for responsible communist behavior may vanish. So the Western motivation for collaboration instead of conflict is strong; all we need is a commonsense perspective on the stakes involved—and the determination to apply it.

The American Approach
to Negotiations

Walter F. Hahn

When President Nixon pronounced, at the beginning of his tenure of office in 1969, that the world is "moving into the era of negotiations," few could suspect that this promise would prove not only prophetic but also an understatement. In late 1973, the world seems to be plunging into negotiations.

The first four and a half years of the "Nixon Doctrine" already have produced a log of diplomacy likely to challenge future historians. Verdicts of success or failure must be left to their eventual judgment and to the longer reach of global forces that the new diplomacy either has mirrored or set in motion.

Meanwhile, however, some generalizations can be hazarded. One is that the Brezhnev visit in Washington in June 1973 probably marked the end of the initial and predominantly bilateral phase of the Nixon-Kissinger diplomacy. The diplomatic efforts by the

75

Administration in the 1969-1973 period were animated by two
basic objectives. The first, and overriding one, was to wrest the
United States free from its debilitating involvement in the Vietnam
War. The second aim, which was linked to Vietnam but drew its
rationale from a broadei global perspective, was to prepare the stage
for a far-reaching reorientation in both the priorities and the substance of America's relationships with traditional allies and
adversaries alike. This quest featured (perhaps necessarily so) the
dramatics of surprise pronouncements and the fanfare of summitry.

The above is not to suggest that the curtain has now descended
with finality upon the Administration's bilateral endeavors. The
summit meetings in Peking, Moscow, and Washington have signaled
more directional intent rather than real substance of new relations.
The general concords that have been so festively signed, particularly
with the Soviet Union, will have to be translated into detailed
agreements in order to acquire meaning. Some tough bilateral
bargaining still lies ahead, especially in such areas as trade and
strategic arms limitations.

Yet, at the same time, a second, multilateral phase in East-West
negotiations is opening. The focus of this phase is on the impending
conclaves in Europe: the Conference on Security and Cooperation
in Europe (CSCE), which is commuting between Helsinki and
Geneva, and the impending negotiations in Vienna on mutual and
(hopefully) balanced force reductions in Europe (MBFR). Furthermore, to the extent that the second round of Strategic Arms Limitation Talks (SALT) between the United States and the Soviet Union
in Geneva progressively interacts with the forementioned negotiations forums, it too is assuming a more multilateral character.

Especially at a time when national and allied negotiating positions are still being fashioned, it would be futile to attempt to
define, in the brief span of this article, the complex tangle of
East-West diplomacy that is emerging, let alone to forecast the flow
of negotiations in the major arenas. Rather, the attempt will be
made (1) to interpret the general philosophy and basic objectives
that appear to be guiding the American approach to the conference
tables, (2) to demark what seem to be the salient American predilections within and among the three principal arenas of negotiations, and (3) to spotlight the major issues and problems that are
likely still to test the indispensable criterion of success in the tricky
diplomatic terrain ahead: namely, the ability of the Western Alliance to transit that terrain in harness.

I. THE NEW AMERICAN DIPLOMACY

The point can be exaggerated, but in many ways the diplomacy that has radiated from Washington in the past four years has signaled an American "coming of age." Some of the specific twists and turns of that diplomacy, as well as certain of its underlying assumptions (to be treated below), may be open to challenge. Yet, as far as style is concerned, the performance in the past four years contrasts sharply with the record of the previous quarter of a century.

The change has come primarily in the conception of diplomacy and its relationship to power. If the scoreboard of U.S. diplomacy in the first two postwar decades was hardly exemplary, this was due perhaps not only to relative American novism on the international stage, but also to a popular definition of diplomacy as, in effect, the antithesis of conflict. A unique history of relatively untrammeled national growth had helped to engender an American perspective of the world in which peace was deemed the normal mode of mankind and conflict an aberration. A corollary view held that so long as men negotiated in good faith, the guns of power would remain not only silent but undrawn and unneeded. Thus, power and diplomacy were considered to be functioning in more or less separate compartments—a view, incidentally, that found its bureaucratic expression in the creation in Washington, unique among major governments, of a separate Arms Control and Disarmament Agency (ACDA) whose principal preoccupation was to prepare for and lead negotiations with the major adversary. Accentuating this separation was an abiding distaste in the United States for the dark practices of power politics that twice in this century had drawn the country into conflagrations not of its choosing.

What has unfolded against this background in the past four years can be described essentially as follows.

A. A Realpolitik American Style

"The test of a statesman," wrote Henry Kissinger in his treatise on Metternich and the Concert of Europe, "is his ability to recognize the real relationship of forces and to make this knowledge serve his ends."[1] Kissinger has brought to his post under President Nixon this concept of the interrelationship of forces, as well as a broad design of strategy in which diplomacy has been given its traditional

---

1. Henry A. Kissinger, *A World Restored* (Boston: Houghton Mifflin, 1957), p. 324.

role as not only the language of power but also the expression of
the constraints upon power.

By the end of the 1960s the constraints upon American power
were fairly evident, even though the perception of them had tended
to be blurred in the previous American Administration by preoccupation in Asia and by the habit of looking upon the world
from confident superiority. The new and sobering realities, as
President Nixon expressed them in his second report to the nation,
included the advent of nuclear-strategic parity between the United
States and the Soviet Union, the diffusion of power marked by the
Sino-Soviet split, and the emergence of new power centers in
Western Europe and Japan.[2] The new realities called for the triad of
priorities that have since become a kind of litany of the Nixon
Doctrine: strength, partnership, and negotiations.

Yet, another stark reality faced the Nixon Administration in its
first four years: the war in Vietnam. Nixon had campaigned with
the promise to end the war, and retrospect shows how heavily the
shadow of this objective played upon the foreign policy endeavors
of the Administration. Nixon and Kissinger realized from the beginning that the road to Hanoi had to lead via Moscow and Peking.

The "Vietnam determinism" of the Nixon-Kissinger diplomacy
of 1969-1972 can be overblown. Thus, for example, the theory,
popular particularly in Western Europe, that the U.S. sale of wheat
to the Soviet Union in 1972 represented in effect an American
payoff to Moscow for the latter's circumspection during America's
military escalation against Hanoi seems a gross exaggeration. Clearly
the larger stakes of American diplomacy in Moscow and Peking
have transcended, and continue to transcend, the interests of the
United States in Southeast Asia. Yet, there is little question that the
imperative of a Vietnam settlement strongly influenced at least the
tempo of American initiatives in Moscow and Peking. In the process, it contributed to a situation in which, as President Nixon
himself admitted, "our relations with our allies appeared for a
period of several months to be somewhat out of phase with the
innovations taken in our relations with our adversaries."[3]

---

2. *U.S. Foreign Policy for the 1970's: The Emerging Structure of Peace*, A
Report to the Congress by Richard Nixon, President of the United States, 9
February 1972 (Washington, D.C.: U.S. Government Printing Office, 1972), p.
3.

3. *Ibid.*, p. 9.

The shadow of Vietnam is dwindling, as is hopefully the "out-of-phaseness" referred to by Nixon in America's relations with adversaries and allies. It behooves America's allies, however, to recognize that the new American diplomacy, based on a hard definition of U.S. interests, will continue to be brought to bear not only in the arenas of East-West negotiations but also in the forums of the Alliance.

B. A New Personal Diplomacy

There is little question that American diplomacy during the last four years and American foreign policy more generally have been "personalized" to a degree unmatched in American history since perhaps the era of Franklin Delano Roosevelt.

The trend reflects in part the personalities of the President and of his principal foreign policy advisor, and in part the imperatives which confronted the first administration of Richard Nixon. The tasks of unraveling the Vietnam tangle and of staging such dramatic turns in American policy as the rapprochement with Peking clearly placed a premium on secrecy and "lonely decision-making."

There is another aspect here which needs to be addressed because it bears meaningfully upon the future conduct of American diplomacy, particularly in the formal arenas of complex negotiations ahead. The complaint has pervaded Washington officialdom that the centralized decision-making and personal diplomacy of the Nixon Administration reflect essentially a distrust by the President and his principal advisor of the governmental bureaucracy and therefore, in tune with the principle that knowledge is power, the attempt to keep the policy machinery as much as possible in the dark and away from the steering wheels of policy formulation.

It is difficult for someone outside the bureaucratic battlefields of Washington to test the validity of this charge. Certainly Nixon and Kissinger have been reported variously as expressing their impatience at the alleged resistance and even hostility of the bureaucratic apparatus in Washington (much of it still populated by men appointed under Democratic administrations) to the innovative changes of the new leadership. On the other hand, there is evidence, particularly in the multilateral negotiations context, that the Administration has given reasonable leeway in discretionary power to negotiating teams; this seemed to be the case in the 1971 Four-Power negotiations for a Berlin agreement and more recently in the preparatory talks in Helsinki for the European security conference.

In any event, it seems clear that as the United States moves deeper into the thickets of simultaneous negotiations along a broad front, whatever distance may separate the Administration and its supporting bureaucracy will have to be narrowed. Henry Kissinger, as imaginative and resourceful as he is, cannot do it all by himself. The Administration will have to draw greater portions of the bureaucratic structure into its confidence with respect to both the grand design of its strategy and its execution.

C. A "Strategy of Linkages"

Precisely because the Nixon strategy has been played so "close to the vest" (and banked so heavily on the element of surprise), it can be interpreted only at one's own risk. Yet the patterns of statements and actions during the past four years do trace some salient assumptions and objectives.

In his much-cited treatise on the Concert of Europe, Henry Kissinger despaired over the likelihood of doing diplomatic business with a revolutionary power:

It is a mistake to assume that diplomacy can always settle international disputes if there is "good faith" and "willingness" to come to an agreement. For in a revolutionary international order, each power will seem to his opponent to lack precisely these qualities. Diplomats can still meet but they cannot persuade, for they have ceased to speak the same language.[4]

The fact that Kissinger has been very actively negotiating in Moscow suggests that, by his criteria at least, the Soviet Union is no longer the revolutionary power that it once was. Indeed, the view of a gradual metamorphosis in the generators of Soviet foreign policy seems to be one of the central assumptions behind the Nixon Doctrine.

This point should not be exaggerated. Despite the convivial atmosphere of recent U.S.-Soviet summits, the optimism in Washington seems to be a guarded one. It is difficult to impute to a sober analyst like Kissinger the belief that the Soviet Union has suddenly jettisoned its revolutionary legacy as well as its time-honored expansionist aims. Yet the pronouncements of the White House do reflect the hope, justified or not, that the mainsprings of ideology in the Kremlin are giving way to the principles of expediency and enlightened self-interest. The implication is that the Soviets can be

4. Kissinger, *op. cit.*, p. 2.

bargained with, and their abiding adversary relationship notwithstanding, the United States and the Soviet Union can find some *selective* grounds of cooperation, particularly in the fields of trade and arms control.

This view seems to have been strengthened by recent U.S.-Soviet accords and by evidence of certain Soviet circumspection. It is also to be shored up by a perception in Washington of a changing nature of the Soviet leadership. Henry Kissinger seems to have gained from his dealing with the Kremlin chieftains the impression that we face today in the Soviet Union a leadership that, in contrast with the personal concentrations of power in the past, is highly "bureaucratized." It follows that a major task of U.S. diplomacy vis-à-vis the Soviet Union should be to prevent the kind of contingency that would help the wrong people in Moscow to capture policy and to steer it back into dangerous directions.

In positive terms, this translates itself into what may be termed a "strategy of linkages" designed to create an "interdependence of vested interests." Kissinger described this strategy in his briefing to members of Congress following the return from the Moscow summit in 1972:

Past experience has amply shown that much heralded changes in atmospherics, but not buttressed by concrete progress, will revert to previous patterns at the first subsequent clash of interests. We have, instead, sought to move forward across a broad range of issues so that progress in one area would add momentum to the progress of other areas. We hoped that the Soviet Union would acquire a stake in a wide spectrum of negotiations and that it would become convinced that its interests would be best served if the entire process unfolded. We have sought, in short, to create a vested interest in mutual restraint.[5]

The statement implies both method and objective. The method is to foster a mutual reinforcement of progress in negotiations over a wide spectrum of U.S.-Soviet relations. This applies to linkages not only in one functional field—e.g., between CSCE and MBFR—but across functional boundaries. Thus the theory is that if the Soviets want to enjoy the fruits of intensified trade and technology transfer, they will have to demonstrate their cooperative intent in SALT and MBFR, and vice versa. The objective is to build an interlocking structure of agreements that can be tampered with only at the risk of bringing the entire edifice crashing down.

---

5. White House Press Release, June 15, 1972.

II. THE DIPLOMACY OF PARTNERSHIP

Negotiations with the Soviet Union undoubtedly still occupy center stage in the global screenplay of the Nixon Administration, but they do not necessarily dominate that stage. Indeed, it seems to be the sincere objective of the Nixon strategy to give more stature and power to the other actors in the drama.

The grand design of the Nixon Doctrine has been variously interpreted, and it need not preoccupy us here. Suffice it to note that a basic denominator of the Doctrine is the notion that the fundamentally precarious bipolar balance that dominated the post-war period should be cushioned by the emergence of other power centers. Perhaps too much thought has been expended on the "pentagonal balance" ostensibly aspired to by the Doctrine (involving, in addition to the United States and the Soviet Union, China, Western Europe, and Japan) and on how, given the enormous and seemingly unbridgeable disparities between the superpowers and the lesser contenders, such a new balance is supposed to function. It could be that the simple premise of the Nixon Doctrine is that of a "stability through complexity"—the notion that the greater the number of independent actors on the stage, the more difficult it becomes for each of the two superpowers to devote exclusive and paranoid attention to the other and to the question of who is ahead and by how much.

All this presupposes a certain loosening of old ties and new and dynamic relationships. And it places into bold relief the question of the future of the U.S.-West European relationship and of the diplomacy of partnership.

Nixon's remark, cited earlier, about alliance relations being "out of phase" with initiatives vis-à-vis adversaries clearly referred to the problem of priorities. The Nixon Administration, in endeavoring to recast its relations with China and the Soviet Union, felt that it had to move boldly. As has been noted, an additional goad was the urgency of a Vietnam settlement. In the process, allies were left reeling in confusion, and in some specific cases (prominently Taiwan) their interests were stepped on.

The dramatic first act having been concluded and the pace having slowed, the gap of American diplomatic priorities vis-à-vis adversaries and allies has narrowed somewhat. Yet the problems of reconciling and phasing these priorities remain. America's national interests sweep the globe, while those of its European allies are largely confined to continental dimensions (to a parochial degree, many Americans contend). In the direct context of East-West negotiations, the "strategy of linkages" pursued by the United States implies the balancing of objectives and tactics over the broad course of multilateral and bilateral negotiations with the Soviet Union. For the Europeans, immediate and vital interests are directly at stake in such forums as CSCE and MBFR.

But the dilemma is more profound. The U.S. Administration recognized that its prescription of partnership entails measures of competitiveness as well as cooperation by a more independent and vibrant Western Europe, but by no means is it willing to accept the ground rules of the relationship that Europeans seem to be espousing. These ground rules, as perceived in Washington, appear to read that cooperation should be continued in the military domain of the Alliance—meaning that the United States should continue to shoulder the major part of the NATO burden—whereas competition in the economic realm should continue relatively unrestricted.

The alleged penchant by Europeans for thus "having their cake and eating it too" has provoked growing impatience in Washington, an impatience that was easily discernible between the lines of Kissinger's call for a "new Atlantic Charter" in April 1973. Kissinger's manifesto amounted essentially to a rejection of these implicit ground rules and the summons toward a new and, from the American vantage point, a more "equitable" definition of the transatlantic relationship.

The critical reaction to Kissinger's "invitation" in Europe gave testimony to the magnitude of the divisive problems that face the Alliance in the "era of negotiations."

A. The Hazards in the Upcoming Negotiations

The most telling charge that can be leveled against the Kissinger summons is that it has been sounded somewhat late in the season. It presumably attempted to set the agenda for a spate of meetings between President Nixon and European heads-of-state. These meetings may yet yield a general catalogue of principles on which rough agreement may be reached. It is extremely doubtful, however, that a new and binding definition of the transatlantic relationship can be hammered out before the Alliance plunges into the hard bargaining of the multilateral conference in Europe.

The prospects point, therefore, to a protracted and often sharp transatlantic dialogue even while the Alliance attempts to muster a united front in Helsinki, Vienna, and Geneva. Not only might this produce intolerable strains on allied cohesion and negotiations management, but it portends an even greater danger namely, an enhanced ability by the Soviet Union not only to accelerate her divisive strategy against NATO but also to become in effect a partner to the transatlantic dialogue. This latter danger will grow commensurate with the inability of the Alliance to reach common grounds outside the conference halls (e.g., with respect to an optimal future NATO posture and burden sharing) and the consequent temptation by the Alliance to leave the solution of nettlesome problems to the crucible of East-West negotiations (e.g., MBFR).

Clearly, the Alliance will face in the negotiations forums an imposing array of contentious issues. The following seem to be the salient ones.

1. SALT

The second round of SALT is underway. There is the sober realization that SALT II will be an immensely more difficult undertaking than its predecessor. The United States must first arrive at its own criteria of how strategic nuclear "equality" might be measured and implemented in terms of numbers and types of weapons systems, and it must decide whether and to what extent a SALT II agreement should try to restrict technological improvements of existing weapons, improvements that could be difficult to detect and police but could well tip a numerical balance of power. Any hard positions that may have emerged on these questions in the U.S. Government are not yet visible.

Other than in underscoring strategic nuclear parity and its implications, SALT I and its outcome did not grate too harshly on U.S.-European relations. For one thing, in the SALT context (if not in some others, such as the preparations for the Moscow Summit) America's consultations with its allies were fairly scrupulous. Also, no palpable NATO interests as such were relinquished in SALT I. Many Europeans looked askance at the inferiority in numbers of weapons systems which the United States seemingly accepted in SALT I, but they generally deemed these essentially American "losses," with only marginal implications for NATO.

This does not relieve anxieties in Western Europe about the

ing increasingly clear that the disparate timing of the two conclaves is not likely to allow for such a linkage. More importantly, however, the United States recognizes the risk that a linkage between CSCE and MBFR might assume substantive dimensions. It fears that any deliberations in CSCE of hard questions of military security (beyond so-called confidence building measures) might not only undermine MBFR but also open U.S. and Alliance interests to the meddling of nations whose narrow (if legitimate) security concerns would muddy the waters of agreement.

The question is whether the new optimism concerning CSCE is warranted. To the extent that it is gauged to assumed Soviet discomfiture, it may be somewhat premature: observers at the preparatory talks noted how quickly the East European nations formed ranks behind the Soviet Union when it came to questions like the principles championed by the West of free movement of people and ideas across European boundaries. No one can yet discern with confidence the objectives and expectations with which the Soviets are entering the Conference. It may well turn out, for example, that more than simply "détente atmospherics" and official Western blessings on the status quo in Central and Eastern Europe, Soviet motives are still focused on the creation by the Conference of a "permanent all-European organ" that would be expected to acquire a life of its own and to dangle more powerfully before NATO and the European Economic Community the alternative of an all-European security and economic system.

3. Mutual and Balanced Force Reductions (MBFR)

The frictions that have marred the approach by the Western allies to the conference tables in Vienna—and which attended in particular the concessions of the Soviet Union on Hungary's status at the Conference—are a stark portent of the difficulties that will badger NATO if and when the actual negotiations get underway. Unless NATO first reaches the new and comprehensive consensus that Kissinger has summoned, MBFR cannot but accentuate the disparate national and regional interests in the Alliance.

The disparateness relates to fundamental investments in the Conference. For the United States, MBFR represents, probably in this order, (1) domestic necessity, (2) plausible exit from the dilemma of its burdens in Europe, and (3) a link in its broader negotiations strategy vis-à-vis the Soviet Union (particularly in SALT). The

motives combine to lend a definite urgency to the negotiations and
to their outcome.

The European partners, on the other hand, approach MBFR with
at best varying degrees of apprehension. They are leery of a U.S.-
Soviet arrangement that would simply place cosmetic coloring on
an American retrenchment from Europe. They see the issues at
stake not in a global context, but rather as national and regional
questions of life and death. To the extent that they contemplate
direct national investments in MBFR (e.g., possible reductions in
their own national forces), they know that these tend to be
frowned upon by the United States.

The dilemma is deepened by the imponderableness of Soviet
intentions and by the thorny nature of the subject of negotiations.
At the risk of oversimplification, one can see two alternative MBFR
scenarios. One would feature an essentially political bargain where-
by American and Soviet stationed forces are cut by some arbitrary
percentage, with only marginal attention paid to the factors of true
balance and asymmetry. The alternative scenario would be comprehensive negotiations covering the entire spectrum of the opposing
postures in Europe. This alternative not only boggles the imagina-
tion, but also entails the prospect of a tortuous process of bargaining probably spanning years. There is the serious question whether
national positions, even if harnessed in a common Alliance approach, could be maintained over time in the face of growingly
impatient domestic pressures and budget constrictions. This is not
to speak of the minefields of divisive issues that the Alliance will
have to navigate.

B. The Dilemmas of Partnership and Negotiations

This article might be faulted for undue pessimism. It will be argued
that the advantages in the "era of negotiations" are not stacked on
one side, and the bargaining will not be a "zero-sum game." The
unfolding negotiations may uncover Soviet and Warsaw Pact vulnerabilities. Even if this should turn out to be the case, however,
exploitation of the opponents' weaknesses would require the kind
of comprehensive, cohesive, and concerted Western strategy that
seems to be conspicuous by its absence.

American diplomacy, it has been stressed, has matured. With the
sobering recognition of new realities abroad and at home, U.S.
policy has descended from the high perch of moralism and confident

supremacy that often marked its approach to the world in the first two postwar decades, and has begun to see the globe more realistically and with a more sober definition of American national interests. It has attuned diplomacy to this realism and to a more comprehensive design. The design, however, has yet to be unveiled in its entirety as a compelling blueprint of national consensus and alliance partnership.

It might have been better had 1971 or 1972 been the "Year of Europe" rather than the "Year of Peking" and the "Year of Moscow." Yet, it is easy to second-guess; perhaps from the vantage point of the White House, particularly under the pressure of Vietnam, there was no real alternative to the perceived priority that relations at the superpower level had to be reordered first before alliance relations could be recast.

The legacy, in any event, are the dilemmas of transition and timing. The Alliance faces the task of groping for a new transatlantic relationship at the same time that it must grapple with the immediate issues at stake in the complex negotiations with the East. It confronts this dual task, moreover, at a time when trade and monetary issues are tugging sharply at transatlantic bonds.

It may be, as some argue, that the tasks are not necessarily at odds with one another, that the demands of East-West negotiations will force a more honest self-appraisal in the Alliance. It is contended, for example, that the preparations for MBFR already have yielded a better understanding of the NATO posture and the interrelationships of its components.

But, this optimism is fragile at best. In order for it to have validity, moreover, the improved understanding has to be translated into a common alliance position.

A rational solution to the dilemma would be for the Alliance to place brakes on the "era of negotiations" in order to buy the necessary time to set its own house in order. At this juncture of events, however, given the various national investments in détente, could NATO muster a consensus on even this stratagem? Would our West German allies, for example, be willing to declare a moratorium on *Ostpolitik*? Would Bonn and Paris be willing to slow the pace in CSCE? Would the United States, for that matter, agree to postpone MBFR and protract SALT?

Questions like these (and the likely answers to them) spotlight the basic problem.

A Strategy for the West: An American View

Wynfred Joshua

The key problem of the seventies for America's policy toward Western Europe remains the same as that of the sixties: how to ensure a credible deterrence and defense posture for the Western Alliance. But the strategic and political context has changed and the answer in this decade is likely to differ considerably from the one attempted some ten or twelve years ago.

The 1960s brought to Washington a group of policy-makers determined to reduce NATO's dependence on nuclear weapons and to emphasize instead the conventional dimension of the Western posture. In searching for a more credible defense against a limited attack than the massive retaliation strategy provided, the strategic concept of the sixties called for a largely conventional defense and for postponing the resort to the use of nuclear weapons, including tactical nuclear weapons, as long as possible. A consequence of the requirement of the high nuclear threshold was the need to keep the

91

nuclear weapons available to the Alliance under central American control. Carried to its logical conclusion, the flexible response concept of the sixties also required that the United States oppose the development of national nuclear forces by its allies.

American efforts to put the nuclear genie back into the bottle reflected an understandable concern over Soviet progress in nuclear weapons. The prospects of a Soviet strategic nuclear capability meant that the United States would be vulnerable to a nuclear strike in the event of an armed conflict with its Soviet counterpart. In the eyes of the West Europeans, however, the changing U.S. strategy seemed to place increasing stress on containing a conflict in Europe, if deterrence were to fail. The Kennedy-Johnson approach eventually resulted in 1967 in NATO's reluctant endorsement of the flexible response concept, but it precipitated France's withdrawal from the integrated NATO commands and it left the Alliance in a protracted crisis which threatens to undermine the very sinews of American-allied cohesion.

I. CHALLENGE OF THE SEVENTIES

Although there are indications that the U.S. version of flexible response has shifted, no clear new concept has been promulgated in Washington. The interpretation of flexible response—loosely worded as it is—remains ambiguous and dependent on the political bias of the interpreter. Yet a number of factors render the need for confidence and cohesion in the Alliance and for a generally accepted strategy more compelling than ever.

First, the détente climate notwithstanding, there is no evidence of change in fundamental Soviet objectives in Europe. Soviet long-range goals continue to be (1) the fractionalization of the Western Alliance, (2) the removal of the U.S. strategic umbrella from Europe, (3) the elimination of the U.S. military and political presence, and (4) eventually the creation of such a change in the political climate that the Finlandization of Europe can come within Soviet reach. Nor has Moscow relaxed its efforts to improve the military means to achieve these objectives. Particularly during the last few years the Soviets have steadily improved the quality of their war-fighting potential in Central Europe and substantially expanded their naval power at the flanks of Europe. Their massive manpower, armor, and tactical airpower, combined with Soviet doctrine, which emphasizes blitzkrieg tactics, give them the edge in a conventional conflict on the European continent. As for the strategic nuclear realm, Soviet attainment of strategic parity with the United States has evoked widespread concern in Washington as well as in European capitals that the threat of the U.S. strategic nuclear forces has been neutralized for anything else but a direct attack on the U.S. homeland. The Soviet Union has consistently tried to encourage this perception in Western Europe. Against the background of strategic parity with the United States and conventional superiority in Europe, the Soviet Union has sought to impress the West Europeans with the futility of their defense efforts. In a highly sophisticated manner Moscow is exploiting the political utility of its preponderant conventional forces in Europe for political ends.

Second, the United States is subject to increasing domestic pressures to reduce defense spending and its troop presence abroad, as reflected in the Mansfield Amendment to recall U.S. troops from Europe. Indeed the last Mansfield Amendment, rather than being introduced on the Senate floor, was reported out of the Senate Appropriations Committee—an action which carries more weight and might swing some marginal votes the next time. The pressures for U.S. troop reductions partly emanate from those political circles which advocate a retreat of America's involvement abroad; in part they reflect an effort to alleviate the U.S. balance-of-payments difficulties;[1] and finally, they are inspired by considerations of manpower and budgetary constraints. In short, the trends in the United States for the rest of the decade strongly point toward a reduction of U.S. troops in Europe. Precipitous U.S. troop withdrawals, however, would seriously erode the credibility of the U.S. commitment and would render the European allies vulnerable to Soviet political coercion.

A third factor affecting the Alliance is the efforts in Washington to move from the era of confrontation to that of negotiation. The

---

1. In 1972, one estimate of the actual cost of U.S. forces in Europe and their U.S.-based support was approximately $7 billion per year; direct costs of the U.S. forces stationed in Western Europe were about $4 billion. Of the $4 billion spent in Europe, approximately $1 billion represented a deficit in the U.S. balance of payments. See U.S. Congress, House of Representatives, Special Subcommittee on North Atlantic Treaty Organization Commitments, *The American Commitment to NATO*, H.A.S.C., No. 92-641 (Washington, D.C.: U.S. Government Printing Office, 17 August 1972), pp. 14978ff. There are, however, other lower as well as higher estimates to be found in the literature.

second round of the strategic arms limitation talks (SALT) is in progress; the preparatory phases of the Conference on Security and Cooperation in Europe (CSCE) and the talks on mutual force reductions (MFR) have started. The bilateral and multilateral negotiations with the Soviet Union underscore the urgency for restoring the ties of political cohesion of the Alliance. Without such bonds the establishment of a coordinated approach between the United States and its allies toward SALT II, CSCE, and MFR would be difficult. So would the joint development of a coherent strategy based on an agreed set of objectives that would fit the changed strategic equation. The failure to define clearly such a strategy would make it well-nigh impossible to gauge the political and military utility of the various components of the American and allied forces that are supposed to support that strategy. There would be no strategic and political framework for determining which elements of the forces can be selected as bargaining chips in the negotiations. Nor would it be possible to define what type of posture the Western allies need to undergird the era of negotiation. The Western Alliance finds itself in a profound dilemma at the very time that its objectives of deterrence and defense remain as valid as ever.

Thus, the issue for the West appears to center on the need to restore confidence and cohesion in the Alliance. To ensure West European resilience against Soviet political coercion in the shadow of Moscow's steadily improving military capability, the West must formulate a common strategic concept and supporting force posture that can deter Soviet aggression at any level. This would also help to deter Soviet coercion based on the threat of such aggression. It goes without saying that such a strategic concept would have to be militarily supportable and effective. What is perhaps less readily recognized is that the strategy has to be politically acceptable to the United States and its allies as well. In spite of NATO's official embrace of flexible response, the allies have never fully accepted the original American version of stressing the conventional defense. Flexible response is still in force today, but there continues to be a wide divergence in its interpretation. At the core of the controversy over NATO's strategic concept are divergent perceptions over the role of nuclear weapons, including tactical nuclear weapons. President Nixon highlighted this point when he raised the question: "Beyond their value as a deterrent to war, how should our tactical nuclear weapons in Europe be used to counter specific Warsaw Pact military threats?"[2]

In an effort to contribute to the debate over what posture appears to be appropriate for the West, this paper outlines a strategic concept that seeks to be responsive to the military challenges as well as the political constraints. It tries to take into account the complex thickets of European sensitivities and fears, yet pays heed to the demands voiced in Washington to bring at least some of the American troops home.

II. THE NEED FOR FLEXIBILITY AND UNCERTAINTY

Central to the strategic predilections of the West is the desire for deterrence. The specter of another devastating conflict sweeping across the continent continues to haunt the West European allies. They care little for having to fight a war, long or short. Their concern is in making deterrence as strong as possible, and if deterrence were to fail, to force the Soviet Union to terminate its aggression on terms acceptable to the West in the shortest time and with as little damage to Western Europe as possible.

Deterrence brackets political and military dimensions. The goal is to convince the opponent that the United States and its allies have (1) the military capability, (2) the will to use this capability, and (3) an effective strategy which, if deterrence were to break down, would make it impossible for the enemy to calculate in advance what type of response his contemplated aggression would trigger. The conceivable magnitude of the response would hopefully persuade the Soviet Union that any attack would entail unacceptable risk. This means, therefore, that the Western allies should have available a wide array of options that would permit them to respond at any level to a Soviet attack and induce the Soviet Union to halt its aggression and withdraw. It also means that the *specific* option to be used by the Western allies should not be determined in advance, but should remain uncertain. In short, the strategy for the Western alliance should provide flexibility for the allies and uncertainty for their Warsaw Pact opponents. A viable strategic concept should be based on these fundamental principles.

---

2. *U.S. Foreign Policy for the 1970's: A New Strategy for Peace,* A Report to the Congress by Richard M. Nixon on 18 February 1970 (Washington, D.C.: U.S. Government Printing Office, 1970), p. 33.

III. THE ROLE OF THE AMERICAN STRATEGIC FORCES

Obviously the American nuclear umbrella constitutes a critical element in deterring Soviet aggression. As long as American troops and nuclear forces remain in Europe, the Soviet Union is likely to perceive a continued coupling between the defense of Western Europe and American strategic nuclear power. Soviet perceptions notwithstanding, the United States finds it increasingly difficult to persuade its allies that the American strategic nuclear guarantee still blankets Western Europe in the era of superpower parity. The strategic nuclear relationship between the United States and its allies is a major area in which mutual confidence has faltered and must be restored. On the one hand, it is precisely the existence of parity that makes it imperative to enhance the linkage with the U.S. retaliatory forces; on the other hand, the coupling requirement is central to European strategic predilections.

In light of these considerations, the United States should strengthen that part of its military panoply that can convey the perception of coupling. This implies the need for some counterforce capability in the American strategic forces, so that the threat of the use of these forces remains credible. The May 1972 SALT Interim Agreement on Offensive Missiles does not prevent the United States from adding the necessary refinements to its strategic forces, such as improving its MIRV (multiple independently targeted reentry vehicles) capability with accurate warheads. This does not mean that the United States should try to endow its entire strategic offensive force with accurate MIRVs; nor does it mean that the United States should have a counterforce capability that can cover all Soviet strategic missiles targeted on Western Europe. After all, the British and French strategic nuclear forces also contribute to the strategic deterrence requirements. But the existence of a U.S. counterforce capability should be made obvious to the allies as well as to the Soviet Union.

Beyond the military improvements of the retaliatory forces looms their political credibility. In the final analysis the linkage of the American strategic forces to Western Europe's defense rests on a political commitment. It is for this reason that the United States should once more make it clear—in open foreign policy declarations and in more private consultations—that its nuclear shield remains inexorably linked to the security of its Atlantic partners. In the case of West Germany, a major target of Soviet pressures, such an effort may even have to take the form of a bilateral U.S. commitment to Bonn.

IV. THE ROLE OF THE FRENCH AND BRITISH NUCLEAR CAPABILITIES

The question of Western Europe's strategic nuclear capabilities and their relationship to the American strategic deterrent is complex and fraught with political risk, from the viewpoint of Washington as well as West European capitals. At the same time, however, the trend of events is such that the question can no longer be skirted, let alone ignored, lying as it does at the very core of the transatlantic relationship and its evolution.

The British and French have long argued that national control lends credibility to nuclear forces. Even a modest nuclear force in the hands of a potential victim would be more credible than the nuclear panoply of the most powerful ally, no matter how close that ally. Perhaps more persuasive is the argument that Moscow, in contemplating aggression or extreme pressure against a smaller nuclear power, would have to consider whether its objective would be worth the risk of incurring a nuclear response. There is, moreover, much to be said for the fact that the existence of national nuclear forces under separate national commands seriously compounds the uncertainties and complicates the calculations for the potential aggressor. Effective British and French nuclear forces would help to deter theater-level nuclear war and would, thereby, contribute to the overall deterrence posture of the West.

For Washington the choice is no longer that which dominated American policy councils in the early 1960s and led to the MLF debacle: the choice between exclusive or modified American control of the strategic nuclear capabilities of the alliance. French and British strategic nuclear forces exist and are being improved despite considerable cost in economic resources and independent effort. The choice for the United States is between *laisser faire* and active assistance, within the bounds of domestic constraints and international treaty obligations, to Britain and France in their efforts to create viable nuclear capabilities.

The choice seems pre-empted by the need to strengthen the overall Western posture in Europe and to restore the bonds of mutual trust and confidence between the United States and its major allies. The global considerations of unfolding American long-range policy are another factor. The Nixon Doctrine envisages an American-West European partnership in a multipower world. Partnership, along with Washington's recognition that it has reduced means to support its strategy, requires greater West European self-reliance. Given the weight of nuclear weapons in the scales of power, self-reliance requires that Western Europe obtain and control a credible measure of that power. In light of abiding nationalist tendencies in Western Europe, the most realistic possibility appears to be to concentrate on strengthening the British and French nuclear capabilities. Moreover, in light of strategic nuclear parity, it would be to the advantage of the United States to have some hedge against a decline in the credibility of its nuclear guarantee. Few would doubt that a primary Soviet goal is the removal of U.S. strategic protection from Europe. The existence of meaningful nuclear capabilities in European hands would help to offset the loss of West European confidence if a perception of decoupling were to prevail in European capitals. The gradual development of truly effective nuclear forces with American help could contribute greatly toward neutralizing the effects of that perception and could render the process less dangerous.

To demonstrate allied cohesion and resoluteness vis-à-vis the Soviet-dominated Warsaw Pact, however, the British and French strategic nuclear forces would eventually have to be coordinated within a wider European framework—if not in NATO, then in some type of revived Western European Union structure or within the European Community context. Such coordination is also crucial to soothe West German fears of losing American protection and being relegated to a second rate power vis-à-vis Britain and France. But there is no reason to insist that either France or Britain would have to surrender ultimate national control over its nuclear forces or jettison its own national targeting plans. The American strategic deterrent, before the dawn of nuclear parity, has ably protected the West European continent, yet always remained under undiluted U.S. control. Britain's insistence on such autonomy has similarly been accepted.

One way of enhancing the effectiveness of the British and French forces is through nuclear collaboration. A host of factors, however, makes the outlook for a meaningful Anglo-French nuclear entente far from bright. This is not the place to examine the factors that argue for or against a concerted nuclear effort between the French and British. Suffice it to say that the difference in strategic concepts in London and Paris, the asymmetrical levels in nuclear technology of the two countries, the absence of compelling economic motives, and severe political constraints render the prospects for effective cooperation remote.

A more realistic solution for strengthening British and French nuclear forces can probably · be found in American support of British and French nuclear efforts. Washington may wish to consider expanding the long-standing American-British cooperation in the nuclear field. This would meet with fewer obstacles in the United States than a rapproachement with France would; the latter's withdrawal from NATO's integrated command structure remains a sensitive issue in Washington. But France's insistence on retaining full control over its own forces and avoiding arrangements that would commit it to participate automatically in military operations augurs ill for the possibility of its return to the NATO fold. An American nuclear arrangement with France would, therefore, have to be in a bilateral context outside the NATO framework. The sense of malaise that pervaded French-American relations in the sixties stemmed precisely from the incompatibility between France's nuclear aspirations and America's determination to arrest nuclear proliferation. President Nixon's call for a more meaningful partnership, however, goes beyond a more equitable burden-sharing. It is a major step toward accepting France as a nuclear power. If the Nixon Administration provides effective leadership, it should be able to sway domestic critics, including those from Congressional quarters.

At the very least, the U.S. Administration can stimulate the quest for solution by conveying its readiness to explore the road to cooperation with France. Two tactical considerations should govern the effort: (1) the dialogue should be staged and phased in such a manner as to avoid any impression that U.S. willingness to explore cooperation portends an American intent to sever the strategic nuclear forces from the defense of Western Europe; and (2) the U.S. approach should be low-key, and actual assistance should be very gradual.

In lieu of its assistance with France's nuclear program, the United States should ask France for increased cooperation in the planning of West European defense. As the scope of U.S. aid increases, the

American price tag should go up. To be sure, conditions obviously unacceptable to the French should be avoided. France's sovereignty and its control over its own forces are not negotiable. Its leaders continue to believe that France cannot entrust its ultimate defense to any foreign ally. But the United States can expect an improvement in U.S.-French political relations, which in the long run will help to enhance the overall Western defense posture. Such a result would be a rich reward. By strengthening France's nuclear program and expertise, moreover, the United States would create the conditions in which Anglo-French nuclear cooperation would be possible.

Bruised by the expulsion from France's once hospitable soil and the French shattering of American hopes for NATO military integration and European political union, the United States' reluctance to engage in a nuclear dialogue with France is understandable. Nevertheless, the problem faces the United States now and the swiftly changing strategic scene makes a solution imperative. If France is no longer an integrated ally, it can be a true partner, whose determination to defend the West should be harnessed to a Western solution.

V. THE ROLE OF THE TACTICAL NUCLEAR AND
CONVENTIONAL FORCES

The threat of the U.S. strategic forces and the French and British nuclear forces serves to deter Soviet aggression in general, and, if deterrence were to fail, to deter escalation to the nuclear theater level of war. Contributing to deterrence requirements are the American nuclear systems located in Europe that can reach the Soviet homeland. Currently, the U.S. forward based systems, notably the long-range nuclear armed aircraft, fulfill this role. For the European allies, these aircraft present visible evidence of the American commitment to defend Western Europe. They are the only U.S. nuclear systems in the European theater that can hit Soviet targets. This does not necessarily mean that, if deterrence were to fail, the European allies would wish to strike the Soviet Union immediately; it means that they value the political utility of having a visible system with this capability. For these reasons particularly the quick reaction alert (QRA) aircraft contribute to the cohesion of the Alliance. The widely reported Soviet efforts in SALT I to include the U.S. forward based systems were viewed with great apprehension in allied capitals as another Soviet effort to remove the U.S. nuclear umbrella from the continent.

These aircraft are, however, vulnerable to Soviet pre-emptive attack. Their capability to break through Warsaw Pact air defenses is limited; moreover, the cost of these planes and their maintenance is relatively high. If one day some of the current aircraft would be replaced with other more suitable systems, such as missiles, the allies would have to be carefully prepared and be convinced that such a step would not presage a strategic decoupling from Western Europe. Any substitute systems, moreover, should meet allied demands of being visible to the allies on the continent and having a range sufficient to cover, if necessary, targets in the Soviet Union. Still, the FBS and the American and allied strategic forces alone would not suffice to deter a massive or even a limited conventional aggression.

Moreover, if the Soviets were to believe that, the presence of American forces notwithstanding, the United States no longer had the will to defend and, if necessary, to resort to the use of nuclear weapons, or that the will of the American allies had seriously weakened, they might be tempted to adopt an increasingly belligerent policy. Such a policy could eventually lead, either deliberately or through accident or miscalculation, to armed aggression against Western Europe. Under such circumstances, the most likely Soviet thrust would be conventional rather than nuclear, to avoid unnecessary collateral damage and to capture Europe as intact as possible. To avoid providing the United States with targets suitable for nuclear counterattack, the Soviet Union would probably attack in relatively dispersed formations.

For halting an armed Soviet probe or a limited conventional thrust, it is imperative that the United States and its allies maintain adequate conventional forces. If, however, the Soviet Union persisted in its aggression, the Western allies would need their conventional troops to canalize the enemy's formations into areas more favorable for counterattack and into nuclear targets. If the Soviet Union continued to press on, the Western allies would have to resort to the use of tactical nuclear weapons to liquidate these penetrations. An early recourse to the use of tactical nuclear weapons would be necessary in light of Soviet superiority in conventional forces. A significant increase in conventional power on the part of the Western allies is clearly not possible. The United States, already struggling to contain domestic pressures for reducing man-power commitments abroad, cannot undertake such increases; nei-ther can America's European allies. Besides, the allies want to avoid a protracted conventional war on their continent.

Consistent with the requirement for uncertainty is the necessity for *not* fixing in advance the stage at which the tactical nuclear weapons are to be introduced; this should be determined by the developments of the actual military situation. Tactical nuclear fire-power should be introduced as a supplement to conventional fire-power to stop penetrations before actual or potential breakthroughs are made. The nuclear strikes should be selective and against mili-tary targets, but executed in such a way as to keep collateral damage to a minimum.

In response, the Soviet Union could, of course, consider escala-tion. But then, in view of the demonstrated resolve of the Western allies to use nuclear weapons, the Soviet Union would have to contemplate that it would place its own homeland at risk to a nuclear strike. Unless it had determined to complete the capture of Europe regardless of the consequences, the militarily meaningful use of tactical nuclear weapons by the allies would induce the Soviet Union to halt its aggression and withdraw.

To provide for a more credible tactical nuclear defense, however, the tactical components of the force need to be improved. Accord-ing to a recent analysis,[3] the current U.S. tactical nuclear stockpile is ill-suited to meet European political demands for limiting collat-eral damage, because the fission content of the weapons is high, their yields are too big, and their accuracy is not satisfactory. However, the technology for cleaner and more accurate tactical nuclear weapons is in hand and could help render the Western defense posture on the continent politically more acceptable to the allies and militarily more viable.

The advanced concepts for tactical nuclear weapons include suppressed radiation weapons which can considerably limit the fallout but increase the blast effect. These weapons could be used to strike relatively hard targets, such as storage sites. Enhanced

---

3. For a detailed analysis of the current state of the art for tactical nuclear weapons, see Robert M. Lawrence, "On Tactical Nuclear War. I and II," *Revue Militaire Générale*, January 1971, pp. 46-59, and February 1971, pp. 237-261; and William Beecher, "Over the Threshold," *Army*, July 1972, pp. 17-20.

radiation weapons, on the other hand, limit the blast and heat effects but increase the prompt radiation without producing long-lasting radioactive products. They could be employed as antipersonnel weapons. Another concept calls for induced radioactivity in tactical nuclear weapons to restrict or deny the use of an area to enemy forces for a given time, depending on the military requirements. These weapons produce relatively short-lived radioactivity and reduce problems of long-term contamination. They could be effective in denying key transit areas to the enemy. In short, there is an array of small nuclear weapons that can exploit and vary their effects.

Given the high degree of accuracy in the delivery systems that is now possible through television, laser, and other guidance, the yields of advanced weapons can be greatly reduced. The capability to deliver accurate, concentrated firepower in small units allows for maximum maneuver, decentralization and dispersal, and concealment. As a result, the West would have a greatly enhanced surprise capability which would profoundly compound the problems for the opponent, thereby enhancing the deterrence and defense posture of the West. If introduced in the stockpile, these weapons would help to support a strategy that seeks to offset the Soviet advantage of mass and blitzkrieg tactics.

All this does not imply a strategy which calls for a largely tactical nuclear defense. Such a strategy would clearly be just as unpalatable to America's allies in Europe as the conventional emphasis strategy of the sixties. Nor would it, in all likelihood, be acceptable to the majority of policy-makers in Washington. But the development of a new discriminate and highly accurate tactical nuclear component, balanced with a similarly improved conventional capability, would go far toward meeting the political requirements of limiting collateral damage, yet would give the Western posture the necessary flexibility and effectiveness at the battlefield level.

The fact that the conventional allied forces in Europe can stand improvement has been repeatedly documented. The study by the NATO Defense Planning Committee on "Alliance Defence for the Seventies" ("AD70") reportedly listed a series of deficiencies in the allied forces.[4] Here again, the so-called smart weapons technology

---

4. *Strategic Survey*, 1970 (London: Institute for Strategic Studies, 1971), p. 19.

for highly mobile weapons systems with highly accurate target
acquisition, notably in the area of artillery and antitank and antiaircraft missiles, would go far toward strengthening the quality of the
Western conventional forces.[5] Terminal homing systems fitted to
missiles, artillery, or other weapons would permit a weapon to
strike a target with surgical precision. The impact on cost effective
combat power becomes evident when we consider that it took from
200 to 300 rounds to cause a casualty in World War II and the
Korean war.[6] The optically tracked, wire-guided TOW missile was
already a major advance in antitank systems. Yet the TOW is not
even fitted with a terminal homing device, but depends on launch-
er-to-target operator guidance. It is not difficult to envisage what
the refinement of terminal guidance would do to such a weapon.

To assess the political and military utility of smart weapons and
their implications for manpower and expenditures as well as for
doctrine and strategy requires a great deal of study. At this stage,
however, four tentative conclusions may be drawn. First, because
terminal homing permits a weapon to be placed in the general area
above the target from which it will find its own way, the launchers
and the missile's initial guidance can generally be relatively simple
and inexpensive. Second, as has been mentioned, smart weapons,
because of their sure-hit capability, permit savings in manpower and
weapons, and hence also expenditures. Third, the new technology
promises to offset to some extent the Soviet advantage of massive
quantities with quality. Fourth, precision guided conventional
weapons permit small units, dispersion, mobility, and flexibility.
These characteristics suggest a similar force structure and posture as
for the advanced accurate tactical nuclear weapons. Moreover,
smart conventional weapons and small accurate tactical nuclear
weapons appear to be able to cover complementary targets: the
former would effectively cover many point targets, whereas the
latter would cover the hard fixed targets and many area targets. For
these reasons the dual capability problem that has bedeviled the

---

5. For a discussion of new developments in military technology, including
terminal homing systems and laser-guided and television-guided antitank and
antiaircraft missiles, see Trevor Cliffe, *Military Technology and the European
Balance* (London: Institute for Strategic Studies, 1972) and John T. Burke,
"Smart Weapons: A Coming Revolution in Tactics," *Army*, February 1973, pp.
15ff.

6. Burke, *op. cit.*, p. 16.

military planner since the introduction of tactical nuclear weapons appears now to be nearing solution.

The introduction of precision guided conventional and nuclear weapons in Europe would provide an effective capability against the Soviet armor and tactical air elements, which constitute major dimensions of the Soviet offensive threat. By emphasizing antitank and antiaircraft systems, moreover, the West would maintain a truly defensive posture. Improved precise and clean tactical nuclear weapons would help to deter the Soviet Union from attacking with massed formations and would serve to cover the larger targets. The improved accurate conventional forces would help to deter the Soviet Union from attacking with more dispersed formations, serve to cover the smaller targets, and thus participate in the nuclear defense. Together these two components of the Western posture, if protected by the umbrella of U.S. and European strategic forces, would considerably vitiate the Soviet Union's tactics and its war-fighting capability as an instrument of military as well as political coercion.

Although the deployment of the full array of advanced systems is not expected until the late 1970s,[7] some systems, such as the Maverick and Walleye air-to-surface missile with television homing, have already been used. An increased emphasis on developing smart weapons—conventional and nuclear—will offer a much more viable defense for Western Europe. Implications for manpower and military budgets can then be evaluated. Moreover, the development of smart weapons could strengthen the bargaining position of the West in negotiating troop reductions with the Soviet Union without degrading the Western deterrence and defense position.

So far the focus has been primarily on the problems of Western Europe; the need for retaining an effective posture on Europe's northern and southern flanks should not be forgotten. Geographical and terrain factors inhibit an effective local defense of the northern periphery. So do political factors. Neither Norway nor Denmark permits the stationing of foreign troops or nuclear weapons on its territory, although the Danish army has Honest John surface-to-surface missile systems in its weapons inventory.[8] Denmark, how-

---

7. Cliffe, *op. cit.* p. 20.
8. The nuclear warheads for Denmark's missiles are not stored on Danish soil. See Cliffe, *op. cit.*, p. 35.

ever, is planning to reduce substantially its military forces and
defense spending. Probably more than anywhere else, the northern
flank derives its security from the strength of the Alliance as a
whole.

At the southern flank the American Sixth Fleet is a primary U.S.
instrument for underwriting the Western position. Withdrawal of
the U.S. naval presence would seriously undermine the defense of
the entire southern flank of Western Europe and would leave the
southern allies in the shadow of overwhelming Soviet land and
airpower without the reassurance of any countervailing local deterrence provided by a meaningful U.S. presence. For Greece and
Turkey, moreover, NATO has always been identified with its most
powerful member. From their vantage point, Soviet naval intrusion
in the Mediterranean further underscores the continued need for
the American military presence. The tangible evidence of U.S.
concern, reflected in the visibility of the Sixth Fleet, conveys to the
southern NATO members that an alternative to a neutralist or
pro-Soviet orientation remains. The political coloring of the current
Greek regime notwithstanding, the U.S. homeporting agreement
with Greece strengthens the earnestness of the American commitment in allied eyes. For the seventies there appears to be no
substitute for the U.S. maritime presence in the plans for the
security of the southern flank.

VI. PROSPECTS FOR THE SEVENTIES

Although the Atlantic Alliance is beset with problems of diminishing allied cohesion and growing Soviet military capabilities and
political initiatives, a viable strategy for the Alliance can still be
found. Such a strategy would structure into a coherent whole the
roles of the American strategic nuclear forces, the British and
French nuclear deterrents, and the tactical nuclear and conventional
forces within the theater as well as the naval elements at the flanks.
To strengthen the perception of coupling, the American strategic
forces should maintain some measure of counterforce capability. To
enhance the overall posture, the British and French nuclear capabilities should be strengthened—an effort which may have to occur
outside the NATO framework. To strengthen the credibility of
defense further, improvements and modifications in the tactical
nuclear and conventional components must be made.

The combination of these modifications could permit the United

States to reduce part of its forces in Europe. The prospects of precision guided weapons in particular would eventually permit a reduction in troops. The actual level of U.S. troop strength, as well as any contemplated changes in the type of forces, however, are clearly issues that should be negotiated in an American-allied forum before they are discussed with the Soviet Union.

However, the possibility of large-scale U.S. troop withdrawals without the serious compromise of the Western deterrence and defense posture is remote. If Western Europe is to be preserved as the frontier of Western, including American, security, then there is no alternative to a continued U.S. military involvement in Western Europe. Shaped by wise and far-sighted American leaders, the American commitment to Western Europe reflects the abiding U.S. interest in maintaining a reasonable balance of politico-military power with the Soviet Union in Europe. The perceived climate of détente does not invalidate this commitment.

America, Russia, and Europe
in the Light
of the Nixon Doctrine

Richard Pipes

In Solzhenitsyn's *August 1914*, among the hordes of incompetent officers leading the imperial Russian armies to their doom, one figure stands out, that of Colonel Vorotyntsev. He alone has his wits about him as he rushes from one sector of the wobbling front to another, querying generals and common soldiers, studying the topography, observing enemy dispositions, and, in the end, guiding back to Russian lines a small band of retreating soldiers. All along, Vorotyntsev sees what needs to be done with a lucidity of which those actually entrusted with the responsibility for decisions are entirely incapable; and had someone like him been in charge, Russian troops surely would not have suffered the debacle of Tannenberg. Exasperated by the obtuseness of his superiors, at one point he asks himself: "Pochemu PONIMANIE vsegda sloitsia nizhe VLASTI?"—Why does understanding always lie beneath authority?

Why, indeed? If I could converse with the colonel or his creator, I would suggest the following answer: Because understanding, being a product of intellectual processes, concerns itself primarily with ends, with what needs to be done; authority, on the other hand, involving as it does management of men, belongs to the realm of applied arts, and tends to become preoccupied with means. Sometimes this preoccupation grows so obsessive that those in power lose sight of the whole purpose to which power has been given them. The more ambitious an undertaking, the more people involved in it, the greater the likelihood that overconcern with the means will produce stupendous mismanagement. (Hence Santayana's definition of fanaticism as "redoubling one's efforts after one has forgotten one's aims.")

All of which is meant to explain my temerity in presenting a critique of policies of statesmen whose intentions are no worse than mine, but who also happen to have access to information that is inaccessible to me. The great merit of free public opinion is that it acts as a corrective to statesmanship by raising questions of purpose, all too often obscured by concerns with implementation.

The so-called Nixon Doctrine appears to be the product of two factors: the steady growth of Soviet military power and the concurrent decline of the American public's willingness to continue bearing a heavy load of international obligations. In some ways these two factors are causally related, but it is safe to say that of itself neither would have produced the kind of change in foreign policy that the Nixon Doctrine entails. The inevitability of some kind of disengagement from the Truman Doctrine had become apparent even before Mr. Nixon assumed office. In an essay published in 1968, Mr. Kissinger outlined the principles of foreign policy which the Republican Administration has been following ever since. He called for a new world "order," one of whose features would be a more equitable spread of responsibilities among all the major powers:

Our deepest challenge will be to evoke the creativity of a pluralistic world, to base order on political multipolarity even though the overwhelming military strength will remain with the two superpowers. . . . A more pluralistic world . . . is profoundly in our long-term interest.[1]

1. Henry A. Kissinger, "Central Issues of American Foreign Policy," in Kermit Gordon, ed., *Agenda for the Nation* (Washington, D.C.: The Brookings Institution, 1968), pp. 589, and 599.

This basic idea became subsequently elaborated into the Nixon Doctrine which—like the historic causes giving rise to it—rests on two principles:

1. In regard to the Soviet Union, America's only serious military rival, "confrontation" is to give way to "negotiation." Rather than attempt at every point of the globe to match and frustrate Soviet challenges with countermoves of its own, as the theory of containment had demanded, the United States will concentrate on locating areas of agreement between the two superpowers. No matter how insignificant or even trivial these agreements may be from the politico-military point of view (so the theory runs), they create a climate of mutual trust conducive to the solution of major differences. Concurrently, through increased trade, the USSR is to be enmeshed in a "web of interests" through which it will gain a greater stake in world stability.

2. In order to make foreign policy burdens lighter and more acceptable to its public, the United States will insist that its allies and friends exert more effort on their own behalf. Peace—and, hopefully, freedom—are everyone's concern.[2] The United States will be willing to help those whose security is threatened, but it will no longer rush to bail them out. In particular, Western Europe and Japan must be weaned from their overdependence on U.S. military strength, and must invest a larger share of their national product in defense.

Like every statesman in our history-obsessed age, Mr. Nixon is anxious to win for himself a secure place in history books, for which reason he is given to wild exaggerations of both the novelty and the significance of his policies. Undoubtedly, the Nixon Doctrine marks a major departure from the foreign policy pursued by the United States since 1948. Whether it indeed inaugurates a "new era" in international relations, as we are insistently told, remains to be seen; such attributions are better left to the historian. As to its alleged novelty, here too the historian may be permitted a skeptical attitude. In terms of diplomatic practice, the Nixon Doctrine introduces nothing new; it merely combines two well-known and tested methods of handling international rivalries, the idea of the "con-

---

2. I say "hopefully" because in recent years, responding to the Soviet "peaceful coexistence" propaganda policy, the United States has allowed the cause of peace to overshadow completely that of freedom, in which the USSR, of course, has no interest. It is certainly easier to search for peace at any price than on stated conditions.

cert" of great powers (the United States and the Soviet Union) and the idea of the balance of power (the United States and the rest of the world). The two elements of the Nixon Doctrine are not correlated in any apparent way, with the result that the present administration pursues two separate policies.

To raise questions about its originality or historic significance is not to reject the Nixon Doctrine. Given the realities of the international and domestic situation in the late 1960s, it is difficult to see how the policy of containment could have been maintained. The only conceivable alternative—complete abandonment of world responsibilities—would have been much worse for the United States and its friends. The conduct of foreign policy under President Nixon has been, on the whole, more skillful than under his immediate predecessors. The weakness of the Doctrine seems to me to lie in its theoretical underpinnings and it is these that I wish to question. Are its basic assumptions realistic? Are they mutually compatible? A frankly pragmatic foreign policy would be immune to such critical analysis. A policy based on a view of a new world "order," one which promises to usher in a new "era," is not. Doctrines have a tendency to acquire a life of their own, to produce action in their own support. Such was the fate of the policy of containment: conceived and formulated on the basis of a realistic appraisal of Communist intentions and American capabilities, it eventually degenerated into something corresponding to neither.

The Nixon Doctrine rests on a theoretical conception of Communism and the Soviet regime. If one can judge by Mr. Nixon's public pronouncements, it is his view that the adversary which he as President faces is an ideological force strongly tinged with fanaticism. This view may be a legacy of his early political career, launched when the anti-Communist hysteria in the United States was at its height. It may also reflect his superficial education. Whatever the reason, there is nothing in President Nixon's speeches that indicates a rudimentary acquaintance with the histories of Russia and its Communist Party, or with the political, economic, and social realities of the contemporary Soviet Union. Apparently he is unaware that the rulers of the Soviet Union and other Communist states have a material interest in the preservation and expansion of their system and that therefore their commitment to it is not merely or even primarily due to an ideologically inspired set of attitudes.

Attitudes can be changed, and it is this prospect that underlies Mr. Nixon's apparently genuine optimism about future Russo-American relations. He seems persuaded that the logic of events requires the world, especially the industrialized nations headed by the United States and the Soviet Union, to draw closer to one another and to learn to cooperate in the solution of common human problems, such as the quality of the environment and the application of science, to mention but two. However, from the reasonable premise that nations *ought to* engage in such cooperation, Mr. Nixon imperceptibly slips into the conclusion that they *will* in fact do so. He is remarkably prone to change the conditional mood of a verb into an indicative one. By means of rhetorical devices, "should" turns into "shall" in his public pronouncements, and, one suspects, in the privacy of his mind.

What makes this faulty logic doubly dangerous is that it is bolstered by a more sophisticated but no less fallacious conviction of Mr. Kissinger's that in modern times territorial expansion has become an anachronism:

In the past, stability has always presupposed the existence of an equilibrium of power which prevented one state from imposing its will on the others. The traditional criteria for the balance of power were territorial. A state could gain overwhelming superiority only by conquest.... In the contemporary period, this is no longer true. Some conquests add little to effective military strength; major increases in power *are possible* entirely through developments within the territory of a sovereign state.... If the Soviet Union had occupied Western Europe but had remained without nuclear weapons, it would be less powerful than it is now with its existing nuclear arsenal within its present borders.[3]

Mr. Kissinger does not tell us what would be the effect on its power status if the Soviet Union had *both* its nuclear arsenal and Western Europe. One suspects that his views on the matter may have undergone some modification as a result of personal experiences with the unappeasable North Vietnamese appetite for territory. Nevertheless, the notion that expansion is no longer profitable does underlie much of the Nixon Doctrine in theory and in practice, reinforcing the related view of great power conflict as out of date. Here too the conditional shades into the affirmative apparently without the author's awareness of the transition.

The political instinct of Mr. Nixon and the historical convictions

3. Kissinger, *op. cit.*, p. 590; the emphasis is mine.

of Mr. Kissinger lead them to the same conclusion: modern conditions impel mankind toward cooperation and render obsolete the spirit of rivalry, aggressiveness, and expansion, as well as the politico-military techniques derived from it. In accordance with this premise, conflict with the Soviet Union is to be de-emphasized and the maximum effort put into seeking out areas of mutual agreement. Personal contacts with Soviet leaders have amply demonstrated that they are anything but fanatical ideologues, and have thus strengthened the President's and his aides' belief in their responsiveness to pragmatic arguments.

Assuming that this analysis is correct, it is difficult to know where to begin the critique of the Nixon Doctrine, which is so riddled with misconceptions and inconsistencies. To begin with, the equation modernity = peace goes back at least a century and a half, to Saint-Simon and the Saint-Simonians, and, somewhat later, Herbert Spencer, who had confidently predicted that the age of "industrialism" would soon replace that of "militarism." The two global wars waged not by the so-called backward but by the most industrialized nations of the world should have laid this appealing equation permanently to rest, but this apparently has not happened. Much of Mr. Nixon's optimism has a pronounced Wilsonian ring, although, according to Henry Brandon, a sympathetic historian of his administration, Mr. Nixon regards Wilson's "idealism" with suspicion. [4] Many of his ideas concerning the need to create a new order to prevent future conflict also remind one of General Smuts and his 1919 blueprints for the League of Nations.

Let us now turn briefly to some specific fallacies:

1. Communism is not merely or even primarily an ideology; nor has fanaticism ever played a decisive role in it. True, Communist movements prior to seizure of power attract ideologues and fanatics; but these are promptly gotten rid of after power has been acquired. Lenin began to slough off his ideological allies almost immediately after he had overthrown the Provisional Government. By accepting the extremely onerous peace terms of Brest Litovsk, he gave his recalcitrant followers an unforgettable lesson in political pragmatism. The readiness of the Soviet regime to sacrifice any element in its doctrine for the sake of preserving and enhancing its power is a fact so well established historically that one is embar-

---

4. *The Retreat of American Power* (New York: Doubleday, 1973), p. 21.

rassed even to have to mention it. There has never been a political doctrine or a government with a keener sense of the realities of power relationships (*sootnoshenie sil*) than the Soviet one. The Soviet system is and always has been distinguished by extreme pragmatism. It is indeed a classic example of authority which, facing gigantic tasks of harnessing human resources, has utterly lost sight of its original aims.

2. This being the case, it is groundless to expect that the Soviet regime will turn more pragmatic. If the Soviet government has agreed to a partial détente with the United States—indeed, has initiated and insisted on it—the reason must be sought not in a growing awareness among its leaders that humanity shares a common destiny, but in factors having to do with international power relationships. The Russians, it must be emphasized, interpret the "balance of power" much more broadly than do Western strategists, who tend to restrict it to military matters: the former include and weigh under this rubric economic, social, and psychological factors. Thus, they may be aggressive when the military balance happens to favor their opponents (e.g., 1946-1950), and conciliatory when it is evenly distributed (the present time), factors other than military ones playing a decisive part in the calculation. The Soviet government launched the détente policy in 1956 for two reasons: because it desired a breathing spell for its population, which twenty-five years of Stalinism and World War II had left exhausted, and because it wished to extricate itself from the isolation into which Stalin's foreign policy had driven it. Since then other considerations have come into play. The primary consideration today is the conflict with China, which compels the Soviet Union to reduce tension on the Western front. Second, there are economic difficulties and the need for Western technology and credits. Paradoxically, having attained nuclear parity, the Soviet Union has a greater interest in a détente with the United States than it had when it was vulnerable to nuclear destruction. This is a practical decision. There is no evidence whatever in Soviet statements intended for internal consumption that the Soviet Union shares President Nixon's and Mr. Kissinger's ideas about the nature of contemporary international diplomacy. The adamant refusal to call off or even to restrain the "ideological war" is not a minor issue, as the White House appears to think; it signifies that from Moscow's point of view the détente is a temporary expedient. Internally, the Soviet media ascribe the

improvement in relations with the United States to a shift in the balance of power in Russia's favor. The United States is depicted, as it was in Stalin's day, as the central bastion of world imperialism and the principal backer of "fascist" regimes. There are no delusions *there* about the United States having experienced a change of heart; America's new policy is said to be the result exclusively of the realities of the power relationship. The unwillingness of the Soviet Union to participate in the "new era" of international diplomacy is clearly demonstrated by the continued jamming of the Voice of America broadcasts. Because he regards Communism primarily as an ideology, Mr. Nixon prefers to disregard these facts, which he probably views as a kind of anachronism and as a practical politician tends to dismiss. If, however, he approached the Soviet Union as a congeries of institutions designed to protect the special interests of the ruling elite, he would take a much more serious view of the Soviet insistence on the right to continue the "ideological" war.

Anyone who reads the President's annual reports to Congress cannot help being struck by one glaring inconsistency. In the theoretical parts, which explain the premises of the Administration's foreign policy, everything is sunny. But as soon as it is time to deal with the specifics, dark clouds appear. It is as if we were listening to an opera, the first half of which was composed by Mozart and the second by Wagner: suddenly Pamino begins to sing the *Götterdämmerung*. The Soviet Union, which is supposed to be evolving from fanaticism to pragmatism and entering into a common partnership with the rest of the world, unaccountably arms itself at a pace and in a style which cannot be explained solely in terms of its security needs. The bewilderment of the President with this evidence is apparent in his 1972 address, where he speaks of "developments in 1971 which make it unclear whether we are witnessing a permanent change in Soviet policy or only a passing phase concerned more with tactics than with a fundamental commitment to a stable international system." Among these developments the President lists the Soviet Union's manufacture and deployment of weapons, its arms policy in the Middle East, its behavior during the India-Pakistan crisis, and "the expansionist implications of Soviet naval activities."[5] This is quite a list. Since

5. *U.S. Foreign Policy for the 1970's: The Emerging Structure for Peace*, A Report to the Congress by Richard Nixon, President of the United States, 9 February 1972 (Washington, D.C.: U.S. Government Printing Office, 9 February 1972), pp. 5-6.

these facts raise basic questions about Soviet intentions, one would expect some analysis of their significance to ensue. In vain. In the next paragraph of the President's 1972 speech all these doubts are brushed aside as the catalogue of "positive developments" is resumed. One can only conclude that the present Administration, while aware of evidence contrary to its premises, chooses to ignore it. The result is that the two superpowers cooperate in combating heart disease and protecting walruses off the Aleutians while at the same time competing in the perfection of the most lethal kinds of weapons. The White House, bent on accentuating the positive, sees nothing worrisome in this.

Another of the glaring inconsistencies in President Nixon's foreign policy is the failure to link in any evident manner the Russo-American détente with his demands on Western Europe concerning its security. In his recent keynote address (23 April 1973) Mr. Kissinger strongly stressed the need for Europe to contribute more to its own defense, the necessity for Europeans to rethink their defense strategy, and the importance of keeping American troops in Europe, but he said nothing about the reasons behind these requests. The enemy is never mentioned. Against whom are all these measures intended? If the Soviet Union is indeed becoming a responsible power genuinely interested in maintaining world stability, then so much emphasis on military preparedness seems misplaced. Or are these contingency measures? There is a serious gap between U.S. policy toward Russia and that toward Europe, one result of which is that Europeans do not take very seriously American exhortations about the need for a greater defense effort on their part.

The importance of Western Europe to the United States is such that in the event of Russia's direct onslaught the United States would certainly react in an appropriate manner. President Nixon is as much aware as his predecessors have been of the fatal consequences that would ensue if West European talent and resources were to come under Soviet control. But for this very reason a direct military attack on Western Europe by the Red Army seems highly improbable. Not only do the Russians have no wish to trigger a nuclear exchange, but they also have less apocalyptic reasons for caution: the desire to maintain good working relations with the United States; lack of experience with coordinated offensive operations on hostile foreign territory; mistrust of satellite armies, and fear of disorders in the event of military reverses. The development by the United States of "smart weapons" capable of disorganizing the enemy logistic lines without recourse to nuclear warheads further weakens the offensive capacity of the Russians in Europe. True, the Soviet Union maintains very large troop concentrations in Europe—it has chosen not to weaken them in order to build up its Chinese front—and it has shown little interest in reasonable mutual force reductions. But from this it does not follow that the Soviet High Command seriously envisages the deployment of its European troops in massive offensive operations. The primary purpose of the Soviet divisions stationed in Europe is to intimidate. They are to preclude nationalist uprisings in Eastern Europe, and to remind Western Europe that over it always hangs the threat of a devastating war.

In view of these considerations, which seem to me to have a high degree of plausibility, the heavy stress laid by Western planners on major military conflict with the Soviet Union appears misplaced. Far too much effort goes into thinking and rethinking the possible Western responses to Soviet offensive operations against Western Europe, and far too little thought is devoted to other, more probable contingencies. On the military front, for example, some action may well take the form of intervention on the periphery of Western Europe—for instance, in Yugoslavia or Greece, where external aggression could be preceded and assisted by internal subversion. Does "flexible response" provide realistic countermoves for this possibility? For example, would NATO units credibly threaten East Germany or Czechoslovakia in order to deflect Soviet operations in the Balkans, should such be undertaken?

The West seems even less prepared to cope with what seems the most realistic threat to its integrity, namely, slow, patient, piecemeal disintegration of Western Europe by a combination of external and internal pressures. The Russian elite has unrivaled experience in uprooting neighboring powers in just such a manner: it is thus that the Russian state has traditionally extended its frontiers and managed to attain the highest rate of territorial expansion ever recorded. Anyone interested in these methods would do well to study the history of the Russian conquest of Novgorod (fifteenth century), Kazan (sixteenth century), and Poland (eighteenth century). The Ottoman Empire might well have fallen victim to the same process in the nineteenth century had it not been for resolute British action on its behalf. Nor should it be forgotten that the scramble for "concessions" in late imperial China, which only the outbreak of World War I prevented from ending in the dismemberment of that country by the great powers, had also been initiated by Russia (Manchuria, 1896 ff.). What we have here is a traditional manner of doing things, admirably suited to Russia's geopolitical situation and to its cumbersome, centralized political machine.

The first step in the eventual absorption of Europe by the Soviet Union has been taken. After a quarter century, the West has finally come to acknowledge the Russian occupation of Eastern Europe not only de facto but also de jure. The recent accords with West Germany mean, in effect, that the West has reconciled itself to Eastern Europe passing permanently into the Soviet sphere of influence and joining the rest of the Soviet empire.

The next step—control of Western Europe—is, of course, incomparably more difficult to accomplish. And yet preliminary measures must soon be taken by Russia to neutralize Europe's military threat for reasons which, in the first instance, have to do with its difficulties with China.

The Soviet Union is not at all pleased with President Nixon's balance-of-power policy, and denigrates it as dangerous to world stability. Why? A "pentagonal" world, envisaged by President Nixon, confronts Russia with the prospect of a two-front war with two potential hostile blocs: Western Europe acting in concert with the United States, and China allied with Japan. The prospect of a European-East Asian military entente, whatever its likelihood, must be a nightmare to Soviet statesmen and strategists. To counter it, the Soviet Union is vigorously pressing an alternative policy— namely, "collective security"—which it would like applied first to Europe and then to Asia. The purpose of such arrangements seems to be to prevent the formation of potential anti-Soviet blocs by the introduction of the principle that no major political or military decisions anywhere in the world can be taken without the Soviet Union's direct participation. This is one reason the Soviet Union lays such emphasis on the development of a navy, a force which has always served great powers as an instrument of "world politics."

Essentially, the Soviet Union hopes to neutralize the damage to its interests implied in the balance-of-power principle by establishing its physical (military) presence in every major strategic area of the globe and demanding a senior voice in all regional politico-military arrangements. A "collective security" pact in Europe

should enable the Soviet Union to nip in the bud any designs of
NATO to exert pressure on it should Russia become militarily
engaged in the Far East. Similarly, an Asian "collective security"
pact (Russia, America, India, Japan, etc.) could be used to isolate
and contain China.

It is difficult to believe that the Soviet Union will get away with
a scheme that so transparently serves its own interests and offers
the others nothing in return but a limitation of options. It is
impossible to see the purpose of a European "security pact" of
which the Soviet Union would be an active partner. Either the
Soviet Union is a threat to Western Europe, in which case it should
no more participate in European security arrangements than a wolf
be invited to join a self-defense organization of lambs, or it is not
such a threat, in which case there is no need for collective security.
Certainly the Soviet Union has no need to fear offensive actions
from NATO; past experience demonstrates that NATO does not
exploit Soviet difficulties. Nor does Western Europe confront a
military threat from any other source than the Soviet Union. One
must conclude, therefore, that the immediate purpose of Soviet
collective security proposals is to guarantee a dependable western
flank and to free its hands for possible action in East Asia.

Such is the immediate aim of Soviet security proposals, but
beyond them lurk long-term goals which carry ominous prospects
for Europe. Russian participation in the politico-military institutions regulating Western Europe—without, needless to add, corresponding opportunities being granted Western Europe in Europe's
Eastern half—will provide Russia with a framework within which to
initiate a process of internal disintegration of the kind mentioned
above. The basic tactic would be to divide in every country the
"peace" party from the "war" party, to pit one state against
another (especially France against Germany), to weaken economic
unity by deals with individual member states of the EEC, and, over
the long run, to detach Europe from the United States.

Realism requires one to recognize that this policy has much
better chances of success than one would have believed possible a
decade ago. The essential point, in my opinion, is that postwar
Europe has undergone a veritable social revolution which has decreased its willingness (although not its ability) to meet the kind of
threat the Soviet Union poses to its political existence. Until World
War II, Europe had been socially a highly stratified continent in

which the lower orders, as it were, "knew their place." Consumer goods beyond the essential ones, travel, most sports, spectacles, and luxuries were outside the range of their pocketbooks and even of their vision. Leadership positions in the diplomatic and military services were reserved for descendants of the "feudal" class and the propertied groups assimilated to it. Now, with the help of American military protection and investments, this situation has undergone radical change. The rise of wages accompanying advances in industrialization and the savings made on defense outlays with the attendant lowering of costs of consumer products have given the mass of Europeans for the first time in history access to goods and activities previously considered the exclusive domain of the elite. At the same time the old "feudal" class has dwindled in influence, partly because its past performance has discredited it and partly because the social democratization of Europe has diminished the awe in which it had been held traditionally. Western Europe is in the throes of a consumer orgy which, with each passing year, diminishes its appetite for an active foreign policy and a major defense effort. The West Europeans do not seem to wish to assume the responsibility for their political and military self-preservation and, deep in their hearts, they see no need to do so, being convinced that the United States cannot afford to let them fall into Russian hands. The policy of détente toward Russia pursued by the United States reinforces this belief, and so does the Russian peace offensive.

Realistically speaking, the best chance of preventing future Russian encroachments in Europe and in Asia seems to lie in a coordination of West European and Chinese diplomacies and (eventually) military strategies. The Chinese seem fully to realize the advantages which would accrue to them from such a policy. But they are not strong enough at this time to carry any weight, nor can they assure Europe of significant relief in the event Europe should be menaced by the Russians. American diplomacy for its part seems strangely to ignore this possibility, whether because it does not wish to alarm the Russians or because it believes that such a policy is impractical. However, ultimately this line seems more promising than the notion of an "Atlantic Community" pressed on Europe by the Nixon Administration. There is a curious inability in the White House to perceive the global ramifications of foreign policy, to understand that the détente with the Soviet Union produces effects on Euro-

pean attitudes toward Russia, and that the opening of American
-Chinese relations could in turn affect Russian behavior toward
Europe. The balance-of-power element in the Nixon Doctrine cannot be made workable if an exception is made for the Soviet Union
on the grounds of a special relationship between the two superpowers. If balance-of-power politics is to be pursued in earnest,
then Russia must be considered a factor in it; and once that is done
it will become obvious that the American-European relationship
also involves China and possibly Japan.

The Soviet Union
and Western Europe

Leopold Labedz

If the proverbial visitor from Mars were to try to understand the
present Soviet policy toward Europe, he would be puzzled by both
the Soviet explanations of it and the Western attitudes toward it.
He would immediately notice a number of strange juxtapositions
and incongruencies. The first would be the coincidence of Soviet
détente policy and the simultaneous Soviet strategic buildup which
resulted in the acknowledgment of Soviet nuclear parity with the
United States. The Martian visitor would notice that the Soviet
naval and air force expansion programs were vigorously pursued at
the time when the United States was reducing its global commitments, and that while the Soviet Union was extending them, it was
assiduously following a policy of what it called "constructive dialogue" with the Americans. What was it that Soviet policy was
trying to achieve for which it was prepared to disregard the bomb-

ing of Hanoi, to suspend the ransom tax on Jewish emigrants, to abstain from criticism of President Nixon, and to perform many other seemingly unnatural acts—from Brezhnev's speech in Tiflis (which helped the Administration defeat the Mansfield amendment) to the discretion of the Soviet press on the Watergate affair? This unusual self-restraint, whatever its interpretation by the "American imperialists," would indeed be difficult for our visitor to understand.

Looking for its motives, he would no doubt discover that in his speech at the 24th Congress of the CPSU Mr. Brezhnev declared:

The revolutionary slogans which we proclaim to the people are not empty words. Even when whole decades pass between the sowing and the harvest . . . the Soviet Communist Party will continue to pursue a policy in international affairs which will lead to the furtherance of the world-wide anti-imperialist struggle.

The Martian would find that the interpretation of "peaceful coexistence with the capitalist countries" is no different under Brezhnev than under his predecessors. "It 'cancels' only one type of struggle—war as a means of settling international issues."[1] The only innovation codified in theory is that intrabloc affairs are to be settled on the basis of the Brezhnev Doctrine. In his research the Martian would come across the resolution adopted at the meeting of the Central Committee of the CPSU on 27 April which noted Brezhnev's "great personal contribution" to Soviet foreign policy.

From his more objective stance, he might be a little less euphoric than Western commentators about the significance of the April 1973 reshuffle in the *Politburo*. Many of them found it positively heartening and declared that the new members would strengthen détente. Peregrine Worsthorne wrote in the *Sunday Telegraph* (29 April) that this is the assumption which "rightly or wrongly" was made in Western Europe. According to Nicholas Carroll in the *Sunday Times* (29 April), the faithful representative of Stalin and Khrushchev at the time of the Berlin and Cuba crises, Andrei Gromyko, is "widely admired in Western foreign ministries as a skilled and determined negotiator blessed with a dour sense of humour." Jonathon Steele commented on the inclusion of Marshal Grechko, whose tanks rolled to Berlin in 1953 and to Czechoslovakia in 1968, in an article in *The Guardian* (28 April) headed

---

1. *Leninism Today* (Moscow, 1970), p. 133.

"Brezhnev Sacks Peace Critics from *Politburo.*" According to Dev Murarka in *The Observer* (29 April), the promotion of Yuri Andropov, the head of the political police, who is busily stamping out Soviet intellectual dissent, "denotes that the KGB has been sufficiently tamed as well as rehabilitated to be given this accolade." Indeed Andropov may deserve it.

Our Martian visitor would already have noticed that, contrary to original Western expectations, détente did not produce an internal relaxation in the countries of the Soviet bloc but, in striking contrast to the arguments rationalizing the new *Ostpolitik*, resulted in the general tightening of political and cultural controls in the Soviet Union and Eastern Europe. There was a conscious effort over the whole area to counter prophylactically the risks involved in détente by a more rigid internal policy. If our visitor from Mars were to ask an American official for an explanation of these coincidences, he would hear that "the era of confrontation is over"—that, as President Nixon said in his Report to Congress on 1 June 1972, we have entered a period of negotiations through which we would be "forming habits of cooperation and strengthening institutional ties in areas of peaceful enterprise," so as to "create on both sides a steadily growing vested interest in the maintenance of good relations" between the United States and the Soviet Union.

If he were to ask about Western Europe, our Martian would find the situation "curiouser and curiouser." He would register diametrically opposite opinions about its political condition and prospects. Peregrine Worsthorne declared:

Today Western Europe is being courted on all sides, by the Soviet Union, by China and not only by the United States. The European Community is a court card which all the superpowers would like in their hand, and are prepared to pay a high price for. After the last war Western Europe was desperate for American protection. Today it still wants that protection, but not nearly so desperately, and not without being conscious that far from having to beg for it, it can probably go on getting it on any terms it wants.[2]

This is hardly a conclusion which will recommend itself to the Americans. On the other side of the Atlantic the political implications of the recovery of Europe are exaggerated for precisely the opposite reason. George Kennan wrote that "as the strength, self-confidence and unity of the West European community grow, the

2. Peregrine Worsthorne, *Sunday Telegraph*, 29 April 1973.

importance of the American involvement naturally declines."[3] The
political diagnosis of Walter Laqueur is more likely to be nearer the
mark: "The present state of West-East relations . . . tends to aggravate the paralysis of will now obtaining in Europe." Although the
risks in this situation are obviously more direct for Europe than for
the United States, it should be clear to any observer—even one from
Mars—that Western Europe is disinclined to face the implications
for itself of the coincidence between the Soviet policy of détente
and the "Nixon Doctrine." The simple truth is that in the last
decade a decline in the political will in the West has occurred, in the
United States and in Europe. Squabbles over defense costs are
merely a reflection of this. The policy of détente provides an outlet
for Western wishful thinking which is never far from the surface.

It is unfashionable to mention risks, much less to insist that
unless they are faced they may sooner or later turn into positive
dangers. Yet it is necessary to stress that the reasons that have
impelled the Soviet Union to seek détente—China, consolidation of
the Soviet hold over Eastern Europe, the need to import Western
technology—do not exclude the possibility that the Soviet Union
may also be pursuing more long-term goals, and if political developments present it with more opportunities in Europe, it is more than
likely that it would seize them in order to shift the balance of
power in the Soviet Union's favor. So far it has always done just
that. It is embarrassing to make such elementary points, but in the
present Western political context they do need repeating. Détente is
by definition a transitional period and the question of what follows
it is of cardinal importance. The Martian visitor would certainly ask
it, even if so few analysts and press commentators are inclined to do
so.

The assumption that the Soviet Union is now a status quo power
is questionable. In any case it would seem a prudent policy to avoid
leading it into temptation. Virtue, in morals and politics, may
consist of a chronic lack of opportunity. But such opportunity may
arise. If détente leads to American withdrawal from Western Europe, if Western Europe is unable to fill the gap resulting from
contraction of American power, thus leaving each West European
country to deal with the Soviet Union on a bilateral basis, the road

---

3. George F. Kennan, "After the Cold War," *Foreign Affairs*, October
1972, p. 214.

will be open to the "Finlandization" of the whole area. Even at
present one could give our Martian visitor names of several likely
candidates for the role of Kekkonen in various West European
countries.

Moreover, this comparison is unfair. What the Finns are doing is
dictated by circumstances largely beyond their control, whereas
Europeans would be in this situation on a more voluntary basis. It is
a melancholy thought that during the Khrushchev period many East
Europeans hoped eventually to reach the status of Finland. They
have not achieved it. And now the prospect is no longer excluded
that it is the West European nations which may eventually find
themselves in this position (without having Finnish *sisu* to cope
with it). Anti-Americanism parading as pro-Europeanism, squabbles
over agricultural prices with small regard for wider political considerations, concealed and unconcealed neutralist tendencies—all these
may lead to West European nonalignment rather than to West
European unity. The French policy of being in and out of NATO at
one and the same time; the "Scandinavian" attitude of Norway,
Denmark, and Iceland; German illusions about *Ostpolitik;* the internal malaise of Italy and Great Britain—all these West European
political and economic weaknesses provide opportunity targets for
Soviet policy, and Soviet leaders are only too well aware of this.
"Exploiting the contradictions among the imperialists" is an old
Leninist tradition. The Soviet and East European press constantly
harp on the differences over trade and monetary policies which are
occurring between the United States, the EEC, and Japan.

There may be room for argument on the long-term evolution of
Soviet political perceptions of the changing world, but there cannot
be any doubt that on the more immediate level of strategy and
tactics they retain certain ingrained characteristics which include subordination of strategic decisions to political considerations, the
pursuit of political goals by stages, concentration on the erosion of
the political will of the adversary, "salami tactics," etc. These
characteristics all derive from the historicist nature of Soviet ideology and, however misplaced the Soviet historical interpretation may
be, it confers on Soviet policy advantages of long-term consistency
and cohesion vis-à-vis the "pragmatism" of the Western adversaries
who so frequently confuse short-sightedness with pragmatism.

Whether this historicist cohesion can be maintained in the face of
historical developments which daily contradict the hallowed dog-

mas of Soviet ideology is indeed another question. But Soviet theoreticians perform incredible dialectical acrobatics in order to rationalize such developments. In international relations they have to square the circle by arguing that the Soviet Union is for détente and for "peaceful coexistence" with the American imperialists and their West European capitalist allies, and that it is promoting the principles of an "anti-imperialist" policy, unlike its Chinese rivals who have betrayed their earlier revolutionary posture:

Recently the bourgeois press has been making a great hue and cry about the invented question of the direction of change in the contemporary world, whether it be bi-polar (USA-USSR), triangular (USA-USSR-China), or multi-polar. . . . It has become fashionable at present to talk about a pentagonal world (USA, USSR, China, Western Europe and Japan). . . . This futile approach leads to an obvious misrepresentation of the real picture of the world with its two social poles—socialism and capitalism. The essence of the "bi-polar" or "multi-polar" conceptions is that they derive the development of international relations not from the class basis of the participating countries, but from narrow nationalist interests. . . . The Chinese version of the "two superpowers" (USA-USSR), allegedly trying to divide the world into their spheres of influence, fits appropriately into this scheme. Both "bi-polar" and "multi-polar" conceptions are directed against the foreign policy line of the Soviet Union and other socialist countries. . . . The principle of peaceful coexistence is first and foremost concerned with the creation of favourable international conditions for the building of socialism and communism, with the strengthening of international unity and cohesion of the socialist common-wealth, with aid to developing countries, with support for all contemporary progressive movements, with the assertion of those principles of international relations which would exclude war as an instrument for solving conflict and which would guarantee non-interference in the internal affairs of other countries, the development of trade and other economic relations between them on the basis of mutual interests and a firm rebuttal of the aggressive forces of imperialism.[4]

This doctrinal farrago can easily be dismissed as a ritual obeisance to obsolete doctrinal pieties, "signifying nothing," yet it does reflect the present Soviet perception of the world and rationalization of its own foreign policy role in it. As such, it is still relevant to note the observation made by Henry Kissinger sixteen years ago:

To our leaders, policy is a series of discrete problems; to the Soviet leaders it is an aspect of a continuing political process. As a result, the contest between us

---

4. W. Kortunow, "Peaceful coexistence and the ideological struggle," *Voprosy Istorii*, KPSS, 1, 1972.

and the Soviet system has had many of the attributes of any contest between a professional and an amateur.[5]

A lot of water has passed under the Potomac, Seine, and Thames since these words were written, and even more since President Roosevelt told Ambassador Bullitt that in his opinion Stalin wanted nothing but security and "that if I give him everything I possibly can and ask nothing in return, noblesse oblige, he won't try to annex anything and will work for a world of security and peace."[6] Now that hopes for détente resemble those earlier expectations of postwar cooperation with the Soviet Union, it may be necessary for our imaginary Martian to learn not only about the role of Marxist historicism in the conditioning of Soviet political strategy and tactics, but also about the lessons, if any, drawn by the West and the Soviet Union from postwar history. Without such a backward glance no innocent Martian could hope to understand the present risks for Europe.

The first thing which he will observe is that in all the current comment on the proposal for a new Atlantic Charter, nobody has questioned what happened to the old one which proclaimed "the right of all peoples to choose the form of Government under which they will live." It is true that Western Europe is not occupied by the Soviet Army as was Eastern Europe at the end of World War II, but it is also true that, in the thirty years that have passed, the question on the historical agenda has moved, as a result of the shift in the balance of power, from a question of the danger to the future freedom of Eastern Europe to one of the risks to the future freedom of Western Europe (not through Soviet occupation but through "Finlandization"). One can only hope that the new Atlantic Charter will be more effective for Western Europe than the old one was for Eastern Europe.

The second thing that our Martian will observe is that this shift has occurred in spite of long-lasting U.S. superiority in military technology.

The third thing he would notice is that when the Soviet Union was relatively weak, Stalin took a hard line in foreign policy

---

5. Henry A. Kissinger, *Nuclear Weapons and Foreign Policy* (New York: Harper, 1957), p. 434.
6. Quoted in John Lukacs, *The Great Powers and Eastern Europe* (New York, 1953), p. 799.

(tempered by caution), and when it had achieved strategic parity and was relatively strong, Brezhnev engaged in a policy of détente in the West. Is the difference to be explained by changes in the internal character of the Soviet Union? This was the predominant argument of Western commentators during the Khrushchev period when "de-Stalinization" provided a semblance of persuasiveness to the idea of a "change of heart" in the Soviet Union, as though foreign policy were simply a matter of heart. Under Brezhnev, there was no "de-Stalinization" but rather a steady return to a "hard" internal policy, a line confirmed at the April 1973 Central Committee Plenum which made it clear that in light of the dangers of "ideological subversion" being increased by détente, there would be extra vigilance and no relaxation of Party controls in the Soviet Union and Eastern Europe.[7] The same Plenum enhanced the status of Soviet foreign policy which has moved nearer the center of Soviet concern at the very time when the United States and the countries of Western Europe have shifted their focus to domestic preoccupations. The Plenum also declared that "the task of holding an all-European Conference on Security and Cooperation has moved to the forefront in European politics" (*Pravda*, 29 April).

If it is still correct that "to the Soviet leaders policy is an aspect of a continuing political process" and not "a series of discrete problems," and I believe it is, then our Martian guest would be entitled to question the political rationale of Soviet policies and the factors which in their architects' perception make these discrete juxtapositions into a cohesive line in "a continuing political process." In order to answer the question, he must notice another point which explains the current shift of direction in Soviet policy toward Europe: the failure of the Khrushchevian strategic perspective about the underdeveloped countries and about the economic race with the West.

In the mid-fifties, the Soviet leadership decided to direct a political offensive toward the Third World, the territory which seemed to hold revolutionary promise and to be prepared to accept the Soviet model of industrialization. The state-inspired rate of economic growth was seen as inexorably carrying the Soviet Union toward its cherished goal of "catching up and overtaking" the most

---

7. *Pravda*, 29 April 1973. Cf. Leopold Labedz, "Shadows over Helsinki," *Encounter*, June 1973.

advanced capitalist country, the United States of America, in labor
productivity—that supreme Marxist criterion of historical progress—as well as in the volume of production and in technological
competition.

The frustrations and reversals in the underdeveloped countries
mitigated the high hopes connected with the strategy directed at
"imperialism's soft underbelly." The conflict with China blocked it,
at least in Asia.

The economic perspective of the Khrushchev era failed no less
obviously. The rate of growth of the Soviet national income has
been falling since 1958 and, as Abram Bergson argues,[8] this was due
to the most sensitive element for Marxists: the decline in the rate of
increase in productivity. During the same time, Japan, Germany,
and Italy achieved higher rates of growth and the United States a
sufficiently high GNP increase to make all the Soviet boasts of the
fifties and early sixties look extremely unreal. Technological competition was even less promising as the Soviet Union had actually
fallen behind in the development of those new industries which are
decisive for what it terms "a scientific-technological revolution."[9]
The lost race to the moon acquired in this respect a symbolic
significance. The promise that the Soviet Union would overtake the
capitalist countries in 1970 in per capita consumption of milk and
butter has been forgotten. Even disregarding the problems concerning the quality and variety of distribution and service facilities,
Soviet per capita consumption is only about one-third that of the
United States and about half that of England. *Radio Erevan*, the
imaginary repository of Soviet unofficial jokes, summed it up in a
reply to a listener's question about the possibility of the building of
socialism in the United States: "Yes, it is possible, comrade, but
where are we going to buy our grain then?"

The collapse of the perspective of the Khrushchev era, in respect
to both political and economic strategy toward the external world,
induced the Soviet leaders to revise it. The new perspective was, of
course, not a result of one grand decision, but emerged through
recognition of new difficulties and a search for new opportunities.

---

8. *Problems of Communism*, March-April 1973, pp. 2-4.
9. In his *Western Technology and Soviet Economic Development,
1945-1965* (Stanford, Calif.: Hoover Institution, Stanford University, 1968)
Antony Sutton argues that "the kind of central planning that guides the Soviet
Union has virtually no capability for self-generated indigenous innovation."

It marked a shift of focus toward Europe, where the possibilities of political gains now seemed greater than before, better than in Asia with its Chinese deadlock and better than in the underdeveloped nations of other continents where fifteen years of Soviet military and economic aid did not bring any commensurate gains.[10]

The logical concomitant of the revised strategy was a modified policy toward the United States, which aimed at the neutralization of its new policy toward China, at involvement in Europe, and, if possible, at getting American credits and technological know-how. Détente was a logical instrument of this new perspective. A more militant strategy would produce the opposite effect: bring the opponents closer, make them more alert, and narrow down the area where "contradictions" between them could be exploited.[11] The results of the new strategy have so far been quite positive from the Soviet point of view, as the *Pravda* editorial of 29 April, summing up the results of the Central Committee Plenum on foreign policy, made clear by using terminology somewhat inappropriate to the détente: "The Soviet Union and the fraternal socialist countries have broken the front of the 'cold war'." The achievement of the Moscow-Bonn agreement was greeted in the Soviet press with an unprecedented outburst of satisfaction. The international recognition of the DDR and the conferment of legitimacy on the Soviet position in Eastern Europe were the cherished goals of Soviet policy for decades. And now, as the London communist *Morning Star* (30 April) reported it, the "security conference is top priority for the Soviet Union."

In contrast with some of his earthly hosts, the visitor from Mars would undoubtedly have acquired by now sufficient knowledge to recognize why this should be so. He would have noticed that Western countries are participating in the Conference reluctantly, that China is very critical of it,[12] and that the Soviet Union can

---

10. Cf. Leopold Labedz, "The Soviet Union in Asia," Adelphi Papers, No. 91.

11. The most recent discussion on the subject can be found in the Winter issue of *Survey* devoted to the international scene in the seventies and current Soviet foreign policy.

12. The Polish *Polityka* (7 April) reported: "We Chinese, said the head of the Chinese legation in Paris, General Huang Chen, are against the Helsinki Conference. The Soviet Union wants to push out the Americans from Europe so as to be able to exert greater pressure on China. . . . Premier Chou En-lai and the head of the Chinese Ministry of Foreign Affairs, Chi Peng-fei, made every

take a cohesive stand in all three conferences (Helsinki, MBFR, SALT II), while for Western countries they represent an occasion to expose their "contradictions."

Even without taking these factors into account, the history of negotiations with the Russians, from Teheran to SALT I, does not inspire confidence in Western perseverance. With few exceptions, like the Austrian Treaty, they usually resulted in political gains for the Soviets, and this time they were not in a position of relative weakness. American shortcomings in negotiating with communist powers are a matter of record which, unfortunately, is neither well-known nor widely understood. The late Professor Philip Mosely described them, and the new director of the Arms Control and Disarmament Agency, Fred Charles Iklé, analyzed them perceptively in a memorandum presented in 1970 to Senator Henry M. Jackson's Subcommittee on National Security and International Operations. What Iklé calls a "semantic infiltration" and what I call "creeping Newspeak" is on the increase at this time of détente and will serve Soviet purposes in negotiations.

Security in Europe is gradually redefined as anything that conforms to Soviet imperial goals. Détente is a matter of "peaceful coexistence" in which the attacks on "imperialism" are to be permitted as "ideological struggle" while criticism of Soviet actions is to be banished as "a return to the spirit of the cold war." "Cultural exchange" is to be determined by the extension of Soviet censorship abroad, and "scientific cooperation" is to be made a vehicle for the acquisition of technological expertise by the Soviet Union.

When it comes to the political side of the negotiations, the Soviet Union knows better than Western countries that accepting a label may already prejudge the outcome of subsequent diplomatic encounters. The West agreed to the title of "Security Conference" in spite of the fact that it was perfectly clear that security could not be the subject of it. But the name remained, contributing to confusion and illusions. The Soviet Union on its part refused in Vienna to recognize the designation MBFR, and rejected it as "Atlantic terminology" (*Magyarorszag*, 18 February) because it did

---

effort to persuade the foreign ministers who visited Peking in 1972-73, M. Schumann from France, W. Scheel from West Germany, A. Douglas-Home from Great Britain, and de Medici from Italy, that their governments should take a more reserved stand at the Conference."

not like the idea of "balanced" reduction of forces as a starting point of negotiations. In this way the Vienna talks, the convening of which was interpreted as implying a Soviet concession to the Western powers for agreeing to come to Helsinki and take part in the Soviet-initiated Security Conference, were neatly converted again to a contentious issue. The Soviet negotiators resist semantic obstacles and are thus free to play their favorite game in which each subsequent compromise is slightly more favorable to themselves than the previous one. In this diplomatic "salami tactic" Soviet representatives have had long experience, and it is not entirely surprising that the procedural compromise reached in Vienna is "substantially along the lines of a Soviet bloc proposal" (*The Times*, 28 April). The West agreed to the Soviet demand that Hungary should not be a full participant but should be limited to observer status. This was described officially as a "compromise," but as the *International Herald Tribune* (5-6 May) reported, it amounted "to acceptance of the Soviet side's position, with the West getting nothing in return."

The substance of the general issue has, of course, been known since the original Rapacki proposal. The Warsaw Pact forces have more than two-to-one superiority over NATO in conventional forces. A symmetrical reduction would only increase this superiority. A simple arithmetic calculation can show that if the process is carried far enough NATO forces would be reduced to zero, while the Warsaw Pact would retain more than half of its forces. The Soviet Union is, of course, well aware that this is a reductio ad absurdum of the idea of negotiations, but it has never been inhibited in bringing forward unacceptable proposals. Sometimes they help to stall the negotiations; at other times, to get a more favorable "compromise"; at still other times, simply to sabotage the negotiations without incurring the odium for breaking them. The rejection of the idea of "balanced" reduction of forces can serve any of these three possibilities.

Even "balanced" reductions may be too risky for the West, yet symmetrical reductions do not take into account the fact that American troops would withdraw beyond the Atlantic and the Soviet ones only beyond the River Bug. Soviet negotiators can afford to wait. They have long been reading in the Western press that negotiations about troop reductions are necessary because American troops will be reduced anyhow. What incentive it gives them to strive for a quick compromise is difficult to imagine, unless they were convinced that the prospect may be reversed.

The preliminary talks at Helsinki have hardly been affected by the developments in Vienna despite the fact that the Russians so quickly retracted their implied quid pro quo. Logically it should have hardened the Western diplomatic stand at Helsinki, particularly on the sensitive, and politically most important, issue there: the question of the "free movement of information, ideas, and people." But in fact the stand of Western powers began to weaken here too. Already in the Davignon Committee which was preparing the platform of the Nine for Helsinki, the French opposed as "provocative" the formulas which would deal explicitly with the "free flow of ideas" and which would implicitly proscribe "the Brezhnev Doctrine." In Helsinki, Romanians got no diplomatic support for their efforts to proclaim an international condemnation of military interventions "whatever the form, whatever the pretext." On "the free flow of ideas and people" the Western powers made a "tactical" retreat from their original position, and at the end of the third round of the preliminary talks they abandoned the original formulation and insisted only on the insertion of "an open formulation" on that subject on the CESC agenda.

The situation is thus not promising for Europe. In Helsinki the Europeans are not sufficiently concerned about their freedom; in Vienna (and outside) they are not sufficiently concerned about their security; it is absent at the Security Conference, and so are the Europeans at SALT II.

What answer could be given to our visitor from Mars if he were to ask about the implication of SALT II for the security of Western Europe? Fears about a "nuclear Yalta" are obviously misplaced; there is still no doubt about the American commitment to European security; but the confirming credibility of the American nuclear deterrent has already come into question.

There is no agreement among the experts about the significance of SALT I. Some considered its results as having increased the security of both the Soviet Union and the United States through the establishment of stability at parity level.[13] Others criticized the U.S. negotiators for going from strategic superiority to strategic

---

13. Cf. Wolfgang Panofsky, "From SALT I to SALT II," *Survey*, 19 (2), Spring 1973, and William R. Kintner and Robert L. Pfaltzgraff, Jr., "Assessing the Moscow SALT Agreements," *Orbis*, 16 (2), Summer 1972.

inferiority by abandoning the 1969 U.S. positions at the beginning of the SALT talks. Dr. William R. Van Cleave, in his testimony before the Jackson Committee, argued that "there was nothing that one could call a coherent national strategy to guide the [American] SALT decisions," that "the terms of agreements themselves are almost the antithesis of stability," and that "future Soviet historians could regard this [result] as the golden age of Soviet negotiation."

Whatever the case in terms of pure military strategy, Dr. Van Cleave is undoubtedly right in saying that "most people in the world do not think like U.S. system analysts." It is the political effect of the perceived strategic situation that matters, and it is in this sense that a shift in the military balance affects the overall balance of power. The question of the credibility of the American commitment to the defense of Western Europe was always, and remains, a question of the credibility of the American nuclear deterrent. There is little doubt that this credibility is being slowly undermined.

Strategic analysts tend to think in terms of consequences of strategic changes in the nuclear balance for the possible conduct of war. The analysts see the logic of the game and assume that the nuclear adversaries, like chess players, would follow it without necessarily testing it on the imaginary nuclear chessboard. But the political consequences follow not only from the actual assessment (which may be right or wrong) of the strategic balance by sophisticated analysts, but from the general perception of the situation by politicians and the unsophisticated public, and this is affected by many factors. There is a striking parallel between the lack of the political component in postwar Western nuclear strategy and its lack in Western strategy during World War II. In the negotiations with the Russians they themselves did not then make and do not now make this mistake. In their approach they always take *politique d'abord*. The Soviet official textbook for diplomats, *The History of Diplomacy*, begins with a quotation from Engels recommending that strategy must be subordinated to politics.

McNamara, his whiz kids, and their descendants never understood this in their technocratic approach to the problem of the strategic balance. The Western "game theory" specialists think the problem is that the Russians have to acquire technical sophistication on nuclear strategy, while the real problem is that it is they who need to become more politically minded.

The relevance of this to the question of European security is
rather obvious. The present troubles between the United States and
Europe can be successfully tackled only through political understanding. The major Western mistakes in the postwar period which
resulted in the shift of the balance of power against the West were
political mistakes and not mistakes of nuclear strategy. Indeed, it is
even arguable that changes in nuclear strategy reflected them without the strategists realizing it. It is certainly ironic that the doctrine
of flexible response, so fully presented by Henry Kissinger in his
book *Nuclear Weapons and Foreign Policy*, did not prevent a
situation in which it may be argued that a limited war in Europe
not being a credible proposition (and it was not a great success in
Vietnam), the United States may soon face a stark dilemma of
either returning to the doctrine of massive retaliation or sacrificing
Europe in a "nuclear Yalta." However, this is not the necessary
logic of development. The credibility of a deterrent is a question of
political psychology and not just of the anticipated moves on an
imaginary nuclear chessboard. It is often argued now that the new
military technology based on lasers—small nuclear weapons—and
the "smart" bombs may fill in the gap caused by the Soviet
preponderance in conventional arms and the prospect of limitation
or withdrawal of American troops from Europe. It is argued that, in
terms of the extent of destruction, "mininukes" do not differ from
more conventional arms. This is an argument, however, which, by
obliterating the sharp distinction between "nuclear" and "conventional" arms, undermines the very basis of deterrence which is
rooted in the general feeling of qualitative difference between the
two. The flexible response may be a necessary element of deterrence and "mininukes" may be a necessary part of it when conventional troops cannot be expected to play this role in the West. But
it will only be "credible" if the distinction is preserved rather than
obliterated in order to facilitate the "selling" of "mininukes" to the
public. As long as it is preserved, the fear of escalation will continue
to provide the psychological underpinning for the deterrent role of
nuclear weapons. It would indeed be paradoxical if, in the search
for their actual "military effectiveness," their deterrent effect were
to be lost in the evolution of military strategy from massive retaliation to "mininukes."

The Russians, who never put much store in the distinction
between a limited and an all-out nuclear war, are better served
politically by their relatively crude strategy. They can escape this

type of dilemma by concentrating on the goal of gradual erosion of the political will of the adversary. If successful in Europe, it will lead to its "Finlandization," i.e., to a situation in which West European countries may become subordinated to the dictates of the Soviet Union's foreign policy and extremely sensitive in their internal political responses to its demands, and in which no politician can play a major role in national politics unless he enjoys the confidence of Moscow. This is not an unrealistic goal for the Soviet Union; it cannot be won by nuclear means. Nuclear strategy can play a role in it only by preserving the central strategic balance. In this perspective, nuclear weapons play a symbolic political role today and are not designed just to play a military role tomorrow. It is the general policy, conceived in its overall political sense, that is of paramount importance in approaching the current problems of Western Europe in its relations with the United States and the Soviet Union. Although the present situation in this respect is understandably causing anxieties, the future is still open.

If our Martian visitor, not being quite able to understand why Europe should be so politically vulnerable in spite of its economic recovery, were to ask how this situation came about in terms of overall political development, he would look closely at the postwar political history of Western Europe. This can be divided into three periods: in the first, Great Britain sabotaged the idea of European unity; in the second, this was done by France; in the third—the present one—the consequences of the previous two periods are becoming apparent, but not learned.

In the postwar history of the United States there is success in its policy of containment in Europe (due to the Marshall Plan and NATO), but not in Asia. The Vietnam War and internal weaknesses in the United States created a mood of withdrawal which impelled American foreign policy to lower its profile and use the Chinese gambit. However, Western Europe remains an area of primordial importance for the United States, and therefore rather obvious contradictions of American policy in Europe must be faced and resolved. They are interrelated.

One contradiction is that a policy asking the Europeans to realize that they must unite and become more involved in their own defense is unlikely to succeed if at the same time it implies no need to worry because "the era of confrontation has ended." Any long-term risks for Europe are then likely to be treated by the

Europeans as nonexistent. Accommodation with the Soviet Union can be achieved through negotiations in a spirit of détente without the need for additional political exertions and military expenditure.

The other contradiction is between American nonproliferation policy and the goal of an independent, though allied, unified Western Europe. A nuclear status for Western Europe is not politically feasible in the near future and, if promoted too forcefully now, it may bring more harm than good. But in the long run, if one accepts the idea of European unification, however distant, one must also accept the idea of an eventual West European responsibility for its own defense which, with the trend away from conscription, must be nuclear in one form or another. It is difficult to imagine it at the moment, but some special Anglo-French-American cooperation in this field seems a necessary prerequisite. Yet as long as France retains its post-Gaullist, anti-Atlantic outlook, fearing the Anglo-Saxons more than the prospect of Finlandization, this will obviously remain an unrealistic proposition.[14] It is sad to recollect that it was de Gaulle who first proposed the idea of the atomic *directoire* and it was the Nassau agreement which finally put an end to this prospect. The present European and American tendency toward unilateralism, which George Ball spoke about and warned against at the Amsterdam Conference, is a legacy of lost opportunities in the past.

But if our Martian visitor thus learns—not from Oxenstierna— "with what little wisdom the affairs of this world are conducted," he will also see that postwar political history reconfirmed the dictum of de Tocqueville that nothing is more difficult for democracies than to have a rational and consistent foreign policy. If this makes him feel too much like Cassandra, he has only to look around to see that, with all the euphoric Pollyannas begotten by détente, it may be useful, if only for reasons of (strategic) balance, to sin on the side of pessimistic realism. To give him some hope one

14. Erick Weit, Gomulka's interpreter, reported in his book *Eyewitness* (London: André Deutsch, 1973, p. 140), a conversation in East Berlin (22 April 1967) between Ulbricht, Gomulka, and Brezhnev, who boasted about the successes of Soviet policy vis-à-vis Gaullist France:

Take de Gaulle. Have we not succeeded, at no risk to ourselves, in driving a breach through the imperialist camp? De Gaulle is our enemy and we all are well aware of it. The French Communist Party was narrow-minded enough to try to stir us up against de Gaulle for their own particular interests. But look at our achievements! We have weakened the American position in the heart of Europe and this weakening will continue.

can point out that rationality is not a conspicuous characteristic of Soviet foreign policy either. In the postwar years, despite its success in achieving superpower status, the Soviet Union had its own troubles and certainly a share of its own mistakes. These often stemmed from ideological blinkers. After all, the two great achievements of postwar American policy—the creation of NATO and the rapprochement with China to redress the weakening balance—were made possible only by the Soviets' militantly abrasive posture and short-sightedness at the time. Internally, the *Machtpolitik* had to be paid for. Although the chronic Soviet troubles with food production may be due to the nature of collectivized agriculture, the relative penury of Soviet consumers is certainly aggravated by the very high spending on defense matters which, according to the Academician Sakharov and to an unofficial samizdat estimate, may amount to 40 percent of the GNP.[15]

It is not surprising that in these circumstances the Soviet Union seeks help from outside for its economic and technological problems and that it is dangling the prospects of trade and profit before American, European, and Japanese businessmen. There is nothing particularly new in the capitalist fascination with the Soviet market. In 1916 an American businessman, Richard Washburn Child, published a book, *Potential Russia*, in which he rhapsodized about the gigantic prospects for trade with this huge country. The revolution put an end to this perspective, but during the Soviet period there were again surges of hope for a sudden astronomical expansion of trade with the Soviet Union. One such surge occurred early in the Depression, another at the end of the last war when Eric Johnson, the president of the U.S. Chamber of Commerce, wrote in the *Nation's Business* (October 1944) that "Russia will be, if not our biggest, at least our most eager customer when the war ends." But there was no steady, much less spectacular, trade expansion either

---

15. This may be too high, but there is a tendency in the West to overestimate the Soviet GNP and to underestimate the military expenditure in it. Precise evaluations are difficult because Soviet spending on military research and development is covered in statistics by "science" and that on other military items is hidden elsewhere. It is pertinent to recollect that when Naum Jasny published his estimates of Soviet agricultural production in the early fifties, his academic critics treated him as a crank. Soviet statistical disclosures in the late fifties revealed that he underestimated agricultural disasters under Stalin. A similar thing happened to the statistical estimates of the prison camps population by Dallin and Nikolayevsky which were later confirmed by samizdat sources.

before or after the war. Once again, President Nixon's Moscow
agreement revived such hopes and Peterson, Hammer, and Pisar
raised them to a high pitch. Yet, as Philip Hanson wrote in the *New
Society* (26 April): "The ballyhoo about Soviet Fiats, American
grain sales to the Soviet Union, and the surrender of Eastern Europe
to Pepsi-Cola can be rather misleading." Until recently, East-West
trade has been small. The share of all communist countries in the
foreign trade of the OECD countries was only 3.3 percent of the
total in 1971. In the same year, the share of the Soviet Union in
American foreign trade was just 0.7 percent.

The prospects for expansion of East-West trade are still limited
for two basic reasons: the restricted ability to pay for imports and
the difficulty of conducting trade between market and centrally
managed economies. The "autarkic" development of such economies made their exports noncompetitive, so that their ability to pay
any large increases in imports depends on credits. Granting these
credits, particularly the long-term ones, may make the creditor
country a hostage to political fortune and could even create internal
pressures on its foreign policy from the investors concerned with
the fate of their investments. In this way, the Nixon-Kissinger idea
of establishing a Soviet vested interest in the status quo through
economic deals may create conditions which would be more favorable to the Soviet than to the American foreign policy, because it is
far easier for interest groups in the United States to pressure the
government and far easier for the government in the Soviet Union
to disregard economic vested interests for political reasons.

Détente is thus fraught with risks for the West. Our Martian
would, however, be right to think that his picture of the situation is
incomplete if he does not learn of the opportunities détente may
hold for the West. Potentially they do exist. The elaborate precautions taken by the Soviet bloc countries to avoid ideological contamination testify to this. If only détente could be used for Western
political goals rather than as a rationalization for Western inability
to pursue them! If the West could master sufficient political will to
exploit détente for its own purposes, rather than follow the Or-
wellian Soviet definition of it! With less risks in détente for the
West and more for the Soviet bloc, Western Europe should be able
to avoid the fate of Finland, provided its relations with the United
States improve rather than deteriorate further. The present American initiative aimed at this met a somewhat lukewarm response in

Europe. In France it evoked outright hostility. One is reluctantly
reminded of the tragic course of prewar Western diplomacy, when
the English and French continued to badger each other at the time
of the rise in power of Nazi Germany. The English proposal for
unification came at the moment of the fall of France and was
rejected.

Surely there is a lesson here for all those Europeans who constantly display anti-American attitudes but continue to count on
American strategic support, and for all those Americans who accept
the observation that the postwar period of American supremacy is
over but who often behave vis-à-vis the Europeans, politically and
diplomatically, as though this were not the case. Applying shock
treatment or creating "shokkus" through inadvertence is not the
most effective way of implementing the new American policy of
rapprochement with Europe and Japan. The Europeans with their
economic strife and the Americans with their loss of political nerve
may yet jeopardize not just the fate of Europe but that of Western
civilization in general.

After 1945, the Eastern half of Europe was lost. Now it is
Western Europe which may face the gradual erosion of its status to
that of a greater Finland or Sweden. Neutralization of Europe can
only be a step in the direction of its eventual subordination to the
Soviet Union. It is only the balance of power in Europe which has
preserved the relative independence of Finland. Once this balance
goes, the fate of Finland and of Western Europe will ultimately be
sealed.

To realize the implications of such a shift in the balance of power
and of the arguments used in the "Indian summer" of the current
détente, one has to recollect that similar arguments were used at the
time when, for the sake of postwar entente, the population of East
European countries was sacrificed. Hopes for peace were more
potent than any sober analysis of postwar prospects. The "theoretical underpinning" of the strategy adopted at Teheran and Yalta was
provided by the analogy with the Vienna Congress and the Metternichian idea of the concert of powers. Professor E. H. Carr provided
it in *The Times*' (10 March 1943) editorial comment in which he
advocated the surrender of Europe "east of Germany" to Soviet
hegemony and the creation of the concert of Great Powers—Great
Britain, the Soviet Union, and the United States—to rule the postwar world. *Où sont les neiges d'antan!* It was hardly a role which

Great Britain was destined to play. As for the idea that the surrender of Eastern Europe to Soviet domination would guarantee a
harmony of interests between Great Powers after the war, it soon
proved to be an illusion. As Bismarck said, "No one will ever be
rich enough to buy his enemies by concessions." Then, as now, the
Vienna Congress provided an incorrect analogy and created a Fool's
Paradise for détente seekers. Our contemporary Metternichs may
find it out when it is too late.

In the meantime, they studiously disregard what risks for Europe
(i.e., its remaining part) the illusions created by this policy entail. It
is ironical that the Soviet magazine *Voprosy Istorii* (No. 3, 1973),
in an article on the American new left "historical revisionists"—
Williams, Kolko, Le Feber, Alperovitz, Horowitz, Bernstein—claims
that they "provided the ideological basis for the recent course of
Washington in the sphere of foreign policy." This is obviously an
exaggeration and a distortion. But this Soviet perception is not
altogether out of place. The illusions of the Nixon Doctrine are
based on the same fallacies as the pre-cold war allied diplomacy.
One can only hope that this time the American negotiators will
remember the lessons of Teheran, where Roosevelt refused to
confer privately with Churchill during the conference and taunted
him in front of Stalin, hoping to establish an intimate relationship
with the latter.

The logic of this attitude led the American officials to disregard
the strategic importance of Eastern Europe. As one of them recol-
lected later:

In our "spheres-of-influence" reasoning, in our anxiety to preserve good
relations with the Soviet Union, my friends and I had hardened our hearts and
in effect condemned Petkov and his like, just as we had consigned the
populations of East Central Europe to communist tyranny.[16]

This time it is the future of Western Europe that is at stake,
however distant that prospect may look now. It would be a disaster
if the new relationship between the United States and Europe were
to be based on old illusions and not on a realistic appreciation of
the risks involved in the shift in the balance of power against the
West which has occurred since the war. This would be a better basis
for establishing continuous U.S.-European collaboration than theat-

---

16. H. Stuart Hughes, "The Second Year of the Cold War, A Memoir and
An Anticipation," *Commentary*, 48 (2), August 1969, p. 31.

rical gestures, like the proclamation of 1973 as the Year of Europe (1960 was the Year of Africa. . .).

Mr. Brezhnev's visit to the United States contributed to the strain between Europe and America. It resulted in new tensions in NATO and created a new displeasure in France. It is ironic that in pursuing his "pentagonal world" idea, Dr. Kissinger managed to produce shocks among the weaker trio: Japan, Europe, and China. In the past, the British balance-of-power policy aimed at strengthening the opponents of the strongest power on the European continent to prevent its domination. The present U.S. policy may achieve precisely the opposite effect; so far it helped to undermine the U.S.-Japanese Treaty, to enfeeble the cohesion of the NATO Alliance, and to impair its new relationship with China. This is hardly the way to strengthen the countervailing powers in the "pentagonal" balance postulated for the future. It is not surprising that Dr. Kissinger has to make all these unplanned additional trips to Japan, China, and Europe to explain away the shocks. The Metternichian concept of the concert of (the super-) powers is not only inapplicable where the powers in question lack a common basis of legitimacy, but also incompatible with the concept of the "pentagonal" balance-of-power policy. This inconsistency may have far-reaching consequences for both the Old and the New World. They may get the worst of both worlds.

Having seen the evidence on the contemporary course of Western powers, the proverbial visitor from Mars cannot but agree that it shows alarming symptoms of political malaise. This is so, even though Western Europe faces only the risks of détente and not the dangers of war. He must come to this conclusion although he is simply an innocent Martian and not a knowledgeable European with a good memory who cannot help having the feeling of déjà vu.

Malaise in Europe:
Diagnosis and Prognosis

Walter Laqueur

I. DIAGNOSIS

The present state of West-East relations, for obvious reasons, tends to aggravate the paralysis of will now obtaining in Europe. It is admittedly even more risky to generalize about Europe than about America: there is no consensus, and the CDU no more sees eye to eye with the SPD in this respect than the British government with the Swedish. The following observations constitute simply an analysis of a mood.

A. Current Political Views

It is widely assumed in Western Europe that the cold war is over (W. Brandt), and that in the age of détente the danger of military attack from the East is virtually nonexistent. (It goes without saying that these views are by no means specifically European; one could easily quote the State Department to similar effect.) According to this school of thought, Soviet attitudes have mellowed for a variety of reasons: economic difficulties at home and hence the need for intensified trade relations with the West, the realization that any attempt to push the Soviet sphere of influence beyond its present borders would at best result in diminishing returns, the acceptance of EEC as a fact of political life. Some Western statesmen have noted "structural changes" inside the Soviet Union (W. Scheel); others have detected a genuine Soviet willingness to improve relations with the West by creating an atmosphere of trust and confidence through the European Security Conference, the MBFR talks, and other means. While not expecting a dramatic reconciliation, they assume with some confidence that following the expansion of West-East trade and cooperation with the Soviet Union in other fields, the gradual erosion of Soviet ideological hostility will be more or less inevitable. Communism, in other words, will still engage in ritual incantations about its impending victory and the demise of the non-Communist political systems, but this will be merely a vision on the distant horizon; as far as West-East relations are concerned it will be quite irrelevant. The danger of Finlandization does not exist; Europe is far too big and powerful to be drawn into the sphere of influence of a power that has already more than enough difficulties with its East European satellites. Thus a status quo plus Europe is envisaged: "free communications between East and West, substantial reductions of troops, foreign as well as indigenous, on both sides ... close contacts between the two pacts and the beginnings of a common security system and de facto invalidation of the Brezhnev doctrine by a diminution of the Soviet Union's fear that her allies would be lured into the opposite camp" (Theo Sommer). Simultaneously, it is expected that the "creation of facilities of mass tourism in both directions, student exchange, all-European television programs, exchange of newspapers and books" (Kaekaser) will lead to an improvement of "contacts between people" and thus ultimately to tangible political results.

The above illustrations have been chosen from West German sources, which is perhaps a little unfair, for they could equally have been selected from the pronouncements of the politicians and political commentators of most other European countries. Mr. Denis Healy, not so long after having announced that the Soviet fleet in the Mediterranean would be bombed out of existence within seconds of the beginning of a military conflict, detected

most profound changes in West-East relations. Others discovered that not only the Soviet Union had changed but the Communists had too. M. Mitterand, answering critics of his Popular Front tactics, announced that, if General de Gaulle included Communist ministers in his government "at the height of the cold war," he himself was surely entitled to cooperate with the PCF at a time of détente. Or, as he said on another occasion somewhat cryptically: "Je sais d'expérience que les dirigeants communistes d'aujourd'hui ont un sens très vif de leur responsabilité . . . "—as if they had not always possessed "un sens très vif de leur responsabilité . . . " whatever that may mean.

B. Implications for European Defense

What follows from these expressions of mood as far as European defense is concerned? Since consolidation is the main Soviet purpose in world affairs—certainly in Europe—it would be the height of folly on the part of Western Europe to spend more than the essential minimum on defense. Unilateral disarmament (within limits) would probably have beneficial effects inasmuch as it would put the Soviet leaders at ease and might induce them to emulate the West. But even if they should not do so and should on the contrary maintain high defense budgets, this would not bring about an essential change in the world balance of power. It would weaken the Soviets economically, and since economics will be the main battleground in the years to come they will suffer for their mistakes. It is not my intention to discuss these arguments in detail. I merely want to draw attention to some glaring omissions which have to be mentioned, however briefly. The present Soviet policy of détente is of course closely connected with the conflict with China. But can it be taken for granted that the conflict will continue forever with the same intensity? If not, what are the repercussions likely to be in Europe? These questions are hardly ever discussed these days. Instead there is a strange preoccupation with the economic performance of the various European countries apparently based on the notion that economic power equals political power. This naturally leads our observers into belittling the political brittleness of Western Europe as a whole and the weakness and instability of its components. The famous prediction of the Hudson Institute for French economic development in the decades to come may serve as an illustration: as if one could engage in economic futurology irrespective of political developments.

C. Progress toward Political Integration

1. History

There is an unfortunate tendency to forget the fact that since the
end of World War II Europe has been living on borrowed time;
America was the main lender until recently, and in recent years
something like a Sino-American umbrella has come into being. If
this fortunate constellation should continue for a very long time, it
is not inconceivable that Europe could overcome its present paralysis of will and a common political and military framework be
established. But if history provides any yardstick, this is a process
which may take many decades. History quickens its pace during or
immediately after a war or a similar major shock; otherwise it
usually moves very slowly. It took thirty-six years from the year the
German *Zollverein* was founded to the establishment of the German
Reich (it also took Bismarck and his three wars). In Italy the
process was even longer, not to mention Mazzini, Cavour, Garibaldi,
and several minor campaigns of national liberation. It took Germany and Italy so long despite the fact that each country had a
common creed, traditions, culture, and language. Is it surprising
that European integration should proceed even more slowly? If
during the fifties a clear and present military danger was perceived,
there is no such feeling now. American competition may or may
not hasten European economic integration, but it will hardly result
in European political integration or the shaping of a common
defense policy.

2. Present Status

The achievements so far have been meager. It took seven years from
1954 (when the French Parliament turned down EDC) to the Bonn
meeting of the heads of the six EEC states. That meeting produced
the Fouchet Plan, only to be buried two years later. Again six years
passed until in 1969 the foreign ministers were asked to prepare a
new plan. Under the new formula France has tried (unsuccessfully
so far) to bring the other EEC countries in line with its Middle
Eastern policy, and there were consultations about the recognition
of Bangla Desh and North Vietnam. Since all resolutions have to be
unanimous, it is not altogether unfair to compare West European
political decision-making with the procedures prevailing in the old
Polish Sejm with its *liberum veto*. The foreign ministers now meet

four times a year for consultations, which can do little harm; whether it will do any good remains to be seen. There has been little progress in European defense planning beyond and above the existence of the Eurogroup within NATO. But even the Eurogroup has been more effective in persuading America not to engage in unilateral troop withdrawal from Europe than in its two main assignments—namely, to make the European defense effort more effective and coordinated and to consult on all specific European problems before they come up in NATO. If the nations of Western Europe were faced in the near future with a sudden major military threat, would they muster the will to resist? Even if this will existed, the present process of decision-making and consultation is still so cumbersome that but for America's leading role in NATO an enemy initiative could achieve its aim well before a decision was passed. In all probability Europe will be spared any such test in the near future. But there should be no illusions about Europe's strength and unity.

D. European Attitudes toward Defense

1. Experts versus Parliaments

The present brief survey deals with European attitudes toward defense. It is not concerned with the views of the experts, which are well known, but with the general climate prevailing in the various European countries, which of course has a direct bearing on the policies pursued by the governments. The general reaction, not to mince words, is one of boredom and repugnance. Boredom exists because military affairs have become more and more complicated. It would be interesting to know how many European parliamentarians know what NPG is about or why WEU was founded, why it still exists, and what its present functions are. True, a great many specialized studies are published, but these are written by experts for experts; their impact as far as public opinion is concerned is nearly nil. Furthermore, the amount of literature produced unfortunately is in inverse ratio to the degree of progress made in European defense. Attendance in the debates on defense affairs in all West European parliaments is weak, sometimes unbelievably weak, and this too is quite significant as far as current attitudes are concerned.

Defense is a repugnant topic because it involves substantial ex-

things which will never be used and which in any case will be out of date a few years hence. This traditional repugnance is reinforced by doubts as to whether these expenses can still be justified in what is thought to be a totally changed world situation. If Western leaders have announced that the age of confrontation is over, that the danger of military attack is nonexistent, that new centers have come into being which affect the overall balance of power, it is only natural that popular opinion should draw the conclusion that a new era of peaceful collaboration has been ushered in. If so, substantial reductions in defense spending are a prerequisite for the improvement of relations between West and East. Western military experts will of course argue that détente has come about precisely as a result of a certain military balance and that if this balance were upset détente might give way to a less agreeable political constellation as far as Western Europe is concerned. But such fears are likely to be dismissed as manifestations of worst-case analysis reflecting the fears and suspicions of a bygone age.

2. Détente

a. Varying Interpretations. This leads one back to the different interpretations of détente and peaceful coexistence in West and East. While Western politicians and commentators talk about the establishment of close human contacts, in the East this is denounced as an imperialist provocation. While Western spokesmen extol the virtues of "bridge building," in the Soviet political dictionary this is "the infusion of the old poisonous brew into freshly labelled bottles." If Western socialists and trade unionists believe that the time has come for establishing closer collaboration with the Soviet Union, Russian commentators simply note that "imperialism has been making ever more active use of such trustworthy imperialist faithfuls as right-wing Social Democracy and various brands of reformism against the socialist countries." This is still the official Soviet line; it is of course well known to Soviet experts in the West, but the general public usually does not want to hear about it, for it does not fit into the Western concept of détente. To be a Soviet expert is by itself now slightly disreputable in the West, which reminds one of the resistance encountered by Freud and his school in the early days: If the psychoanalysts were thought to be somehow oversexed, in view of their constant preoccupation with the libido, Soviet experts in the West are thought to have a vested interest in proving Soviet bad faith.

b. Effect on the Soviet Union. Détente admittedly imposes restraints on the Soviet and Communist leadership vis-à-vis the West, and this may well constitute a serious problem in the long run. Historically they have always needed a major enemy to justify the state-of-siege structure of the Soviet system. But at present there is only China left as a major danger (and the Soviets prefer not to talk too much about the subject); Israel doesn't quite qualify for the role of encircling the Soviet bloc. However, since Soviet defense spending (unlike Western) is not influenced by public opinion, one should perhaps not make too much of the difficulties faced by the Soviet Union during détente, certainly not in the short run.

E. Pressures toward Accommodation

In certain West European countries the temptation to get a "free ride" seems strong, and it is reinforced by the advice coming from overseas. An American writer recently noted that "the experience of the neutral countries in Europe is also of some relevance to the prospects for continued deterrence ... Sweden and Austria have survived without the necessity of any basic accommodation to the Soviet Union detrimental to American interests in those countries." And the obvious conclusion: If those countries can stand firm without any American troops within the borders, surely the others could too?[1] (Equally, it could have been argued that Luxembourg spends less than 1 percent of its GNP on defense and Monaco spends nothing at all.) Another American writer, admittedly writing from the distance of 4,000 miles, has extolled the virtues of Finlandization, both as a good solution for Europe per se and as a policy corresponding to the desires of most Europeans.

1. In Relation to American Troop Reductions

The wish on the part of public opinion to get a free ride coincides with the near certainty that the number of American troops in Europe will be reduced, perhaps drastically, during the years to come. The importance of the American troop reductions (to quote

---

1. Robert A. Paul, *American Military Commitments Abroad* (New Brunswick, N.J.: Rutgers University Press, 1973). The author was chief counsel to the Symington Committee on U.S. security agreements abroad.

David Owen) does not lie in endless arguments about the actual
number of troops to be withdrawn, but in the fact that to many
Europeans any American troop reductions will be seen as the
prelude to total withdrawal. These Europeans see the arguments
that lie behind reducing American force levels as basically reflecting
a growing American belief that the defense of Western Europe is
not a vital national interest. Such a change in American priorities, if
it were to take place, would completely undermine the credibility
of the existing American nuclear guarantee.[2] These fears may be
exaggerated, but they are not altogether groundless. For in any case
a greater effort on the part of the European states will be demanded
in the future, and this precisely at a time when the public is
psychologically least prepared for it. The French, the German, and
the British governments may see the necessity but they face a
hostile environment. Parliaments and public opinion could be gal-
vanized into action by a breakdown of the détente (say as the result
of Soviet interests in Yugoslavia or Romania) or by a sudden
breakdown inside a major European country which would put the
whole European defense effort into question. An American an-
nouncement that U.S. troops were to be reduced over a certain
period could have a salutary effect, but then it might not. In
medicine the application of shock therapy is indicated in some cases
(depression) but definitely contraindicated in others (anxiety neu-
rosis or a cardiac condition). My own feeling is that a shock would
probably do some good, but I say this without any particular
assurance; we do not really know enough about the sickness of
Europe, our patient. It may lead to a long overdue reappraisal of
Europe's defense responsibilities and a willingness to do something
about it. On the other hand, the shock may lead Europeans to
believe that since they can no longer rely on U.S. protection they
must accommodate themselves to the superpower that is geographically nearer to them.

Obviously it is not beyond the physical ability of Western Europe
to replace American troops and conventional equipment. The decisive issue is whether the will to do so (and the ability to coordinate the efforts of the various countries) still exists. This takes
us back to the domestic situation in the major European countries,
which will be of decisive importance in this context during the

2. David Owen, *The Politics of Defence* (London, 1972).

years to come. Other things being equal (and it seems most unlikely
that the East will somehow outproduce the West in the seventies or
that it will gain a sudden, decisive military advantage), the key to
Europe's future will be on the domestic scene.

2. In Relation to the Domestic-Political Consensus

a. Political Shifts in General. It is, of course, an open secret that
there is no correlation between economic performance and the
domestic-political consensus. The center of gravity in West European politics has shifted to the left in recent years in the major
European countries. In Italy a government which does not provide
an opening to the left of some kind seems unlikely to last. In West
Germany and France the process is obvious; the disintegration of
Gaullism may proceed at a slower rate than many observers
thought, but the trend is unmistakable. Britain has a Conservative
government, but there too a leftward trend seems evident. (The fact
that Communists gain in parliamentary elections no more than
forty or fifty thousand votes is quite irrelevant, for they are firmly
entrenched in key positions in the trade unions and, as recent
events in Britain have shown, this is where much of the negative
power is. They cannot, of course, run the country, but no government can rule against them.)

Having noted the trend to the left, it would be misleading to
regard "left wing" necessarily as a synonym for "anti-European" or
"antidefense." The West German government is more eager to
strengthen the Western Alliance than the French; even the German
Jusos, with their pronounced anti-NATOism, would probably consider themselves good Europeans, even though their Europeanism is
not that of the multinational companies. They advocate socialist
reforms in an all-European framework, some of them quite radical
in character. The Italian Communists (and the trade unions dominated by them) no longer attack Europe as a capitalist-imperialist
conspiracy. The French Communists have done so albeit with much
less conviction, probably for tactical reasons. In Britain one of the
most effective critiques of anti-Europeanism has come from the
para-Trotskyite *New Left Review*. On the other hand, many fervent
opponents of European unity in Britain are on the right of the
political spectrum, and the part played by orthodox Gaullism in
thwarting a common European defense effort is still vividly remem-
bered. It may well be that Europe has less to fear from the

revolutionaries who want to change it from within than from the
superpatriots who disrupt it by haggling forever, by not being
willing to concede an inch of national sovereignty, by effectively
torpedoing any move toward closer political union. In other words,
Europe has as much (if not more) to fear from the mentality of
small shopkeepers (in high places and low) than from the enthusiasm of the revolutionaries.

While British Laborites are in opposition, they always make
neutralist noises; but basically their defense policy is not as irresponsible as the extremists make it appear. They favor a European
nuclear deterrent (in which America will be involved) with some
multinational control system including other European nations.
They doubt whether an independent Anglo-French deterrent without American participation is a practical proposition, be it only for
financial reasons.

The French left—I refer to M. Mitterand and his friends—have
said that they will favor NATO until something better evolves. I do
not know how deeply this attachment is rooted. On the other hand,
we have M. Debré who has said that in his view "defense policy is
only valid as a function of a nation's patriotism," and since there is
no European patriotism there can be no political unity, and hence
also no common strategy, certainly not in the nuclear field. France
has retreated from its anti-NATO line, but to an outside observer
the difference between the Gaullist and the Socialist policy as far as
the defense of Europe is concerned does not seem very striking. To
what extent the Socialists would be able to assert their views against
their Communist partners in a Popular Front is admittedly a different proposition.

b. Political Attitudes of European Youth. At this point a brief
note on the attitudes of the younger generation seems to be
necessary. European youth are on the whole much freer of nationalist passions than the generation of their parents, not to mention
their grandparents. The nation state has become largely meaningless
for them; it is no longer something to fight for, let alone die for.
But at the same time they have by no means developed a new
"European" consciousness. To oversimplify a complex situation:
They are far more preoccupied with domestic affairs and a desire to
change the quality of life than with foreign policy. Having grown up
in a relatively peaceful age, they fail to see the need for spending a

substantial part of the national resources on defense, either of their
own country or of Europe. Defense spending seems a cold war relic,
a conditioned reflex dating back to the time when a military threat
may (or may not) have existed. Nor do they see any reason to waste
a year or more of their lives in the army, hence the growing number
of conscientious objectors. The youth of Europe, *grosso modo*, no
longer think in national categories, but this has made them more
parochial rather than more internationalist in outlook.

II. PROGNOSIS

A. Prospects for an Effective European Defense Policy

Whether there will be an effective European defense policy depends
much less on the ability of the experts to work out ingenious
formulas than on the existence—or absence—of a political will.
Economic performance can easily be measured. It is more difficult
to compare the military strength of countries. But how does one
measure political will, the general mood, and other such imponder-
ables?

1. Scandinavia

Scandinavia is at present Europe's weakest link, both because
NATO forces are greatly outnumbered in that region and because
willingness to cooperate in European defense is least developed
there. Swedish attitudes are known and need not be discussed in
detail. The opposition to Western Europe ("monopoly capitalism in
its search for greater profits") and America is by no means limited
to Communists and left-wing Social Democrats; it also counts
among its followers (as in Britain) the liberal youth organizations
and the Agrarian party which, as in Norway, is anti-European. While
Sweden made a major effort in the fifties and early sixties to back
up its neutrality with substantial defense spending (it was as high as
in NATO Europe), in recent years there has been a considerable
drop. Since in a few years Sweden will be able to offer no more
than token resistance to an invader, it is not surprising that the
debate about civil resistance has had a new lease on life in Sweden.
The merits of such a policy are not readily obvious if applied
against a determined superpower with much experience in putting
down popular uprisings; it would merely cause misery to the population. A stronger case could probably be made for active collabora-

tion with the invader, but then the danger of invasion seems remote (and considering the course of Swedish foreign policy, perhaps rightly so); Soviet ambitions may well not want to go beyond the Swedenization of Europe.

In Denmark the Seidenfaden Report has made the point strongly that Nordic (and Western) defense should not be neglected. But this has not prevented the Social Democrats from pressing for radical cuts which in the view of NATO circles would make it virtually impossible to defend Denmark. (The country did spend 2.4 percent of its GNP on defense, but this is regarded by the critics as an intolerable burden on the national economy.)

While Norway is a member of NATO, like Denmark it adheres to the "base and ban policy": no foreign bases on its territory and no nuclear weapons. Norway's vote against EEC did reflect the anti-European sentiment rampant in this country, and though this decision should not be regarded as irreversible, it will take time before a more cooperative attitude prevails, and it is doubtful whether Norway's entry will involve greater willingness to contribute to a common defense policy.

Swedish neutrality has become more and more one-sided; it is now even more one-sided than in 1939 when the then Swedish Prime Minister declared that the country was not just politically but also "spiritually" neutral. Swedish public opinion today is certainly not "spiritually" neutral. Denmark and Norway have not on the whole followed the Swedish lead in this respect, certainly not in its more extreme manifestations, but they have been among the first to respond favorably to the Soviet idea of a European Security Conference. I find it difficult to believe that Norwegian and Danish official circles can possibly have thought that the ESC would bring real peace any nearer; they probably assumed (as did Romania and Yugoslavia) that ESC would go on for a very long time, and that while it lasted the Russians would do nothing to diminish the general euphoria.

2. West Germany

The decisive question as far as West Germany is concerned is, of course, whether the *Ostpolitik* will inhibit the programs of political and military integration with Western Europe. My own feeling is that Germany's relations with Eastern Europe should have been normalized ten years ago; what causes misgivings at present is not so much the *Ostpolitik* but the illusions surrounding it, the feeling—at least in some German circles—that nothing should be done to jeopardize the new rapprochement with the East. But the honeymoon seems already to be over; the DDR has a vested interest in preventing a real rapprochement between Bonn and the Soviet bloc. This is one of the essential facts of life in Central Europe which even the Jusos will have to accept sooner or later. As far as the hopes of German industry for an enormous growth of trade with the East are concerned, this is a periodically recurring *fata morgana;* promises of contracts dangled in front of Western capitalist exporters always have a magic effect. But unless the deal is concluded the effect evaporates sooner or later. The publicity given to the unlimited vista of *Osthandel* is in inverse ratio to the amount of trade done. In 1932 German exports to Russia were proportionately six times those in 1972, and even in 1940 under Hitler and Stalin they were four times as much. *Ostpolitik* apart, Germany is no doubt among the more stable European countries. The two main dangers are the political effects of an economic recession; the fear of a depression and its consequences are more deeply rooted in Germany than in any other country. The other danger is the radicalization of the universities which went much further in Germany than in any other European country and had a much deeper impact, not just in academic life but as a major political factor—*vide* the activities of the Jusos.

3. *Britain*

The present state of Britain is bound to remind the historian of 1914, a year which also witnessed the outbreak of several crises at one and the same time. Again there is the Irish question, a small minority more or less successfully disrupting normal life in part of the United Kingdom. Last year Britain lost almost twice as many working days as the result of strikes as Italy, which is next in line. The political consensus on certain essential issues which distinguished British life no longer exists, and the pessimists maintain that the country has become ungovernable. As far as its defense policy is concerned, Britain no longer aspires to a world political role; it sees its function almost entirely in a European context. The present British government has fewer illusions than others in Europe about the character and the extent of the present détente, and it recognizes the need for greater political unity in Western

Europe. A Labor government would normally have pursued a foreign policy not very dissimilar, but in view of the polarization which has affected Labor in recent years, one hesitates to speculate now about the future. The British malaise is deep-seated, but it is in some respects deceptive. Galsworthy, a British writer who has gained considerable posthumous fame all over Europe through television, wrote in the preface to one of his novels that no people in the world seems openly less sure of itself; no people is secretly more sure. This inner sureness may be by now altogether divorced from reality, an outdated conditioned reflex, but to some extent it still exists and it may help the British people to muddle through.

4. France

It ill behooves a foreigner to analyze the French political scene at a meeting which takes place in France and with so many French experts present. One hopes that such an analysis will be provided by one of them, for outside observers are bound to feel genuinely baffled by the inner contradictions of Gaullism and whatever it is that has succeeded it. France is the main pillar of European unity, yet at the same time most of the issues that have divided Europe (and Europe from America) have their origins in France. Nor has an impressive economic growth rate been of much help to the party in power; it would be interesting to hear about the causes in some detail. As far as a common policy on defense is concerned, there have been vague promises for the future, the general assumption being that the time is not ripe yet to discuss defense.

5. Spain

Spain has not figured prominently in the headlines for many years now, but it may well be that this period is drawing to an end. It is no doubt an inevitable process, but as far as the outside world is concerned it may mean one more problem on top of all those troubling us.

6. Italy

Four years of stagflation have aggravated the political situation in Italy and triggered off, as in England, a multiple crisis: a shift of middle-class voters to the extreme right, a students' revolt, growing unemployment, resentment of domination by an ever-growing bureaucracy, and increasing disaffection of the working class which manifests itself in much greater militancy, especially among younger workers. In these circumstances Italy is very much preoccupied with problems of survival; foreign affairs and defense cannot possibly be given high priority.

B. Prospects for the Future of Europe

This briefest of surveys of the European scene is bound to result in pessimistic conclusions, and unfortunately there is no reason to assume that a less superficial study would lead to more cheerful results. The lack of purpose, of vision and initiative seems to be all-pervasive; the dead weight of the forces of inertia seems to prevent any major departure. It could of course be argued that in essence the condition of Europe has never been better since 1945, and that for a long time it was considerably worse. Europe has survived, not owing to its own exertions, and it will in all probability somehow survive the years to come, assuming that America and China prevent the Soviet Union from fully asserting itself as Europe's strongest power. But the idea of Europe as one of the new centers of world power, as it figures in the visions of the advocates of the concept of a multipolar (or pentagonal) world, is simply ridiculous. What is so frustrating about it is the fact that Europe *could* be such a center of power; the material basis exists, and if it were not for the paralysis of will the divisive factors in Europe could be overcome. Europe could be defended by the Europeans with an essential minimum of American help. But it is the doubt about Europe's will that is at the bottom both of European neutralism and of its excessive dependence on the United States.

There is no known cure for weakness of the will, individual or national, and there remains only the comforting thought that national will, like the national mood, is subject to change, sometimes suddenly and usually without any apparent reason. Perhaps a shock will have a salutary effect as far as Europe is concerned; perhaps time—albeit a lot of it—will do the trick. Perhaps the long-term dangers facing Europe will suddenly disappear. Nevertheless, strong nerves and a great deal of faith are needed to keep one from despairing of Europe.

Northern Europe
in the Process
of European Security

Johan J. Holst

I. SECURITY IN THE NORTHERN CORNER OF EUROPE

We normally discuss the problems of European security from the point of view of the center. The dominant political and territorial disputes have, of course, been concentrated in the center and to a lesser degree in the soft underbelly of Europe. In Northern Europe the territorial status quo has not been under challenge since World War II. The pattern of alignment and nonalignment has provided a rather stable configuration of political interdependence. Interpenetration and mutual involvement, coupled with a high degree of cultural and social homogeneity, have lent coherence and cohesion to the pattern of intersocietal politics in Northern Europe, particularly in the core area of Denmark, Norway, and Sweden. Scandinavianism has, however, never constituted a sufficient reason and foundation for the security policy of the Scandinavian states. Northern Europe is still Europe, and the stability of the northern corner is inextricably linked with the continued tranquility of the center.

Conflicts involving Germany constitute the *casus foederis* of the Fenno-Soviet Treaty of Friendship and Mutual Assistance. Swedish defense planning is focused on the problem of designing against spillovers from a conflict in Central Europe. From the point of view of strategy Denmark is a German appendix and is linked to the Federal Republic through the Command Baltic Approaches (COMBALTAP). Norway's position is more ambiguous as its links with Europe pass through an Anglo-Saxon filter. The security of Norway is inextricably linked with the security of the sea lanes of the Northeast Atlantic. American and British naval power constitutes the only relevant counterforce to the Soviet Northern Fleet.

The Norwegian security problems are caused primarily by the proximity to the Soviet naval base area on the Kola Peninsula. There is no way Norway could mobilize an indigenous counterforce. The problems are compounded by the fact that the technology of the central balance has driven the Arctic regions into the center stage of power adjustments. Thus the problem of protecting against the fallout from the superpower competition is added to the panoply of Norwegian security problems. The "solution" has been sought in a European anchorage for the transatlantic ties. Norway has not permitted the stationing of foreign troops on its territory during peacetime but has sought instead to acquire security by linking the integrity of Norway to the political integrity of Western Europe. Alas, this particular construction received a major blow in the recent referendum which turned down Norwegian membership in the European Community.

It has often been suggested that the policy of not permitting the stationing of foreign troops or nuclear weapons under dual control in time of peace amounts to a unilateral concession vis-à-vis the Soviet Union. The matter is more complex. The unilateral restraints are observed primarily because they are believed to contribute to Norwegian security. Small border states always have to tread a fine line between deterrence and reassurance in order to avoid a loss of security through provocation or appeasement. Also there is always the problem of preserving the balance at home.

In Northern Norway the maintenance of a stable settlement around a viable economic infrastructure is a serious and difficult problem. The transformation of traditional ways and patterns of life which is taking place as employment in the primary trades of fishing and agriculture recedes, is causing problems of alienation and dissociation. In a country where distances are great and the large centers are few, conflicts emerging along the center-periphery axis are particularly intractable.

II. THE SOVIET NORTHWEST CORNER

The struggle to maintain a competitive set of opportunities in Northern Norway takes place also in the shadows of a massive and impressive Soviet policy of directed colonization of the Kola Peninsula area. The population of Murmanskaya Oblast' was only 14,300 in 1920. It rose to 320,000 by 1939. In 1962 the figure was 625,000, and the 1970 population was around 815,000. Of the population on the Kola Peninsula, 89 percent live in urban areas. There are altogether twelve cities and towns concentrated in the area along the Murmansk Railroad on the Kola Peninsula, with a total population of 625,000.

The volume of industrial production has grown significantly. Based on a 1940 index equaling 100, the output was 474 in 1960 and 833 in 1967. The fishing industry is of particular importance. The Murmanskaya Oblast' accounts for more than one-fifth of the total output of fish products in the Soviet Union. The trawling fleet comprises more than 460 vessels. They are modern and capable of operation on the oceans of the world. Of the catch, however, 60 percent is taken in the Barents Sea. There is an important production of alloy metals, and the raw materials for more than half the total Soviet production of fertilizers originate on the Kola Peninsula.

There is, in other words, an important Soviet strategic stake in the area apart from the purely military one. But the military one is formidable.

There are two motorized infantry divisions on the Kola Peninsula between the Murmansk Railroad and the Norwegian border. They are supported by army support units including heavy artillery and missile units. They have a high degree of mobility and are maintained in a high state of readiness. The two divisions are part of the forces of the Leningrad Military District. The total force of the

Leningrad and Baltic MDs is in the range of 15 to 18 divisions. There is in addition an airborne division in each of the districts. The border troops under the Ministry of the Interior amount to 10,000 men in the area against Scandinavia.

A naval infantry brigade of 2,000 is garrisoned due east of the Norwegian border at Pechenga. It is equipped with modern landing ships of the *Alligator* and *Polocny* class as well as amphibious tanks.

There are two MRBM bases south of Murmansk.

The Kola Peninsula is part of the Archangelsk Air Defense District. Because of the importance of the area from the point of view of forward continental defense, the air defense activities are quite extensive. The infrastructure includes perimeter acquisition radars for the Moscow ABM system.

The tactical air force of the Leningrad MD includes some 500 units. The normal deployment of aircraft to airfields on the Kola Peninsula is about 300 aircraft and helicopters. The infrastructure, which includes 40 airfields, half of which have runways in excess of 1,300 meters, could support a much larger force. There are five airfields with runways larger than 1,800 meters and another two with 1,600-meter runways in Northern Norway.

The major military instrument is, however, the Northern Fleet, which comprises some 500 vessels and 100,000 men. The fleet includes 170 submarines of which 70 to 80 are nuclear powered. A large number of the 45 Soviet Y-class submarines are operating with the Northern Fleet. They carry 16 missiles of the SS-N-6 (1,500 n.m.) variety. A modified version, the D-class, is equipped with 12 missiles of the SS-N-8 (4,000 n.m.) type. The surface fleet includes some 30 cruisers and destroyers, 35 ocean-going escorts, 25 landing ships, 25 missile-carrying patrol boats, and 150 to 200 smaller vessels.

III. THE SOVIET NAVAL EXPANSION AND ASSOCIATED
     INSTABILITIES

In 1949, when Norway and Denmark joined NATO, the British and American navies were unchallenged in their supremacy in the Northeast Atlantic. During the 1960s a basic change occurred in the security environment of Northern Europe as the Soviet Navy became a potential and visible challenge to the dominance of the traditional naval powers in the Norwegian Sea. Norway is still trying to comprehend and gauge the implications of the Soviet power for interposition and interdiction at sea, particularly as the potentiality of military action may cast shadows over the politics of the littoral states.

Since 1963 a pattern of Soviet naval maneuvers has emerged based on two major exercises per year, one in the fall and another in the spring. The area of operations extends to all of the Norwegian Sea, and occasionally into the central portions of the Atlantic as well. The exercises indicate that Soviet naval planners may look at the Greenland-Iceland-Faroes gap as their forward defense zone covering the access routes to and from the Atlantic.

The major tasks of the Soviet Navy in the Northeast Atlantic include the following:

- to counter Polaris/Poseidon submarines,
- to neutralize U.S. strike carriers prior to aircraft launch,
- to ensure control of the fleet areas,
- to assure access for Soviet SSBNs to stations off the East Coast of the United States,
- to intercept NATO lines of communication and supply,
- to provide maritime fleet support for land operations in contiguous coastal areas,
- to create and sustain impressions of Soviet power and reduce the perceived efficacy of American guarantees to Northern Europe.

Neither of the two superpowers seems to have opted for a policy of command of the Norwegian Sea by means of a steady state deployment there. Rather, they appear to have opted for a policy of reciprocal "command denial." However, the interest in reciprocal denial of access and command may not differ significantly from a prescription for preponderance. The waves from such a competition would certainly wash against the Norwegian shores.

The Russians lack air cover for naval operations over large areas of the North Atlantic. The recent launching of the first *Kiev*-class aircraft carrier may herald the eventual rectification of this deficiency. In the short run, however, the lack of air cover will constitute a constraint. The Soviet fleet has no home bases or indirect supporting points on the Norwegian Sea. In a war they must reckon with allied airpower operating out of Norwegian and Icelandic airfields or pre-empt the threat from materializing.

Because of the constraints imposed by climate and weather, the Soviet Union has concentrated a large portion of its naval support facilities in the Baltic area. But the Soviet Union does not control access to and from the Baltic in peacetime. The concentration of the Northern Fleet in the very small area around the Kola Fjord makes it extremely vulnerable to strategic air attacks. The Soviet lack of carriers may be compensated for to some extent by missile protection and offensive missile power, particularly of the cruise missile variety. The Russians have opted for a configuration of small compact vessels with heavy firepower. The land-based long-range bombers of the Soviet naval air force can mount a serious threat to Western surface forces in the Northeast Atlantic. A similar denial capability is represented by the formidable submarine force. The Soviet navy is in many ways, however, ill suited for a protracted campaign for the control of the Norwegian Sea.

It can be argued that the deficiencies and structural characteristics of the Soviet naval posture in the North imply elements of pre-emptive instability on the strategic as well as operational levels. Since Soviet naval vessels would need to exit from the Baltic and Barents Seas in order to take up forward defense positions, or simply to avoid concentration in a vulnerable target area, Soviet decision-makers would presumably be subject to considerable pressures for an early deployment of the fleet in a crisis.

Access to harbors and air cover from Norwegian territory could alleviate some of these pressures. The Russians possess a demonstrated capacity for the rapid seizure of contiguous coastal areas, and they could project a formidable screen against intervention.

The integration of the cumulative effects of changed circumstances on the security situation in Northern Europe is an extremely difficult undertaking at this point. In the following I shall attempt only to identify and distinguish some of the major problems and perspectives.

IV. THE TRANSATLANTIC BRIDGES

The structure of Norwegian defense arrangements is such as to presume the potential availability of outside reinforcements in an emergency, particularly from North America. It is based on the further assumption that there will be sufficient warning of impending danger to permit the transfer of forces to Norway and the mobilization and transportation of Norwegian forces from Southern to Northern Norway. Most of the transatlantic reinforcements, particularly the heavy equipment, would have to come by sea. The Soviet naval expansion increases the potential dangers of escalation in an emergency, and by rapid deployment the Russians may be able to transfer the onus of conflict initiation to the Western powers attempting to reinforce the northern flank of NATO, in the same way the American Navy could exploit its local superiority during the crisis in the Caribbean in 1962. Thus the risk calculus would change in Oslo as well as in Washington and the credibility of the transatlantic guarantees could suffer a major blow.

Potentially there are several ways of designing around the problem. Heavy equipment could be stored in Norway and portions of the Atlantic fleet could be home-ported to Northern Germany, Holland, or Great Britain. It is unfortunate, of course, that the uncertainties in regard to American capabilities should coincide with growing doubts about American judgment and competence which have been fed by the war in Southeast Asia and the declining stature of American authority and integrity at the highest level of decision-making which has been caused by the Watergate affair. North Europeans have to consider also that the United States may have to grant priority to protecting the sea lanes in the South Atlantic to the Persian Gulf in the context of the expected energy crisis toward the end of this decade.

A forward naval strategy in the Northeast Atlantic will constitute an important element in the future defense of Europe. It needs to be supported by a forward base system (Scapa Flow?) and a concerted European effort involving the North Sea powers in NATO. The prospective offshore oil drilling in the North Sea and further north will create new interests in need of joint protection. There is a need also to realign the NATO command structure so as to bring it into consonance with the emerging strategic situation, particularly in regard to the relationship between SACLANT and SACEUR.

The superpower rapprochement that has taken place over the last few years and is symbolized most dramatically perhaps in the SALT I agreements carries portents of reciprocal concessions for purposes of stabilizing and managing the central balance. As the dramatic improvements in missile guidance and miniaturization promise to make the fixed land-based missile obsolescent and intolerably vulnerable, the major foundation of the central balance may be moving to sea. Such a turn of events could intensify the competitive nature of the Soviet and American naval operations in the Northeast Atlantic. However, as the range of the Poseidons has reduced the importance of the Norwegian Sea as a deployment area for U.S. strategic missile submarines, the range of the Soviet SS-N-8 may make the Russians less dependent on exiting from the Norwegian Sea in order to threaten targets in North America. In such a situation an arrangement could conceivably be made for the purpose of ensuring reciprocal first-strike invulnerability by conceding preferential presence in certain ocean areas. The shadows that such an arrangement might cast over the politics of Northern Europe need not be elaborated upon.

The newfound fascination with balance-of-power politics in Washington, the mobility that is inferred from the objective of maintaining better relations with Moscow than does China and better relations with Peking than does the Soviet Union, the propensity to view the world in terms of a pentagonal structure to which it refuses to conform—all point toward the need to work on a reformation of the structure of U.S.-European as well as U.S.-Japanese relations. A new Atlantic charter may provide a useful watermark, but it cannot substitute for the need to realign and establish institutions that will permit a transatlantic bargain to be struck involving compromise and concessions from both sides across the total spectrum of relations extending from money to troops. American patronage can no longer enfold the political order in Western Europe. But an American commitment to and involvement in the security of Europe remains a *conditio sine qua non* for the viability of the order. Hence, the transatlantic bargain should permit a stabilization of the U.S. commitment to maintain troops in Europe. The level of troops may have to be reduced, but the stabilization of the commitment is essential. The Atlantic security structures cannot retain their viability with the constant threat of a Senate majority forcing through a unilateral American reduction hanging over it like the sword of Damocles. The politically stabilizing impact of a bipartisan American renewal of the political and military commitment to the defense of Europe would be such as to alleviate latent fears of impotence which could lead to a race for, or intransigence against, détente with the East. It would have a particularly salutary effect in Northern Europe, where the pattern of politics is tied so closely to the evolution of superpower relations.

V. THE INDIVISIBILITY OF THE EUROPEAN PEACE

For a peripheral country like Norway, security has to a large extent inhered in a political linkage to the integrity of Western Europe. The security arrangements in NATO have given expression to the notion that peace in Europe is indivisible. The current era of East-West negotiations in Europe may produce some "internal frontiers" which will tend to erode this fundamental notion.

It is clear by now that any agreement on force limitations in Europe will be concentrated in Central Europe, thus producing distance to Northern and Southern Europe which would not be included in the area of force limitations. It is clear also that France will refuse to be party to any arms limitations scheme and that Great Britain will be affected only through the troops it maintains on the continent of Europe. The internal frontiers thus produced could be particularly undesirable at a time when, in the wake of the expansion of the European Community, some new effort may be made to give political coherence to the cooperation and commitments of the Nine. For Norway an arms limitation scheme which is confined to Central Europe would add to the isolation and distance which will be the inevitable results of the refusal to join the EEC—a refusal which I believe to be temporary only.

We can look at a force limitation agreement from two different perspectives: (1) as a means of accomplishing defense policy goals and (2) as a means of furthering wider security policy objectives. These are distinguishable but not mutually exclusive objectives.

A force limitation agreement that aimed at a reduction of the force levels in Europe would serve the purposes *inter alia* of accommodating domestic pressures for reduced burdens and a reallocation of efforts and resources. It could provide an impetus also for a reconfiguration of the NATO defense effort. Such implications should not be the subject of East-West discussions, but we need to be aware of the options that must be maintained so as not to foreclose preferred West-West reconstructions on the level of East-West negotiations. The readjustments of the NATO posture would perhaps include an expansion of territorial forces, fortifications, modern antitank weapons, etc. They should probably encompass also the introduction and sharing of advanced technology such as precision guided munitions, which promise to increase significantly the fighting power of modern armies and, most importantly, to raise the nuclear threshold.

The social benefits from reductions should ideally be widely shared. Preferential reductions of stationed forces may produce intra-Alliance problems. However, the reductions are unlikely to be of a magnitude that would permit significant cuts in budgets or conscription in the short term.

The security policy objectives of force limitation arrangements would focus on the role of military force in European politics, insulating to some degree the political process against military pressure. Such a perspective directs attention at limitation of force movements rather than force levels. Limitation of force movements would, in the context of European security, apply first of all to stationed forces. They might include constraints on reinforcements as well as on redeployments. Here the arrangements for the center would also have a direct bearing on the security predicaments prevailing on the flanks, as they might protect against a relocation and transfer of pressures.

The situation in regard to ground forces and air power in Northern Europe is not such as to provide the Russians with strong motives to agree to reductions down to balanced levels within the region. Percentage reductions would cut into a margin which is already too slim on the Western side. However, a symbolic cut or the introduction of a freeze could provide an important link to the total structure of East-West arrangements in Europe. It could serve as a means of counteracting a fragmentation of the security infrastructure of the political order in Europe. Second, it is only in the context of a broad European arrangement that a balance of the asymmetries prevailing in Europe can be struck. Preferential reductions on the Kola Peninsula are conceivable only within a framework of a broad bargain covering large parts of the European continent and where the totality of trade-offs can be made to balance.

The security policy objectives would focus also on the pattern of force employments. Constraints in this context would lend precision to the general commitment to renounce the use or threat of force and to respect the inviolability of national frontiers. They could encompass measures such as:

- preannouncement of military maneuvers,
- prohibition of maneuvers in border regions,
- exchange of liaison missions at divisional and army headquarters,

- exchange of fixed and mobile observation posts,
- prohibition of crossing national frontiers with military forces except as part of routine rotations and maneuvers,
- prohibition of the establishment of foreign bases in more countries in Europe.

A system containing such elements would serve to reduce the convertibility of military force into valid political currency. It could provide a basis for a pan-European arrangement linking the various security zones of the European political order and thus could lend renewed substance and coherence to the notion of the indivisibility of the peace in Europe.

VI. THE NUCLEAR ENIGMA

The nuclear weapon does not, of course, lend itself to disinvention. The security of Europe is inextricably linked with nuclear peace. The perennial problem in NATO has been to arrange for "special drawing rights" on the American nuclear deterrent. Britain and France have, of course, taken out their own insurance against future uncertainties. In the years ahead it may well be that a closer cooperation in nuclear matters, based on the complementarities of British and French achievements, will develop between London and Paris. It seems important to me, however, that such a nuclear entente not have any formal link to the European Community. Such a link could make the possession of nuclear weapons into a scale of comparative status and influence. It could open the nuclear issue in Germany, or alternatively, affect the relative priorities of *Ostpolitik* and *Westpolitik* in ways which could dampen German enthusiasm for community building in Western Europe. In any event the position of Germany is endemic to the basic problem of nuclear management in Europe.

It should be recognized by now that neither Paris nor London is about to dispense with its nuclear deterrents. It is quite obvious also that such forces make at least some marginal contribution to overall deterrence via the residual uncertainties. And, we should recall, uncertainties extend also to the future of transatlantic relations. To hold the British and French forces in trust for Europe does seem to me a reasonably prudent course of action. It does not mean, however, that they can be instruments in the construction of Europe. But they do constitute to some degree instruments for the protection of that construction should the American guarantee prove less viable under a future President and in altered circumstances.

NATO's tactical nuclear posture in Europe contains important elements of pre-emptive instability which would become salient if a serious crisis were to occur. The quick-reaction aircraft, for example, constitute vulnerable targets which might invite and precipitate disarming attacks. In my view, the present panoply of so-called tactical nuclear weapons in Europe defies inclusion in any coherent strategy. These weapons promise to destroy rather than defend Europe and thus to deter the possessor as much as or more than the aggressor. The posture is in some sense one of pre-emptive surrender in the event that deterrence should fail. And nobody can issue absolute guarantees that it will not fail.

The present generation of TNWs should be replaced by the new generation of small precision weapons which permit a high measure of deliberate control and target discrimination. They should be brought into the inventory in reasonable but not excessive numbers. The weapons are needed not as a means for reflex escalation but rather as a link in a continuous chain of options. Some of the tasks of the TNWs today could be transferred to precision guided munitions with high explosives, and others could be transferred to high-accuracy MIRVed strategic missiles. Tactical nuclear weapons do not obviate the need for effective conventional defense in Europe. For very good reasons statesmen are going to be extremely reluctant to transgress the nuclear threshold. There is always the problem of Soviet retaliation and pre-emption. We shall never be in the position of being able to fight highly controlled antiseptic nuclear wars with high-confidence assurance against dirty and disastrous eruptions. From the point of view of world order as well as the solidification of deterrence in Europe, it is important to maintain the saliency of the nuclear threshold.

We have come to a dead end in the search for a reasonable doctrine upon which to build a stable balance of nuclear deterrence. The doctrine of "mutual assured destruction" just is not a viable expression of our best efforts to attain security in the nuclear age. Men of conscience and humanity and with a sense of esthetics will want to transcend the twisted logic of the present state of affairs. Deterrence is a psychological variable that cannot be expressed in numbers of dead citizens and percentages of industry destroyed. Strategy has parted with political objectives when the deliberate

destruction of civilians becomes a means of dissuading and influencing decision-makers who are not invariably sensitive to the needs
and wants of those civilians. The divorce is caused also by the calls
for massive and prompt retaliation on the basis of incomplete
evidence about the objectives and the intentions of the adversary.
The technological improvements that permit a much broader range
of discrimination and deliberate control in the exercise of military
power promise to provide a basis for a realignment of strategy,
politics, and ethics. That basic distinction between combatants and
noncombatants that provided the structuring element for the laws
of warfare is in dire need of resurrection. It was eradicated by
strategic bombing in World War II, and it has been forgotten almost
completely by all sides in the conflict in Southeast Asia. Any
serious policy of arms control will have to be concerned with the
reconfirmation of the distinction between counterforce and coun-
tervalue attacks. Too many distinctions have been fuzzied and
buried in partisan orthodoxy. Such was the fate of the distinction
between counterforce and first-strike strategies.

The long-term challenge is to construct a more rational order that
is consistent with political objectives and human compassion. Some
of the structural elements in such an order would include a shift of
emphasis away from punitive deterrence and toward active and
passive defenses. A long-range policy for dealing with the problem
of nuclear proliferation would have to include a strategy of nuclear
de-emphasis on the part of the nuclear powers. Nuclear weapons
produce some of the most intractable existential problems of our
time. The deficiency of the current arrangements provides no excuse for continued inattention, complacency, or abdication of
responsibility.

A View from the Southern Tier

Duilio Sergio Fanali

I. THE PROBLEM

The present era is characterized by the transition from a period of
cold war, armaments races, and bitter confrontation to a period of
negotiations.

Negotiations in SALT for the reduction of strategic armaments,
in CSCE for the security of European states, in MBFR for the
revision and reduction of armaments (which logically should be
linked to CSCE), and in the Disarmament Conference as well as the
personal top-level meetings and agreements are the most convincing
proof that "negotiations" tend to be considered a new method of
resolving crises and safeguarding interests in an atmosphere of
lessened tension.

However, it must be noted that these negotiations, which on each
occasion have assumed new aspects, have not yet succeeded in
checking or attenuating the dynamic force of Soviet expansion.
This expansion has been Russia's political and strategic aim, pur-

sued for a considerable time and with unflinching tenacity within European and non-European countries. This leads us to wonder whether the above top-level negotiations will really be a prelude to a new era of general and sincere agreement, or whether they will tend to allow the Soviets (who have also serious and urgent internal problems to solve) the time necessary to consolidate certain positions and to develop their programs at greater ease. Not the least important of these programs might very well be that of applying multiple warheads to its missiles (already more potent and numerous than those of the United States), with the result that the United States' present qualitative advantage would be eliminated. If these are the true Soviet motives in the negotiations, the consequences for U.S. friends and allies as well for American public opinion, in which dangerous antimilitary and neoisolationist tendencies are already present, would certainly be negative. Certainly negotiations, agreements, direct contacts, and top-level meetings are a considerable achievement, and it is to be hoped that they will be able to avert disaster; however, they must be conducted with great caution. It is necessary to play one's cards with extreme skill, never for one moment losing sight of what the opponent's final aim might be.

After two world conflicts, the victors laid the foundations of a bipolar equilibrium by dividing Europe roughly into two parts, each in the sphere of influence of one or the other protagonist. In this world, security was no longer linked to a multiple equilibrium in the name of law and civil solidarity, but to a global opposition imposed in the name of a "democracy" obsessed with ideological contrasts and factors of power. There is no doubt that, so far, the bipolar balance has precluded the possibility of a third world war, due in part to the unacceptable risk involved in nuclear arms. There is no doubt either that Western Europe, behind the atomic shield of the Atlantic Pact, has enjoyed a privileged position which has safeguarded some of its essential interests. At the same time one must admit that from the system of security resulting from the above equilibrium, no real solidarity has arisen in either bloc, and no effective collaboration has emerged between the two. The lessened tension may yet lead to unpleasant surprises.

What is certainly not very edifying for Europeans is the fact that the most important negotiations seem to be carried on "over the head of Europe" and are probably concerned with the division of the world into zones of influence (taking into due account the role of China, Japan, India, and the Third World in future settlements). In particular, they set out to guarantee for the USSR the strengthening of its influence in Europe, while the United States might be forced into a gradual withdrawal. Moreover, time seems to work in favor of the Soviet Union. The world today is driven by material necessities (hunger, overpopulation, etc.), by the desire for ever-increasing presumed well-being and by the illusions—so well fostered and utilized by the Soviets—concerning the struggle against capitalism (at least in the Mediterranean and most certainly in Italy). It is highly improbable that such a world will be able to resist materialistic pressure and ideologies, or that it will choose the path of self-control and restriction of instincts, and of sacrifice and duty imposed by the necessity of respecting the dignity and rights of others.

The situation in the Mediterranean is, moreover, far more critical when compared with that of the rest of Europe. The voice of the Mediterranean peoples—far more divided and fed by material conflicts of interests as well as by permanent instability due to conflicts in the Middle East and troubles in the Pan Arabian world—becomes weaker and weaker, in Europe, in America, and throughout the world.

The global role undertaken by the United States in 1945 has obliged U.S. leaders to make a continuous effort to keep the bipolar equilibrium stable in spite of Soviet boat-rocking. The destiny of Hungary and Czechoslovakia has clearly shown that Dulles' "rolling back," Kennedy's "new frontiers," and then Johnson's "bridge building" have not brought all the results their sponsors hoped to achieve. Furthermore, the United States has also had to assume the role of policeman to hold back, or attempt to hold back, further Soviet encroachments. But this role, already in itself untenable, has gradually deteriorated for obvious reasons, including the increasing intolerance manifested by U.S. public opinion. However, the gradual abandonment of the thankless role of policeman does not affect the bipolar nuclear reality. The United States, at least for the moment, has accepted the least costly solution, that of parity.

Western Europe, or rather the geographical collection of European nations, is still very far, in fact much too far, from unity. After the illusions of the fifties, still faced with only two alternatives and anxious to find a better security, Western Europe committed a series of very grave mistakes, the first of which was to forget the real benefits obtained from the Atlantic agreement. It has not taken into account the fact that security was, and still is, linked to a "status quo" containing several contradictions which have rendered the system precarious ever since its foundation. If the alliance projects are to continue, the present situation is still prey to new phases of instability, particularly in the bipolar nuclear field. If Mr. Nixon maintains his current foreign policy designs, this might turn out to be detrimental to European security.

If in some way Moscow succeeded in influencing U.S. public opinion as to the uselessness of tactical and theater nuclear forces presently deployed in Europe, current negotiations might lead to disastrous conclusions for European security. If Europe, politically divided and militarily vulnerable, is deprived of decisive American support, it could present little or no opposition against overwhelming Soviet superiority.

It is well known that Kremlin policy aims at the elimination of blocs. Once NATO has been eliminated, with the bilateral agreements between Moscow and its satellites remaining unaltered (apart from the effective Soviet domination of Eastern Europe), an intact Soviet empire would be found on the borders of Western Europe.

II. THE MEDITERRANEAN

The Mediterranean is inseparable from Europe, and in the present world situation it constitutes one of the most delicate and urgent problems. A series of problems of world-wide dimensions—complex, multiform, and very often dramatic—are centered there in a relatively small area.

The Mediterranean Sea directly influences the lives of about 300 million inhabitants, divided into as many as 19 coastline countries, or even 22, if we are disposed to accept the Soviet opinion that the Black Sea is an integral part of the Mediterranean. (If we accept this opinion the number of inhabitants is roughly increased by a further 150 million.) It is true that three of the European countries—Spain, France, and the Soviet Union—have other sea outlets, but this does not alter the fact that traffic in the Mediterranean is very heavy. In proportion to its size—1,200 ocean ships (400 Soviet) under flags of all nations transit there daily—the Mediterranean traffic is probably greater than that of any other sea.

So there are 19 countries with citizens of diverse origin, race, languages, interests, tendencies, and religions. These are all factors which throughout the centuries have contributed to a disunion within the territories concerned. However, at the same time, the fact of having a sea in common has always united these peoples in their commerce and trade, thus allowing the rise and the consolidation of an age-old but vibrant civilization.

During the last meeting of the Atlantic Council held in Brussels at the beginning of December 1972, certain foreign ministers raised the problem of the Mediterranean when discussing the larger problem of European security. Emphasis was placed on the Soviet penetration in this sea, which is becoming more and more pronounced. If there should be a reduction of forces in the Central European region, this might constitute a vital threat to the flank of the continent, or the "soft underbelly" of Europe, as Churchill called it.

Another aspect to be seriously considered is that across the Mediterranean pass enormous and increasingly indispensable quantities of Middle Eastern and African petroleum destined to supply the countries of Western Europe and the United States. The other petroleum route, that of the Indian Ocean, is certainly no safer.

The most important event characterizing the politico-military situation in the Mediterranean in recent times is the expulsion of Soviet military advisers as well as Soviet combat troops from Egypt. It is obvious that this attitude and the successive assumption of full powers by President Sadat go beyond the military field, in the strict sense of the term, and have consequences in the political and economic fields. However, the "break" cannot be termed final even if, from the political point of view, Soviet prestige has perhaps been weakened in the eyes of Egypt and the whole Arab world.

For the time being, Moscow has accepted Sadat's ultimatum with apparent calm. While still maintaining in Egypt the naval bases obtained previously and increasing in that country the number of civilian, technical, and economic advisers, Moscow has, at the same time, taken steps to broaden its relations with Syria and Iraq. Certainly the apparent loss of air bases in Egypt may, at least temporarily, have weakened the operational capacity of the Soviet fleet in the Mediterranean. However, in case of necessity, and provided pre-stocking has been made possible, a redeployment of air units would be a question of only a very few hours. This loss then cannot be considered significant or decisive.

In considering the Mediterranean it might be useful to examine briefly those countries which have an ideology that is similar, if not identical, to that of the Soviet Union.

Yugoslavia is going through a particularly difficult phase in the political as well as the economic field. It may be assumed that the Soviet Union will not fail to take advantage of this particular crisis by intensifying its influence within the country in order to prepare the way for post-Tito interference. This leads us to the consideration that the relationship between the Kremlin and Yugoslavia has, in reality, changed, and that the four years of apparent carefree independence from Soviet influence are gradually coming to an end. The recent grant of a loan of $500 million by the Soviet Union for the modernization and amplification of Yugoslav industries and shipyards, together with the request to obtain the use of installations in the Yugoslav naval bases along the Adriatic, indicates the change in Yugoslavia's policy of independence.

Albania's internal situation is slowly deteriorating as a result of the gradual cooling of this country's relations with China. This deterioration is increasing its isolation in the international field. It is possible that the Kremlin has already taken advantage of this isolation, because the existence of small pro-Soviet groups in Albania has been noted.

Therefore, conditions appear favorable for a further development of Soviet strategy in the Mediterranean. The Soviet Union (which, as mentioned earlier, considers itself to be a Mediterranean border country, since it declares that the Black Sea is part of the Mediterranean) is now making its presence felt more and more in this sea. The quality of Soviet methods and means is increasingly improving. As a result, the Soviet presence constitutes a real threat, against which "close vigilance" is certainly not sufficient.

III. SOVIET POLITICAL INTENTIONS AND STRATEGY

Often many forget the world-wide nature of the bipolar equilibrium. All over the world, Russia has played a clever, uninhibited game to achieve its aims, each one in tune with the role of power which the bipolar balance confers on it and befitting the Tsarist imperial tradition. The game carried on in one corner of the immense chessboard is not intended as an end in itself, but is connected with moves in other corners where, simultaneously and in an articulate manner, foreseen and facilitated repercussions make themselves felt. Operating on multiple levels, the Soviet Union has been able to extend to its own advantage the factors of power which influence the international equilibrium.

The Soviet Union is using conventional means as well as subversive tactics. But what has counted more than anything else is the close relationship within the international Communist movement. After the parenthesis of the Khrushchev period, the "Troika" reemphasized the right of force, proclaiming, on the one hand, the Brezhnev Doctrine and placing, on the other, global strategic objectives.

New situations of power have resulted in the following:

- Soviet predominance in Asia, where Moscow has alternated pressure (by means of huge military installations on the borders of China and massive aid which have fostered and prolonged the Indo-Chinese conflict) with agreements which, in the case of India, have changed the strategic configuration of this subcontinent in favor of the Soviet Union;

- Soviet capability to engage in blackmail in the Middle East, source of European and U.S. petroleum supplies, hinge of three continents, and starting point for the encirclement of NATO from the south across the Mediterranean;

- Soviet strategic capability to obstruct—with naval and aero-naval means scattered in the North Sea, in the Mediterranean, and even in American waters—the intercontinental strategy of the United States;

- Soviet competitive technological advancement which forces the United States to choose between a ruinous arms race and acceptance of a state of parity. The latter choice would perpetuate a security system based on force and arbitrary decisions.

In particular, in regard to the European NATO members, the Soviet Union has sought to achieve the following aims:

- through a necessary period of lessened tension, to endeavor to absorb the most advanced Western technologies, especially in the economic and agricultural fields;

- to consolidate its predominance in Eastern Europe, especially now that the Soviet Union has succeeded in obtaining official

recognition of the German Democratic Republic by the West
and, particularly, by the Federal Republic of Germany;

- most important of all, to bring about a relaxation of tensions
and thus of the West's precautionary measures. This would
certainly facilitate long-term Soviet designs to extend its
sphere of influence in the rest of the European continent from
which it expects great technological and labor resources.

These openly subversive attitudes, this continuous penetration,
which is now assuming disquieting proportions, still find the responsible European organizations and diplomatic circles hesitant and
passive. The Europeans are faced with a situation which, if it is to
be translated into terms of real and permanent security, involves all
the support of the United States.

IV. POSSIBILITIES OF DEFENSE

Having outlined the general political situation and that of Western
Europe, with special emphasis on the Mediterranean and its bordering countries, we must examine the possibilities of defense
against the danger of Europe becoming "Sovietized."

It is useless to hide the fact that the situation is becoming more
and more difficult each day. Time works in favor of those who
have already experimented with a plan and who have a tenacious
and efficient organization. Therefore, before any other steps are
taken, it is essential to establish a genuine international collaboration; this cannot be brought about by threats or by the unbearable
weight of a useless device, but rather by the conviction that the risk
of a war does not offer the advantages attainable through negotiations founded on guarantees and international law. The task of
decisive force in the present strategic contest ends up by placing the
international community at the mercy of the most unscrupulous or
the most irresponsible power. All this emphasizes that security is
already governed by force and arbitrary decisions which promote
permanent instability instead of harmony and collaboration.

The nations of Western Europe cannot neglect these characteristics and this global aspect at the very moment that, at Soviet
suggestion, a security conference is being convened. Moscow has
made this move, convinced that the Soviet Union will be able to
play its cards in such a way as to exploit the nuclear factor in its
own favor.

The U.S. weapons located in Europe are the ones that are at stake. The Soviet Union will try to show the United States that these arms are useless for American security. To the Europeans, the Kremlin will say that it is in their interests to eliminate any possibility of their territory becoming a nuclear battlefield.

Faced with this situation, what is the exact strategic change that must be opposed?

The strategy of NATO is presently based on reacting to an act of aggression against its territory. However, the margin of security is considered to be wider in the United States than in Europe. Today, the European states—either non-nuclear or with limited nuclear capability—have no possibility of defending themselves independently. Therefore, the will and the decisive power to identify aggression are the responsibility of the United States. From will and decisive power taken together emerges the "credibility" that must be presented with regard to both war and peace. This credibility—American and Atlantic at the same time—must not be weakened in any way.

Neither should we forget a series of factors unique to nuclear strategy.

First, there is the time factor, which means that when it is finally recognized that there is a threat that requires a specific response, it may already be too late.

Second, the degree of superpower political leverage may be increased at the expense of third parties and without violating any limitations agreements. This can be done as a result of technological development, which allows the multiplication of military, political, and psychological forms of aggression.

In the third place, the Soviet Union's strategy of penetration and expansion no longer requires either total warfare or armed conflict of significant proportions; in fact, since 1945 the Soviet Union has committed many acts of indirect aggression, and the indecisive Atlantic attitude has allowed force to prevail by accepting the *fait accompli*.

Even the nuclear stalemate may be identified with Atlantic incapacity to translate U.S. nuclear power into terms of political leverage. Meanwhile, Russia has been taking steps to expand its control everywhere and to threaten even the United States with its technological progress. European security still depends on whether U.S. nuclear armament will continue to be deployed in Europe.

This security would be further guaranteed by better Atlantic and European cooperation and by agreements which could result from the envisaged SALT negotiations.

War and peace are not separate and contradictory terms; the former is a military phase and the latter a political one, especially since—in accordance with the present conception of "permanent struggle" imposed by Soviet strategy—it is difficult to find a clear distinction between these two terms. If the security of the West European nations were to be based on a single option of defense, namely the conventional one, then this would lead not to peace but to unconditional surrender to force and arbitrary action.

Let us now consider, in particular, the Mediterranean situation. In the Mediterranean, the Soviet fleet has established and consolidated its presence in such a way that the strength of its position cannot be denied. After the Cuban setback, the Soviet Union, at an ever-increasing pace and in an unprecedented manner, augmented its maritime power, building up with feverish haste a merchant and military fleet which today equals those of the leading Western nations. Each year, for missile-launching submarines of the Yankee class alone, the Soviet Union spends a larger sum of money than that which the United States assigns to the construction of the total number of its new naval units. Today, the Soviet Navy is in a position to exert pressures capable of putting the United States in a grave and embarrassing political situation. In less than ten years it has almost completed the encirclement of the northern and southern flanks of NATO.

In the Mediterranean the locations of Soviet bases are well known. They have been reinforced in Syria and Egypt, even if Sadat's recent attitude might give us the illusion of a pause in progressive penetration. The bases probably exist along the entire African coast, where the presence of technicians has been noted for some time and seems to have been recently increased. In the Red Sea, in preparation for the day when the Suez Canal will be reopened, the Soviet presence is noted at Hodeida in Yemen, at Berbera in Somalia, and at Aden in South Yemen, as well as on the Island of Socotra. All this activity takes place in addition to renewed Soviet efforts to approach Yugoslavia and to expand commercial relations with Iran.

These developments lead us to suspect that the Soviet Union is seeking to achieve vitally important aims in Europe and the Atlantic

Alliance in the short run, and on a world-wide basis in the long run. It is well known, in fact, that major petroleum routes must necessarily pass through the Mediterranean and the Indian Ocean. The presence in this ocean of Soviet naval units, as well as the penetration—for the moment apparently commercial—in Iraq, is beginning to worry the Far Eastern countries that import petroleum. World requirements for petroleum today are about 2,400 million tons, and it is envisaged that by 1980 they will have reached 4,500 million tons. Europe imports 90 percent of its requirements, Japan 99 percent, and the United States is now becoming a prominent importer. All this proves that the Mediterranean is of vital importance to Europe and to the Atlantic Alliance.

But what should be done to check and neutralize this massive Soviet penetration in the Mediterranean? Without losing further time it would seem necessary to take advantage of the particular political situations that have recently arisen and of the indecision that characterizes the behavior of certain Mediterranean bordering states. These nations still appear hesitant to decide whether or not to accept Soviet attempts at infiltration. It is a known fact that no fleet can act freely or efficiently unless it has adequate air and aero-naval support. It is true that at the present moment the Sixth Fleet is probably able to protect itself and the Mediterranean nations, but will it still be able to do so if the air bases located along the entire length of the North African coast receive significant Soviet air force reinforcement by means of a rapid and unexpected redeployment?

The loss of the Mediterranean would lead to the breakdown of the NATO defensive system and eventually the overthrow of Western civilization.

This categorical truth must sink in deeply, not only in the states bordering the Mediterranean, but in all European nations and not just those in NATO. All must be convinced that it is necessary to oppose this penetration with every means possible, as it may very well restrict our Lebensraum and deprive us of our ability to survive as a civilization. It does not mean that such opposition would involve armed conflicts. It would be sufficient to use the same methods as the Soviet Union. It has been seen that the military defense of the Mediterranean depends not only on an indispensable political solidarity and peacetime strategy but also on the ability to counterbalance the actions of the Soviet air forces. These units, if redeployed in sufficient quantities or deployed on new bases in North Africa and the Middle East, could paralyze all types of military and maritime operations. The Sixth Fleet, which up to now has safeguarded the security of the European Mediterranean countries, could then no longer ensure their defense, because it would be preoccupied with the task of its own survival when faced with a predominant Soviet air force.

Should such a situation arise (and this is not at all an unlikely supposition), it would first and foremost be necessary:

- to set up an efficient counteroffensive instrument capable of neutralizing any offensive attempt on the part of the Soviet fleet;

- to establish suitable air bases in all the countries bordering the Mediterranean, sufficient to constitute a deterrent and to limit all movements;

- to employ, where necessary, short or even vertical take-off aircraft, well hidden and protected in caves on the numerous islands still in our safe possession; (Units of V/STOL aircraft would help to solve the problem in an efficient manner until it is possible to create the necessary infrastructure for other types of aircraft. Protection of antisubmarine aircraft and helicopters would also be required. V/STOL aircraft present a limited radius of action. They are continuously being improved, and they could land on most of the ships at sea or on any island which could easily be prepared for such landings. Lastly, the employment of remotely piloted vehicles would constitute an adequate and economic complement to the air forces, especially in electronic warfare, in surveillance, reconnaissance, and certain forms of attack.)

- to reorganize and maintain in a state of readiness the weaponry that already exist;

- to pay particular attention to the task of intensifying training for maritime operations;

- to improve weapons systems for sea warfare;

- to establish special troop units with airlift and airdrop capabilities as well as sea-launched air transport;

- to speed up, without further delay, a real union of Europe (in this connection we must include Spain and other friendly Mediterranean nations);

- to establish a new strategy for the defense of the West, with the aim of regaining the initiative from the adversary;
- to convince ourselves that the struggle must be permanent, integral, and world-wide, and that to carry on this struggle it is not sufficient to use military means only, because of the new and continuously evolving forms that this contest assumes;
- to continue the struggle in all sectors, especially in the ideological field;
- to attempt to regain any positions that might have been lost and to ensure that no further losses occur;
- to create adequate military, civilian, and technological instruments.

Obviously, all this is not an easy task; in fact, it is a very difficult one, demanding above all political farsightedness, the establishment of priorities, tenacity, and a spirit of unity, as well as infinite patience. Cohesion, unity, and stability can only ensue from a common ideal and a common aim.

V. CONCLUSIONS

Europe and the Mediterranean are in crisis because of a lack of cohesion among the various nations that have not yet succeeded in convincing themselves of the absolute necessity of political unity.

The loss of the Mediterranean, or its control by the Soviet Union, would represent a very serious, and probably decisive, danger to the survival of Europe and the West. Such a loss appears to become more probable every day if we tolerate the continuance of the present state of disorder caused by internal malaise and a gradual but inexorable Soviet penetration into the political, ideological, economic, social, and military fields.

The present regime of negotiations and top-level meetings does not improve the European situation. It is not suitable for arresting or attenuating the process of deterioration, cleverly and constantly fostered by Soviet psychological and unorthodox warfare. Neither would a greater presence of European nations, especially Mediterranean—now very scantily represented at the conferences and meetings held chiefly among the Soviet Union, the United States, China, and Japan—improve the present situation. Because of its lack of unity, Europe is always the object of negotiations and only rarely a negotiator itself.

As mentioned earlier, the bipolar equilibrium bears out these conclusions and a tripolar, quadripolar, or pentapolar equilibrium would not alter the situation (at least as long as Europe is not united). It is, therefore, essential that the European nations, and therefore the Mediterranean nations, modify their inert policy of "standing by" and stop waiting for the United States alone to solve the serious problems that concern them. Let them remember that collaboration does not deserve its name unless it is active. They should form an effective political and ideological unity and, with the necessary programs and planning, coordinate their efforts to achieve the single aim of restraining and neutralizing the enlarged Soviet presence in the Mediterranean, which is manifest in every sector.

Above all, let them make their voices heard within Europe, within NATO, and throughout the entire Western world. The present state of passive waiting, of chosen overoptimism and overconfidence in negotiations, does nothing but encourage the strengthening and expansion of Soviet influence among peoples of Western civilization. To the "permanent struggle"—begun and pursued by the Soviet Union with remarkable tenacity and perseverance—it is necessary to oppose with the same tenacity, to take advantage of every favorable circumstance to consolidate our positions, to try to lay the foundations for future advantages, and to stretch out a hand toward nations which are undecided and those which, though having economic possibilities, do not know how to exploit their resources to improve their standard of living. In a word, it is necessary to adopt the same policy of infiltration as the Soviets, even if with different intentions, in order to make our presence felt. By remaining passive, one can never have hopes of victory; by leaving the initiative in the hands of the adversary, sooner or later one succumbs in an inane manner.

Today the situation in the Mediterranean is difficult but not desperate; tomorrow it might definitely be compromised.

The Atlantic Alliance must overstep its present geographical boundaries and admit other nations; it must revise the field of organization and strategy—at present almost exclusively military—and extend it to the political, social, economic, and ideological spheres. Let it convince itself that it is only security in the Mediterranean that can allow an ever-increasing development of the Alliance itself and assure the petroleum and other basic raw material

routes for the future. Because of the global importance of petroleum, the Mediterranean nations, getting weaker and more divided,
will become more and more an object and not the subject in
disputes and negotiations, and their influence on the determination
of their own destiny will continuously diminish.

Therefore, it is necessary to reorganize the strategy (presuming
that such a strategy really exists) for the defense of the Mediterranean. The new strategy should include the complete spectrum of
activities; tasks should be assigned and there should be complete
collaboration. This should involve any necessary degree of sacrifice
and the dedication of all the necessary resources without timidity.
The purpose here should be to make the Mediterranean once more a
European Sea within the sphere of the larger Atlantic Alliance.

Certainly the way is long and difficult and results cannot always
be guaranteed. Nevertheless, it is worthwhile trying, with every
effort and with unity of purpose and by collaborating in close
harmony and cohesion, to create a strategy capable of integrating
and coordinating the various policies which the European and
Atlantic nations deem useful to adopt for their defense and security.

Only in this way will it be possible to achieve a partnership which
will finally give security to Europe and the Mediterranean, thus
guaranteeing the security of the whole Alliance. This security is a
most precious possession which will certainly not come as a gift
from the Soviet Union, but must be earned at the cost of sacrifice,
determination, abnegation, and constant toil.

Strategy for Europe

S. W. B. Menaul

I. INTRODUCTION

The world today is in a state of transition, generating changes more rapid and more far-reaching than anything that has occurred since World War II. The enlargement of the European Economic Community, developments in weapons technology (both conventional and nuclear), strategic nuclear parity between the Soviet Union and the United States, a European Security Conference, and Mutual and Balanced Force Reduction discussions, coupled with the superior conventional capability enjoyed by the Soviet Union and its Warsaw Pact allies, have created a situation in which the whole concept of strategy in Europe should be re-examined. The present Atlantic organization is no longer suitable to meet the challenges of the remainder of this decade.

A. Historical—Grand Strategy and Military Strategy

The prewar military alliances with which Britain entered the 1939-1945 conflict had by 1940 been exposed as totally inadequate

to stem the assault mounted against them by an enemy that had
better equipped armed forces, had superior skill, and had adopted
realistic tactics that exploited the elements of surprise and mobility
to the full. The outcome of the German assault on the West in 1940
was a foregone conclusion, and Japan's initial success in the Far East
followed a similar pattern.

The approach to strategy in pre-World War II days followed the
classical Clausewitzian doctrine that "war is a continuation of
politics by other means," and thus the first essential was to study
national policy, which was said to be inherited from the past and
dependent upon environment, geographical situation, ideology of
the people, and the leaders that arise. The processes of marshalling
the total forces available to a nation—financial, industrial, material,
and economic resources as well as armed forces—were defined as
"grand strategy." Most of the major industrialized nations of the
world, including Germany, adopted this pattern, though the organization of the *Oberkommando der Wehrmacht* and the methods of
conducting military operations were peculiar to the Nazi regime.

Stepping down from the broad considerations involved in marshalling the total resources of a nation to prosecute war (or to deter
a potential aggressor from embarking on adventures that might lead
to war), the next most important requirement was the mobilization,
distribution, organization, direction, and command of fighting forces. In this sphere of activity, strategy was thought of in terms of
specific theaters of war and projected campaigns. The process of
reasoning that governed the imposition of pressure on an enemy by
the employment of armed forces in battle with superior advantage
was called "service strategy." This title was not, however, univer-
sally employed, and it was not uncommon to find the process
referred to as military strategy, combined strategy, or joint strategy.
Most British official documents of the prewar era used the term
"service strategy" or simply "strategy," and were at pains to instill
into students at staff colleges and other military academic institutions that discussion of strategy was not an exotic cult merely
because it was conducted at cabinet or chiefs-of-staff level, but was
in fact no more than common sense applied to war. Unfortunately,
there was a singular lack of common sense, as applied to war, in
most democratic countries in the halcyon days of the 1930s, and so
far as the Western allies were concerned, realization of their plight
came nearly too late.

B. The Nuclear Age

World War II saw the creation of two new, and hitherto untried, elements in war, totally unknown in Clausewitz's day, which were to have a profound effect on the course of the war. The first was the conduct of war in the air—the third dimension—and the second the application of nuclear energy in the form of weapons for delivery from the air. Both have changed the older concepts of strategy, but the transformation has been as slow to develop as that which accompanied the discovery and application of gunpowder. Today we are living in a different world from the one the classical strategists lived in thirty years ago. The concept of applying military pressure to achieve political objectives when other forms of persuasion have failed is vastly different, yet we in the West still appear to be reluctant to acknowledge the transformations that have taken place, and tend to plan for future wars on the assumption that they will be fought on the pattern of the last one. Too many politicians and assorted observers of the contemporary politico-military scene go even further and proclaim that new weapons are more immoral than older ones and should not be introduced into the military arsenals of Western nations. There are no such inhibitions in the Soviet Union or China. New technology and new weapons systems often demand new tactics for their successful applications, and a real breakthrough in the field of defense often demands, though seldom gets, a new approach to strategy. The tendency in the West is to persevere with old and tried national principles even when it can be shown that they are outdated.

Any sovereign state today professing to be wholly independent—which implies the will and ability to resist pressure or intimidation from other states and, if necessary, the means to impose its will on a potential enemy by force—must possess adequate military power as an indispensable element in ensuring the freedom and independence it cherishes. But independent states, with similar philosophies and concepts of freedom, long ago recognized the importance of alliances and the advantages of collective security, though they also learnt to their cost that simple alliances of national states did not always meet the requirements which their architects had hoped for. Such is the complexity of modern means of exerting military pressure that individual European states are today no longer capable of designing an effective strategy or the means to implement it, including the instruments of defense to counter coercion, pressure, or intimidation by the only enemy likely to be ranged against them in Europe. Nor are they capable of protecting their overseas interests by individual national efforts.

Alliances are giving way to political and economic groupings whose collective efforts are necessary to provide security from attack, the threat of attack, or intimidation, thus guaranteeing the freedom of action deemed essential in the preservation of a particular way of life. In Western Europe the move is voluntary but determined, and will of necessity be slow. In Eastern Europe and the Soviet Union there is more compulsion, and already the advantage in military terms, despite economic inferiority, favors the Warsaw Pact—regardless of the success of NATO, from its inception in 1949, in ensuring the security of Western Europe, and under whose protection the EEC has become a reality.

Grand strategy may still be defined as the organization and direction of the political, economic, psychological, and military resources of a nation or community of nations to ensure the survival of the type of society preferred. Military strategy is simply the controlled application of military power either to persuade a potential aggressor to desist from imposing, or threatening to impose, his ideas on another state or group of states, or, if necessary, to compel him to submit to one's own will or suffer the consequences of military action which could result in total military defeat and negotiated surrender, unconditional surrender, or, in the extreme case, the total destruction of the adversary's homeland. The latter event became a frightening possibility with the advent of thermonuclear weapons, though such extreme action has not so far been attempted by any nation as a means of achieving a political aim. It is, however, implicit in the concept of strategic nuclear attack as a last resort in the event of armed conflict between the superpowers and their allies.

In conflicts throughout the world since World War II, conventional weapons, including those in the most sophisticated ranges, have been used by warring factions, some of whom have been actively or passively supported by the nuclear powers; yet the nuclear warhead in all its forms has remained in its leaden casket. There have been few occasions since Hiroshima and Nagasaki when any one of the nuclear powers sought to impose its will on an adversary through the medium of nuclear destruction, though in one or two

cases the possibility of the use of nuclear weapons has been discussed. In the Korean and Vietnamese conflicts there was a noticeable reluctance by Western nations to use the total conventional
military means at their command to achieve their stated political
and military objectives, and this was especially true of the use of air
power by the United States.

Nuclear weapons have not, therefore, deterred either of the
superpowers or China from becoming involved in conventional
conflicts, though the Soviet Union's involvement has invariably
been by proxy. Nuclear weapons have, however, acted as an effective deterrent to hostilities between the superpowers and their
allies, but even in this capacity they have not obviated the need for
both the superpowers and their allies to provide themselves with
conventional weapons of the most sophisticated kind, and it is
unlikely that in the foreseeable future any of the industrialized
nations will forego research and development into even more
sophisticated, manpower-saving conventional weapons, perhaps extending to the partial automation of likely battlegrounds.

In recent years, with the achievement of strategic nuclear parity
between the Soviet Union and the United States, and as nuclear
weapons became more powerful and their accurate delivery more
assured, the tendency has been for the nuclear powers to shrink
from the possibility of strategic nuclear exchange. Nuclear parity
between the two superpowers today means in effect that the
concept of grand strategy, involving the use of thermonuclear
weapons in which each would be responsible for the slaughter of
millions of its own citizens, whom it thought it was its duty to
protect, is less credible than at any time since the concept of
nuclear deterrence was first propounded. The idea of using thermonuclear weapons in the classical concept of imposing one's will
upon an adversary has become virtually impossible.

But even if the state of strategic nuclear parity that exists today
between the superpowers, guaranteeing mutual assured destruction,
makes the prospect of strategic nuclear exchange much less likely, a
war in Europe or the Middle East is still possible in which conventional and tactical nuclear weapons could, and probably would, be
used in the battle without necessarily escalating to nuclear holo-
caust. While the emphasis may now shift to conventional weapons
and new types of tactical nuclear weapons, it is nevertheless still not
possible to eliminate the strategic nuclear weapon entirely from the

argument. It forms part of the whole spectrum of deterrence and defense and may still act as the ultimate deterrent. Thus, in an era in which the balance of power is still basically bipolar though changing, only the superpowers can indulge realistically in the once universal art of grand strategy. Only they have the resources and the means of marshalling them to achieve a given aim, whether it be the imposition of one superpower's will on another superpower or on another nation, or even the deterrence of a potential aggressor from embarking on an adventure, the successful outcome of which would be to the superpower's disadvantage. Individual European nations are no longer in a position to defend themselves against the only possible potential enemy ranged against them in Europe, and even the concept of alliances of national states such as NATO will have to change.

II. CHANGING RELATIONS BETWEEN AMERICA AND EUROPE

The question now being asked by America and her European allies is, to what extent has the U.S. nuclear guarantee been eroded as a result of the attainment of strategic nuclear parity and the bilateral talks on strategic arms limitations currently taking place between the United States and the Soviet Union, and how do Europeans view the attitudes of the American people, members of Congress, and the Senate, who interpret the now familiar Nixon Doctrine in a number of different ways. To these uncertainties must be added the attitudes of European nations themselves to the changing world scene, particularly the members of the new enlarged EEC, eight of whose nine members are also members of the NATO alliance. Their reactions to détente, a European Security Conference, Mutual and Balanced Force Reductions, and the SALT talks vary considerably, and all these problems come at a time when the major European nations are preoccupied with the economic and political problems of the new enlarged Community. In the meantime, the Soviet Union maintains its military posture and extends its conventional superiority over the NATO Alliance, while showing no signs of reducing military service within the Soviet Union or its satellites. The options open to the Warsaw Pact powers are therefore increasing, while those available to NATO and to Europe are diminishing. The Nixon Doctrine makes it abundantly clear that the United States is not going to become involved in the internal affairs of other countries, particularly in the Third World, but it reiterates the resolve of the United States to fulfill its alliance commitments, particularly to Europe. Europe is the number one priority for 1973, or, as Dr. Kissinger has described it, "1973 is the year of Europe." At the same time the United States emphasizes the need for Europe to undertake a greater share of the defense burden. The new Europe of the Nine has the potential to develop into a strong, viable economic and political community which the Nixon Doctrine already identifies as one of the five elements in a potentially multipolar world which will replace the bipolar society we have known since the end of World War II. But there must also be a European identity in defense and a European body with whom the United States can discuss security and defense problems, especially in the light of current discussions in Helsinki and Vienna; Europe must speak with one voice.

The shift to multipolarity involving the United States, the Soviet Union, China, Japan, and Western Europe will take time to reach finality—probably till the end of this decade. Nevertheless, this changing world order is bound to affect relations between the United States and Europe, irrespective of future political changes within the United States itself. On the other hand, it is unlikely that any radical changes will be apparent in Soviet policy despite the European Security Conference and MBFR, even though it is just possible that some agreement might be reached for token reductions in armed forces on both sides. If the EEC does not acknowledge the need for unity in defense and act voluntarily, then it will probably be forced to do so at a later date as it develops closer integration in economic, industrial, and foreign policy. The alternative is to do nothing, but to rely on the existing NATO Alliance of national states and massive U.S. protection in both the nuclear and conventional fields, risking the possibility of U.S. withdrawal, partial or complete, at some future date which would expose Western Europe to Soviet political, economic, and ideological penetration, which would, in the long run, achieve the Soviets' aim of gathering Western Europe within their orbit without recourse to war or conflict of any kind. Already the emergence of factions in certain West European countries advocating policies which go well beyond the aims of détente as currently practiced by West Germany (e.g., a neutral Scandinavian bloc) gives cause for concern, while France pursues a national defense policy outside the military organization of the North Atlantic Treaty, but at the same time actively furthers the aims of a united Europe as symbolized by the enlarged Community.

As the EEC increases in number and expands economically and politically, it has the opportunity to create in parallel its own grand strategy, associated military strategy, and defense capability, not as a superpower but as a more equal partner with the United States in providing the means for the common defense of the Western world, capable of resisting any encroachment by the Soviet Union (or China) into those areas of interest where they could exert political and economic influence which would be in direct conflict with the interests of the United States and Western Europe. Such capability must not be confined to Europe alone, but must extend to the oceans of the world upon which Europe depends for its survival. Middle Eastern oil is one example of an area of vital interest to the Western world which is progressively coming under Soviet influence, yet is not vital to the Soviet economy, at least not yet. Stability and security can be achieved only by a strong Western partnership in which the United States and the new Europe have a similar approach to world problems and in which both are prepared to cooperate in devising grand strategies to achieve their agreed aims, which may be simply stated as the preservation of the freedoms they profess to cherish.

It is unlikely that Western Europe could in the foreseeable future aspire to superpower status, even if this were thought politically desirable, and there is thus no possibility that Western Europe could achieve complete independence from the United States in defense within this decade. Neither can the new Europe dictate to the United States what it considers U.S. contributions to European defense should be. Since the United States has a continuing interest in the security and stability of Western Europe, its contribution to the overall defense of the West should in the future be worked out in collaboration with the EEC, through a representative body under the auspices of the European Parliament empowered to discuss defense and security with the United States in exactly the same way as a similar body discusses economic affairs, including trade, tariffs, investment, and monetary matters. The framework for maintaining military forces in Europe must for the time being, however, be NATO, and even if a new "European Defense Committee" develops, the NATO infrastructure, with its headquarters, communications, and logistics organizations, would have to be utilized. It is of paramount importance that in this era of peace and negotiation rather than confrontation, security considerations should not be relegated to a subordinate place below political, psychological, and economic problems. If this should happen, there is a danger that while the Soviet Union maintains its massive military power, the will of Europe to defend itself could be eroded and ultimately fatally weakened.

The United States is currently examining its foreign policy in the aftermath of the Vietnam War, and in the light of its new relationships with the Soviet Union and China. Europe is now in the forefront of its deliberations, and among the decisions which must be made soon is the future of U.S. military commitments to Europe in the light of the new proposals for partnership between the two pillars of the Atlantic Community and the possibility of this partnership being extended to include Japan.

Throughout most of the 1950s the United States enjoyed near nuclear monopoly, followed in the 1960s by nuclear superiority under which her commitment to Europe and its accompanying military strategy were defined and accepted by the European members of NATO. Confrontation, where it developed (Cuba and Berlin), was handled with relative ease, and the outcome was never really in doubt. This year the United States will attempt to establish a new relationship with the EEC, consistent with its declared intention of honoring its alliance commitments but from a new low-profile posture designed to permit some reduction in U.S. armed forces and a positive reduction in the U.S. defense budget. Political extremists are bound to demand more extensive cuts in the U.S. military contribution to the defense of Europe than the present situation would allow, but on the whole the President and Congress recognize the undesirability of any unilateral reduction in U.S. armed forces in Europe outside agreements which may be reached in MBFR discussions.

III. A NEW STRATEGY FOR EUROPE

In developing new policies for Europe on the basis of partnership as defined in the Nixon Doctrine, the enormous economic, political, and security problems which confront the new enlarged and still growing EEC will need constant analysis. In the evolution of agreed U.S.-European economic and foreign policies leading to meaningful

and effective defense strategies for the years ahead, changes in
current policies will have to be made affecting trade, monetary
affairs, and the NATO Alliance. Obstacles to be overcome are
already proving more difficult to solve than might have been expected. West-West negotiations are currently more urgent than
East-West ones, if the conferences at Helsinki and Vienna are to be
conducted to the West's advantage. Much has already been written
about the European Community and the prospects for future integration in monetary and economic affairs, leading eventually to
complete political unity, and it is not the purpose of this paper to
go over them again. Suffice it to say that the Community's relations
with the United States must not be an extension of previous
bilateral associations but must be based on a Europe speaking with
one voice to a partner with whom we have had a long and friendly
relationship and whose continued support is essential to European
survival and prosperity.

A. Grand Strategy

In attempting to define a new strategy for Europe, reference must
be made to economic and political considerations, since it is now
generally accepted that in the evolving European structure it is not
possible to separate political and economic affairs from security and
defense requirements. The original aim of a united Europe, as stated
by Churchill in 1947, was to eliminate any future possibility of
conflict between major European powers or groupings of such
powers. To all intents and purposes this has been achieved under
the security and stability provided by NATO, to which the United
States has contributed a major share in the military and economic
fields. Since none of the major European powers is in a position to
practice grand strategy in the classical sense, and each provides only
what it considers it must or can reasonably afford as a fair contribution to the NATO Alliance, the concept of simple alliances on
the prewar pattern or, indeed, within the existing NATO framework
will not suffice to ensure the security of the West in the evolving
new multipolar world which may reach fruition in the 1980s.

Nearly all the strategic and tactical nuclear effort and a large
contribution in conventional arms are currently provided by the
United States to the NATO Alliance, and there is no indication that
European countries could or would fill the gap if the U.S. effort
were to be withdrawn or even marginally reduced. Today the sum

total of the military power of the Western Alliance is less than is
necessary to ensure security against the only possible opponent
likely to attempt to disturb the stability and the evolving economic
strength of Western Europe. The Soviet Union, on the other hand,
has become a world power and a superpower and demonstrably
practices grand strategy in the classical manner; it is in an almost
unique position to do so. If further proof were needed it is readily
seen in the political, economic, and military activities of the Soviet
Union world-wide and in the proportion of gross national product
currently devoted to the armed forces of the Soviet Union and its
allies, even though in the past twenty-five years the Soviet Union
has not actively engaged in war operations on anything like the
scale of the United States, Britain, or France.

It is essential, therefore, that the new EEC, as it expands to
include in due time, one would hope, all the members of NATO,
and as it progresses toward economic and political union, should
develop in parallel an identifiable grand strategy to meet its security
requirements. This should be followed by clearly defined military
strategy and tactical doctrine in cooperation with the United States
to ensure the future security of the West and Western interests as a
whole, within which a united Europe could develop political and
economic strength consistent with its natural wealth, population,
and the energies of its people. The EEC is the only organization
that can fulfill this task. It will be responsible for the future
economic and political destiny of Europe, and it must also accept
the obligation for defense. No other organization, such as the
Western European Union (WEU), could adequately fill this role,
though other groups could help to achieve the aim. Fortunately,
there are already signs of a move in this direction. The Eurogroup
ministers have acknowledged that adequate defense in Europe can be
achieved only through a system of collaboration in procurement
which may soon require a common European defense budget.
Indeed there does not appear to be any reasonable alternative. No
European nation can afford all the complicated and costly weapons
systems which science and technology are now offering, and as
collaborative procurement and a common defense budget become
essential, there is bound to be closer coordination in European
defense planning, leading, one would hope, to a fully integrated
European defense organization. The NATO military chiefs have
recently called for greater rationalization of military forces, which

is another step toward closer collaboration and standardization. The alternative is to go backward to national policies with their duplication and waste of effort and resources which could only lead ultimately to fragmentation and final disintegration of what has already been achieved within the concept of a European Economic Community, under the protection of the NATO military organization.

B. Military Strategy—Revised Concept

The current strategy of flexible response in Europe, while basically a tenable strategy, needs revision. It is based more on hope of what the Warsaw Pact might do than on a solid military strategy to meet any or even the most likely contingency. The ability of NATO conventional forces to stem a purely conventional thrust into Western Europe is declining, and the concept of the use of tactical nuclear weapons as a last resort—in the hope, it is claimed, that such a decision would persuade the Warsaw Pact "to halt the aggression and withdraw"—is no longer credible in the light of technological developments in both nuclear and conventional weapons in the last five years. The strategy of flexible response was introduced in 1967 to replace the trip-wire strategy of immediate nuclear response and was based on the theory that tactical nuclear weapons favor the defense and that the Warsaw Pact would cease aggression and withdraw on the threat, or actual use, of current types of tactical nuclear weapons when it became evident that NATO could not contain an incursion by conventional means only. There is, however, nothing in recent statements by Soviet military experts that gives the slightest justification for accepting this proposition at face value. On the contrary, senior officers of the Soviet high command going back to Sokolovsky in 1963 have repeatedly stated that in their view tactical nuclear weapons favor the offensive, and the Warsaw Pact forces practice this concept assiduously in every major exercise, including the most recent "Shield 1972," which was held in Czechoslovakia in the autumn of last year. Current Soviet tactical doctrine for Europe advocates a swift, all-out offensive in which the use of tactical nuclear weapons could (and probably would) be employed in conjunction with conventional forces from the outset of the attack. Warsaw Pact ground and air forces are poised well forward to implement this doctrine; they are capable of advancing up to 70 miles a day, and the terrain in the central region is well suited to this type of attack. The Soviet Union does not need convincing that NATO in the last resort would use tactical nuclear weapons, but it is adopting an offensive strategy that optimizes its superiority in conventional forces, and it believes that in the execution of its tactical plans on the central front, the NATO forces could be prevented from using their existing tactical nuclear forces effectively.

It remains only to examine what new or revised military strategy is required to deter or, if necessary, defeat the only possible threat to Europe in the foreseeable future—namely, the Soviet Union and its Warsaw Pact allies. There is, of course, no indication that the Soviet Union intends to embark on military adventures in Europe in the immediate future, although its intentions and capabilities (which are, and always have been, complementary) continue to underline Soviet long-term aims in Europe. The tactics to achieve those aims may of course vary from time to time. The Warsaw Pact forces' conventional capability is superior to the forces of the NATO Alliance in almost every aspect, and even though the Soviet Union has achieved strategic nuclear parity with the United States, it continues to spend a high proportion of its gross national product on further increasing and substantially improving its conventional military power, which goes far beyond what might reasonably be expected for its own defense, even allowing for the forces which it deems essential in the implementation of the Brezhnev doctrine in its East European empire.

It has long been obvious that European member nations of the NATO Alliance are reluctant to provide large conventional military forces in peacetime, and in recent years some countries have bowed to internal political pressure to reduce their conventional forces below what they must know to be the minimum contribution necessary to the collective defense effort of the Alliance. In the current atmosphere of peace, negotiation, and détente, this situation may well deteriorate further; there never has been and never will be any possibility of the Western nations matching the Warsaw Pact in mass of conventional forces. The only possible alternative is a joint strategy aimed at deterring and, if necessary, defeating any thrust into Western Europe by the Warsaw Pact forces, based on the application of new technology which will provide greater firepower with minimum manpower (and Europe has already reached the manpower minimum) at acceptable cost and which will bridge the firepower gap between existing conventional firepower and current types of tactical nuclear weapons.

This new approach to military strategy in Europe will involve the introduction of new conventional weapons systems such as zero-error bombs ("smart bombs"), missiles, and antitank weapons (particularly those delivered from helicopters) which advances in laser, electro-optical, and infrared technology have made possible; greater mobility for infantry; better communications and surveillance (including the use of remotely piloted vehicles); greater use of modern sensors and electronic countermeasures; and more effective battlefield control and direction of forces. This can only be achieved through centralized procurement based on agreed tactical doctrine formulated from a European concept of grand strategy.

The introduction of small, controllable, mini-nuclear weapons of variable yield could close the gap between purely conventional firepower and the greater intensity which can be achieved with these new nuclear weapons, which have the highly desirable characteristics of optimizing blast or radiation to suit the tactical requirements of the ground battle or, alternatively, greatly reducing the destructive effects on nearby nonmilitary targets through radiation suppression. The introduction of these new nuclear weapons would greatly ease the security, dispersal, and control problems that are currently encountered with existing types of tactical nuclear weapons while at the same time complicating the enemy's problem of achieving their destruction—a course of action that would be high on his priority list in the event of an offensive against the West if worthwhile aims were to be achieved. The degree of firepower and the means of delivery which the application of new techniques could provide would go far to redress the current imbalance of forces on the European continent, thereby adding greatly to the deterrent capability of NATO forces throughout the whole spectrum of defense up to the strategic nuclear forces which would remain as the ultimate deterrent. In the event of failure to deter, more options and more effective tactics would be available to the forces defending Europe, with enormously higher guarantees of destroying enemy invading forces, especially armor, logistics, vital assembly points, and lines of communication. Hence, we would not be submitting friendly territories to the degree of destruction inherent in the current concept of the strategy of flexible response, which envisages resort to tactical nuclear weapons (of higher yield and more destructive in all respects than the new types of weapons which could be made available) if conventional forces failed to stem a Soviet advance. These weapons would be an integral part of the whole spectrum of deterrence and defense. The enemy would be unable to assess the reaction of Western forces or the strength of firepower that he would encounter in retaliation, as he can now. Equally important, the accuracy with which firepower could be brought to bear by existing forces, appropriate to the scale of the invasion, greatly enhances the prospects of stopping an incursion before resort to high-yield nuclear weapons becomes necessary. Thus it is now possible to make the strategy of flexible response meaningful and effective under all conditions of Soviet attack.

The technology required to transform the military forces of Europe, including naval and air forces, is available now, and the United States has shown willingness to make much more information available to Europe; but it cannot be applied effectively in penny packets. Only by collaboration in research and development, design, production, and procurement based on a common, agreed European strategy, a tactical doctrine, a common defense budget, and in collaboration with the United States at every level could these new weapons be acquired in the quantities necessary to meet a revised, realistic strategy. There are already collaborative ventures between European countries, and many U.S. weapons systems are currently in service with European armed forces. Intercollaboration between Europe and the United States must therefore be one of the particular aims in future discussions of modern weapons systems. This would involve close and continuing dialogue between a European weapons program agency, under the auspices of a European Defense Committee responsible to the European Parliament through the Council of Ministers, talking directly with the United States, rather than the present ad hoc system of bilateral negotiations between European members of NATO and the United States, or discussions within NATO itself. Such integration would produce considerable savings in manpower, greater standardization in equipment, more modern weapons systems, and a very considerable increase in the effectiveness of the defense forces of Western Europe.

But France, the only other nuclear power in Europe (with Britain), while a member of the enlarged Community, is outside the NATO military organization (though still a signatory to the North

Atlantic Treaty). If there is to be a new approach to European
strategy and defense requirements, it is essential that France take
part in the discussions as an equal partner with the other members
of the Nine and the existing NATO military organization. Both
Britain and France are rapidly approaching the stage where vital
decisions regarding their nuclear capabilities will have to be taken.
Their current nuclear weapons systems may soon be obsolete and,
since lead time in providing replacements may be anything up to
ten years, these decisions are even now becoming urgent. They must
be discussed in the concept of European defense and not purely
British or French national interests. Neither country is in a position
to defend itself by its own efforts from an attack by the Soviet
Union, and it is difficult to envisage a scenario in which either could
use its nuclear weapons in defense of purely national interests. But
both must maintain nuclear capabilities as contributions to the
overall strategic and tactical nuclear capability of the West. France
must be included in European defense discussions at all levels, and
the most promising initial approach might be through the Eurogroup and the NATO Nuclear Planning Group. All current and
prospective members of EEC should undertake to make a proper
contribution to defense requirements while they enjoy the economic and political advantages which, it is hoped, membership in
the EEC will confer upon them.

The economic wealth of Europe makes it entirely feasible to
provide and maintain an adequate military balance, equitably shared
between European countries and between Europe and America. The
recent agreement between the nine foreign ministers on a timetable
for the European Security Conference (duly accepted by the dele-
gates) is an encouraging example of Europe beginning to speak with
one voice in foreign affairs. There is no reason why it should not
emulate this desirable trend in discussions on defense. But those
who persistently advocate increased conventional forces and diminishing emphasis on tactical nuclear weapons are perpetuating a
myth that no sensible strategist could accept. No European country
today would be prepared to authorize the sort of conventional
forces that would be needed to fight a purely conventional war
against the Warsaw Pact. The cost would be enormous, even assuming that the manpower could be made available, and there is no
evidence whatever that the Soviet Union intends to reduce its
tactical nuclear stockpile or revise its concept of a land battle in

Europe. New technology offers the alternative of smaller forces, more effectively equipped with better conventional and tactical nuclear weapons, which in combination would provide a more effective deterrent force, and in the event of failure to deter, more options including the possibility of containing a Soviet thrust by purely conventional means. But if this too failed, then the enormously higher firepower available from the use of new tactical nuclear weapons, and the highly accurate means of delivery which technology could provide, would offer vastly greater prospects for success on the battlefield than current strategies and equipment offer today. The new strategy, which should be made clear to the Warsaw Pact, would be purely defensive and aimed at *appropriate response* to contain any military adventure into Western Europe by the Warsaw Pact, without destroying vast areas of European territory in the process.

The importance of the central front in Europe has been emphasized because it is there that the bulk of Western and Eastern forces are deployed. It is the most likely battleground and currently the most sensitive area in discussions of defense in general and nuclear defense in particular. But the northern and southern flanks of the NATO Alliance must not be forgotten. It is on the northern flank that the greatest deployment of Soviet maritime power is to be found, and in the Kola Peninsula area at least four Soviet divisions are always available for operations. Opposing them is one Brigade Group, and since Norway (and Denmark) will not permit foreign troops on their soil in peacetime, the Commander-in-Chief must rely on reinforcements from outside to provide the forces needed to stem an assault whether by land, sea, or air. This situation would have to change if the EEC accepts responsibility for future European defense requirements and Norway changes its mind and applies for admission to the Community, which it is likely to do.

Nor can we ignore the dangers on the southern flank, whether direct through Turkey and Greece or by maritime pressure in the Mediterranean using Middle East bases and facilities. Enlargement of the Community to include not only those countries currently members of NATO, but Spain as well, would do much to improve the cohesion of those Western nations interested in the defense of Western Europe and Western interests as a whole.

If a more united, enlarged, and growing EEC and the United States could between them agree to such a strategy and provide the forces necessary to implement it, the security of Europe and the West would be assured. There would be the added bonus of entering the MBFR discussions in the knowledge that limited agreement to reducing forces could be negotiated in the certain knowledge that security would not thereby be diminished but would on the contrary be greatly enhanced.

A German View
of Western Security and Defense

J. A. Graf Kielmansegg

I. THE IMPORTANCE OF THE CENTRAL REGION

When we look at the various subjects of this colloquium it becomes clear that whereas they start with the global aspect they gradually come down to one central focus, a focus which we are considering this afternoon. This is just the same picture we must use as a basis in any consideration of Western security and defense. The geographical center and also the key bastion of defense is, indeed, Central Europe. Except for the outer flanks in the North and South, it is only here that there is direct contact on land with the power of the Soviet Union. Only here can the decisive land battle take place in the event of armed conflict. It is only logical that the main mass of the Soviet and satellite ground forces is directed toward Central Europe, and this has not been altered by the military build-up on the Sino-Soviet frontier. This fact is quite simple and is not new, although sometimes one gets the impression that the West has become so accustomed to this fact over twenty-five years that it has forgotten it.

The focal point of this center of defense is the Federal Republic of Germany, whose eastern frontier is also the front line. For this reason there is no problem of Western security which does not in some way involve the FRG, and similarly there can be no defense of Europe without Germany. And so it is just as well to ask for a German view of Western security and defense. However, I hesitate to give my talk this title. The Federal Republic cannot, under any imaginable circumstances, defend itself alone against the Warsaw Pact, and thus a German view can never be isolated, can never be only German. What I learned when I was Commander-in-Chief, Allied Forces, Central Europe, and I learned it very profoundly, was to see the whole more than its individual parts. It is hardly worth-while to consider the subject in any other way, and certainly not to arrive at the optimum results for security and defense; nearly all the difficulties and weaknesses of Western defense follow as a conse-quence of the fact that in the Alliance there is still much thought and many actions which are not in accordance with this principle.

I should like my remarks to be seen against this background, so that I can now confine myself to pointing out one fact with all the emphasis at my disposal—a fact that decisively influences any Ger-man view of Western security and defense (whatever form it may take in other respects) and which is not applicable to most other NATO partners; only Norway, Greece, and Turkey are at all simi-larly affected, and then not to the same extent.

In an armed conflict between East and West, which would doubtless be global in character, all NATO countries would admit-tedly be subject to a threat from the air, nuclear as well as conventional, as would their naval forces also, since Russian ships are sailing all the seven seas. But Germany alone would be the principal land battlefield—and this from the moment the first shot was fired. This would be a very special kind of contribution to be made by the FRG. It is easy to understand that the number of Germans who are not very happy with this idea is by no means small. It is my impression that their number could increase con-siderably, considerably in the political sense also, if the feeling, which is already noticeable, were to be strengthened that Germany could become not only the battlefield but also the main nuclear killing ground, whereas an "after SALT umbrella" would in fact protect only the United States and the Soviet Union.

II. RECOGNIZING REALITIES

This brings me to the point mentioned in the paper by the Stanford Strategic Studies Center of 23 January 1973, in reference to "the changing strategic environment, the crisis of confidence in the U.S.-European Alliance and the need of a common coherent strategy," and here I take the word "strategy" in both its political and its military senses.

This paper also speaks of "reshaping the Western defense posture." What does this mean, especially when the same paper speaks of being "more realistic"? I am quite in agreement with the call for a more realistic view, but I ask: What must we recognize before we can see reality as it is?

In this context, I should like to make a few points.

1. So far Western security has in practice been based only on the military strength of the Alliance. For some years the West has been striving to strengthen its security by means of treaties and agreements. The terms SALT, CSCE, MBFR, and *Ostpolitik* indicate the areas in which that has been happening. In addition, there are the well-known treaties negotiated in Geneva (nonproliferation, seabed, etc.) which go beyond NATO and the Warsaw Pact. Of course, it is a truism that it is easier and safer to stand on two legs than on one. But the second leg, the political one, becomes even more necessary when the other one, the military one, has been suffering for years from atrophy of some important muscles, as is the case with the West. If this atrophy is not halted, we may easily topple over before we have found a footing with our second leg. Furthermore, in a crisis political settlements alone, if they are not backed up by enough military strength, are usually worth less than the paper they are written on, and they can never be a substitute for our own strength. The view that this is possible—that political security can simply be substituted for military security—is an easygoing, seductive, and popular opinion, but it is a perilous opinion. Nevertheless, it is finding more and more adherents.

2. The decisive factor in the military strength of the West has been and still is the nuclear preponderance that has hitherto lain with the United States. It has made the weakness in conventional arms, particularly that of the land forces, tolerable. But now the

Soviet Union has caught up in the strategic nuclear area, and since
SALT I there has been something like parity in this respect. In this
context it is important to realize that the Soviets regard this parity
not only as a military fact but also as a political principle recognized by the United States. We all know that this parity is doubtful
from the military and technical points of view, and that in any case
it is fragile. We also know that it is an open question how long
Moscow will be interested in recognizing parity as a principle and
observing it in practice. SALT II will, I hope, make us somewhat
wiser in this respect.

3. Although it would be a dangerous error to believe, as many
do, that the use of strategic nuclear weapons would simply be out
of the question from now on, it is on the other hand clear that
parity makes use of the strategic nuclear potential even more
improbable than before. This applies—and we should heed this
point—to the defender even more than to the potential aggressor.
The logical consequence is that, if a war broke out, it should be
expected to take a form short of a strategic nuclear exchange, at
least in its first phase. This in turn makes both the political and the
military roles of tactical nuclear weapons and conventional forces
even more important than before. In the former, the United States
has some preponderance, but in the latter the Warsaw Pact powers
have a great preponderance. Moscow will not give up this superiority, even if it should be possible to reduce the level of conventional
forces on both sides. On the other hand, an increase in the conventional forces of the West cannot be expected—neither for the
European countries nor for the United States. On the contrary, the
danger of further unilateral reduction of forces present at the
Central European Theater (this process of erosion has been under
way since as long ago as 1966), before or even without MBFR
results, cannot be dismissed out of hand. Even in the event of a
reduction that in fact went halfway toward being balanced, the
asymmetry would remain, though on a lower plane. In other words,
the problem would, in essence, be unchanged.

4. Whatever reasons they may have, the Soviets are today doubtless interested in arriving at political agreements with the West and
in achieving cooperation that is useful to them in certain spheres.
All in all, that is a favorable situation that must be used. But no one
knows how long this interest will last. I am not called upon here to
deal with the East-West talks in detail, but I should like to make
one remark on this subject. There are four conference tables—for

SALT, CSCE, MBFR, and *Ostpolitik. Ostpolitik* is still being processed, even though, or rather precisely because, treaties are already in existence. Otherwise, you would not, for example, be seeing shortly the rather pompous state visit of Brezhnev in Bonn. On one side of all the four tables sits the Soviet Union, sometimes with its satellites and sometimes without them. On the other side, the Western side, only the United States sits at the SALT table; while at the CSCE table it is the United States, Canada, the European members of the Alliance (including France), and the rest of Western Europe right down to San Marino. At the MBFR table it is also the two American countries and various as yet undefined European states, not including France, however. And finally at the *Ostpolitik* table it is the FRG alone. So the Western side is a motley array. The great strength of the Soviet Union's position lies in the fact that it is the only power, and at that the hegemonic power in its own bloc, that is sitting at all four tables. It knows this. As far as Moscow is concerned, the rule of classical drama is observed—the unity of time, place, and action. Not so for the West. If the United States and the other Western partners do not, as I mentioned before, set more store by the common whole than by its constituent national parts, if they do not achieve real union in political aims, plans, and tactics at all four conference tables, then Moscow will, quite respectably, bring about effects of fragmentation, dismantlement, and disintegration. So far there are not many signs of a common concept, though we must be gratified that NATO has at least worked out serviceable guidelines for CSCE and MBFR, and has collected a mass of industriously calculated data.

A tendency is visibly growing in public opinion, and even in political circles, in the West to regard the distant aim of bringing about a reliable détente, balanced force reductions, and effective arms control as already a *fait accompli*, thus giving a pretext for reducing expenditures on security. This tendency does not exist in the East and will not exist there in the future, but what does exist is the attempt to promote and exploit Western euphoria by every possible means. The most unwise thing the West could do would be, unilaterally and prematurely, to defer military planning, stop research and development programs, and reduce troops and arms production. But many people consider this wise. They cannot or will not see that Russia is behaving in precisely the opposite way and that it is impossible to bargain if one first offers and gives away one's bargaining counters to the adversary. Furthermore, and this factor is almost completely overlooked, much time and military strength would then be lost and could not be quickly made up if there were a change in the political situation. Although it is very difficult to make accurate prophecies on political developments, one thing can be said with certainty: No political situation is permanent, and the more dictatorial a regime is, the more suddenly and unexpectedly can changes occur. No one living on the coast of a tidal sea would be so silly as to tear down the dikes and seawalls just because the tide happened to be out at the moment.

In this context the presence of American forces, mainly land forces, in Europe is particularly important. They are a military necessity not only because without them there would be gaps in the defense network established to contain the aggressor, but also because American troops—in more than only symbolic strength— simply cannot be replaced by European troops, even if it were possible to raise more forces in Europe. Only American troops can substantiate the American commitment in Europe, with its attendant deterrent effect; only they can prove that the nuclear promise is not an empty one. Moreover, this is a decisive psychological factor not only as regards the Soviet perception concerning the firm determination of the United States to stand up to any threat against the security of NATO Europe, but perhaps even to a greater degree for the corresponding perception of the European NATO partners. In almost all West European states, the inner—i.e., psychical— stability has been shaken, sometimes to a greater and sometimes to a lesser degree. Communist talk of peace has a hypnotic effect on a considerable number of people, as it has sweet-sounding charms. Because of the tempting vision or even illusion of détente that has come about through the East-West talks, many have lost the conviction that anything has to be done about security.

The American participants in the conference, and perhaps others also, know Charles Schulz, the Peanuts cartoonist. In one of his little books he shows what security means. One of the drawings shows a little girl, with a strong boy holding her by the hand. The caption reads: "Security is having a big brother." What do you think the little girl would feel and perhaps do if her big brother suddenly let go of her hand and disappeared from view? His assurance, "I'll be back," would not be much use then.

This is the appropriate place for another remark concerning the political aspect of the American presence in Europe. No European should doubt the justification for this presence, and no American should doubt its necessity for the security of the United States. However, for some time we have seen both types of doubt. In Europe emotional anti-American feeling is flourishing in places, and on the other side of the Atlantic many people have forgotten that America must be defended in Europe, have forgotten that if Western Europe—or even only its centre—transferred its allegiance to the Soviet sphere—no matter how this might come about—it would mean that the Soviet Union would be the sole and undisputed number one world power in all areas. I need not explain here what this would mean in military terms, what a threat the Soviet Union would be to the United States if it were the power controlling the Atlantic coast of Europe, even if without physical possession. Of course, Europeans must realize even more clearly than before that it is an urgent and vital task for Europe to prevent this, but the task is impossible without an American presence.

5. Unless all that we have heard and seen for about the last four years is deceptive, it must be concluded that the political role played by military power is losing its significance to the United States but is becoming more significant to the Soviet Union. I do not think that this correlation is a very reassuring one. As early as 1971, a leading article appeared in a German newspaper under the title: "U.S. gives up leadership role—USSR determined to consolidate their power."

Here it is noteworthy that the Soviet side has recently again and again emphasized self-confidently, and incidentally quite rightly, that, to quote one source, it was "only the shift in the balance of power in favor of the Socialist camp that made it possible to find a new type of relationship." Professor Proektor, from the IMEMO in Moscow, for example, makes the same statement almost word for word in the January edition of the periodical *The Soviet Union Today* and, significantly, adds as further factors favorable to a détente "the need to reduce armaments in the USA and the large European States, which has an economic basis" and also the "anti-imperialistic and anti-war feeling in various strata of the population, which finds expression in activation of social and political forces." It seems to me that this is a very realistic view.

So I have made five points in furtherance of my opening remarks. Their essentials are as follows:

- Military security cannot simply be replaced by political security; political security is worthless unless backed up by military strength.

- We now have something like strategic nuclear parity; we do not know how long it will last.

- As a result, tactical nuclear weapons and conventional forces are more important than ever.

- On one side of all the East-West conference tables sits the Soviet Union. On the other side are sitting different Western states in various combinations and without a common concept. In this context, but not only in this context, American military presence is important and cannot, by its nature, be replaced by any European effort.

- Western conviction of the need for maintaining a strong military defense seems to be wavering; the Soviet Union, on the other hand, sees an increasing significance in military power as a political instrument.

These five points describe the realities I mentioned in my opening remarks. There are other realities: for instance, the fact that it has become an open and difficult problem whether the United States and Western Europe are understanding partners actively assisting one another in the area of commercial, monetary, and economic interests, or whether they are unfriendly opponents and rivals. There is more than a slight danger that this rather unfortunate state of affairs may have repercussions on our common security and defense.

However, the chief basis for a reshaping of the Western defense posture lies in the realities shown in my five points, and they must be considered realistically, more realistically than has so far been the case. To say this is not mere pleonasm, but a consequence of the existence of people who are quite able and willing to treat realities as if they were unreal.

It is of course possible to judge these facts in different ways, but there is no good in ignoring them. They cannot be set aside by intellectual exertion; they cannot be made to disappear by any conjuring trick, except perhaps as a rabbit is concealed in a top hat; you cannot see the rabbit, but it is there just the same. I cannot recommend such self-delusion.

III. DETERRENCE OF THE SOVIET THREAT

It has become increasingly the practice in the West, when decisions regarding security planning and armed forces development are being discussed and made, to start with the quantitative, organizational, and cost-effectiveness aspects, and once this has been done, to try to find an appropriate strategy. It is certainly necessary to examine these aspects carefully and to assess their significance, but they should not be the sole criterion applied, nor should they be the starting point of further thought.

First one must know what one wants to do, and in many situations, what one has to do, then, in the light of this knowledge, examine and assess all circumstances, facts, and figures; and then decide what one can do and how one can do it. The end result of this must be the missions to be given to the armed forces. More briefly, one must know first what results one wishes to achieve.

This principle is often broken, but in such cases military strategy, forces, and missions are not in the necessary equilibrium; their interrelation becomes unstable.

The paramount political aim of the West vis-à-vis the East is nothing else than to preserve the peace and guarantee its own security—security against the possibility that a foreign political will might be imposed on it, in peace or through war. In practical terms, that means that in no event and under no circumstances will the West be the aggressor. Thus far, all is clear and in line with the declared policy of the Alliance. As a logical consequence, the military posture is basically conceived in terms of defense. But here the difficulties begin. There is no uniformity in thought or action with regard to detailed political aims, and the forces do not bear the necessary correct relations to the strategy and assignments or missions.

In order to ascertain what form one's own defense and the missions to be given to one's forces should take, it is necessary first to take a cool, unbiased look at the potential aggressor. I should not mention figures, which I take it are common knowledge at this gathering, and I shall not speak on the old but ever-new question of whether the aggressor should be assessed in terms of his intentions or his capability. To me, the answer is very simple: delete the word "or" and substitute "and," that is, consider both intentions *and* capability. At best, it is only possible to guess at the intentions, which moreover can change overnight; the capability can be measured with a fair degree of accuracy and can change only very gradually.

At this point I want to try to describe briefly the true nature of the danger from the Soviet Union. If it is not understood or its existence is denied, Soviet political aims will never be correctly recognized and Soviet political and diplomatic attitudes will never be correctly understood.

First there is the great military power of the Soviet Union, which is continually growing and improving, is far superior in the conventional field, and is geared to attack by its strength, structure, and doctrine. This fact cannot be taken seriously enough. If there should be armed conflict, the Russians will attack, immediately and rapidly, even when, and precisely when, they subjectively believe that they must defend themselves. That is the strategic and tactical principle on which their forces are constructed and trained. Incidentally, if I were sitting in Moscow, I should not act any differently. Only in this way can the Soviet Union completely exploit the great advantages of initiative, surprise, and selection of the main point or points of attack, which only the attacker can have. The side that has these three advantages can double the force of any military operation; these are advantages that cannot be measured, that cannot be calculated by any computer, but they can perfectly well make the mathematical results of any planning null and void on the battlefield.

The second element in the Soviet danger is its ever-expanding political and military presence throughout the world, which is becoming particularly evident in the use of the Russian Navy, whose political and psychological effect is at least as important as its military impact.

Third, the danger lies in the Communist ideology, which remains expansive, even though at the moment that fact is to a large extent veiled.

Please do not misunderstand me. I do not in any way mean to imply by my remarks that Moscow is now pursuing, or will pursue in the future, a policy that leads straight to the final aim of war. I do not assume the existence in the Kremlin of any such master plan, but warfare has by no means been crossed off the Russian list of political expedients. At the moment, in my opinion, the Soviets do not need to plan a war against the West or part of the West, because they can assume, not without justification, that they can achieve their objective in Europe anyway. This objective is unmistakable—namely, to replace the *pax americana* in Europe by the *pax sovietica*. For the pragmatic grasping of opportunities as well as for all other possible lines of political action based on military strength, for indirect strategy, for alteration of the availability of geographical areas, for political blackmail, and for direct attack—the Kremlin has in its armed forces a powerful, high-quality, and very versatile instrument that it could use at any time.

Therefore the salient point for the West must be both to arrive at political settlements that make the indirect handling of this instrument more difficult, and if possible futile, and to possess military strength of its own that will present direct action with a risk that will seem too great to the Russian way of thinking, which is different from that of the West.

This brings me to the question of the deterrent effect. On this point I should just like to make two remarks, or to be more precise, I should like to state two principles that must not be contravened or overlooked if a deterrent is to be effective.

1. Deterrence is in part a state of mind of the person who is to be deterred from some course of action. In order to ensure that the appropriate state of mind exists, it is not only the deterrent that must be convincing but also the defense into which it would be transformed. Deterrence and defense are complementary and must not be considered or treated separately, as they are in much theoretical thinking. For example, a distinction is drawn between the military capacity to wage war and the capacity to prevent war—which might be different, it is argued. But this overlooks the fact that it is only possible to prevent *the* war that one could, if need be, fight. Deterrence and defense are, so to speak, two states of matter of the same substance, as are, for example, water and steam. If we equate water with defense and steam with deterrence, then it is clear that only so much deterrence can be generated as there is defense present.

Deterrence and defense must contain the same components as those of the military instrument in the hands of the potential aggressor, though they must not necessarily be of the same magnitude. Unless all the links in the chain are present and hold together, the desired success cannot be achieved.

Although Lenin did not know strategic and tactical nuclear weapons, what he said in a pamphlet titled "The Left Radicalism," which appeared in 1920, is well worth reading. The following quotation might have been written specifically on the subject of deterrence and defense and is still valid today. Lenin wrote:

Everyone will admit that it is unwise and even criminal for an army not to prepare to master the use of all weapons and means and methods of warfare that the enemy has, or could have, at his disposal. That applies to politics even more than to warfare. In politics there is even less possibility of knowing in advance what means of action we can take and what will be advantageous to us in this or that set of future circumstances. If we do not have mastery in the use of *all* means of action, we may suffer a severe or even decisive defeat if alterations in the situation that are beyond our control call for a form of action in which we are particularly weak.

I mentioned before that the first thing one must ascertain is the nature of the potential aggressor. The next thing one must know is what one expects from one's own defense, that is, what military missions should be given to the armed forces. Only then can one consider what is possible, and take figures, questions of organization, and cost-effectiveness into one's calculations, thus finally determining what missions can be given, or what must be done in order to make it possible for the desired assignments to be carried out.

As far as the missions are concerned, here, as in almost every sphere, maximum, average, and minimum requirements are theoretically possible. Without going through all the steps of the thinking process I have just outlined, I shall move straight to the conclusions. In the present state of affairs in Western Europe it is unfortunately quite pointless to think in terms of anything but minimum requirements, although NATO's defense mission—that is, the mission given by the governments to the military, which has remained unchanged for seventeen years—is almost a maximum mission. You will remember it: "To preserve and to restore the security and integrity of the NATO territories."

What should we now regard in addition to the deterrent role as a minimum mission for the allied forces, or perhaps rather as a basic mission, which neither can nor may be given up as long as aggression is possible and which, by the way, would be honest? I suggest the following:

- To maintain and strengthen the determination of the governments and the general public to resist all forms of Soviet pressure by ensuring that the forces give the feeling that successful resistance is possible.

- To preserve the cohesion of defense, through establishing and/or maintaining a right relationship of all available forces, both nuclear (strategic, theater, and tactical) and conventional, taking into account the weakness of the latter. This applies to planning as well as to the structure.

- In case of an attack, to obtain a rapid and full indication at the frontiers of the location, type, and extent of the attack; to achieve an initial success on the battlefield by halting the aggressor as far east as possible and in such a manner that he cannot resume his attack without escalation, whether conventional or nuclear; to create conditions that will preserve for NATO the possibility of escalating to a general nuclear response, including allowing time for the decision-making process.

IV. REQUIREMENTS FOR NATO

If we assume that this basic mission is correct and corresponds to political aims, then I consider it to be appropriate and the definitive minimum the West, and particularly my country, can account for not only today but also tomorrow—that is, after the final conclusion of the SALT talks, after a security treaty at the European Security Conference, and after a mutual force reduction, whatever form this may take. I admit that these developments, as well as future weapons developments, can lead to alterations of the defense posture in quality and quantity, but they must not lead to an alteration of this basic mission. This is also valid if nothing like this should happen. A change of this mission would only be conceivable if the Soviet Union became the sixteenth partner in NATO!

What about the practical possibility of carrying out this basic mission? One has certainly heard many doubts as to the fulfillment of the present official NATO mission. But even this basic mission, which is a minimal mission, is by no means as assured as many people assume and even declare. What can be done to improve the situation? What must *not* happen if we are to avoid the successful accomplishment becoming even more questionable?

Much could be said on this subject. The title of this colloquium is "American-Allied Relations in Transition." It is not my task to deal with this specifically, but I should like to state now, before I make definite suggestions, that in my opinion a new basis for sharing the burden between the United States and its European partners is not only a justified American claim but a necessity. Western Europe must surely realize that and act accordingly. However, sharing the burden does not mean a reduction in the American presence in Europe.

Four more points that seem particularly important to me are the following:

1. Many people think that it would be possible to remedy the present unsatisfactory state of affairs by inventing a new strategy. Apart from the fact that a new strategy cannot be invented so easily and the old changed for a new just like changing a shirt, I can only say that this is a fallacy. For the defender in the nuclear age there are only two military strategies: massive retaliation and flexible response, which should rather be called the strategy of flexibility. As far as I am familiar with the various theories regarding so-called new strategies, they are all in fact only modified forms of the flexible response, with fancy new names. However, what must be done is to look for a modified, and more effective, form of flexible response, one that is better adapted to present conditions and advanced technology.

2. On the other hand, what must *not* be changed is the existence of all the links of the chain of deterrence, and their state of being firmly interlocked. Perhaps changes concerning how to act could be made. However, in the West there is, for instance, talk of a nuclear-free zone in Europe, or of a "no-first-use" agreement, or of exclusion of the FBS. In different ways, each of these measures would disturb or destroy the correlation of the allied forces and would disrupt the relationship between nuclear and conventional defense. But primarily it would render Western Europe and particularly Germany almost helpless against Soviet conventional superiority, exposing them to pressure or political coercion in peace and the full brunt of the attack in war. In any case, we should consider very carefully and very critically whether the inevitable disadvantages for the defense posture that would be brought about by such measures could be even approximately compensated for by any political results that might thereby be achieved. Those affected—that is, the Central European NATO partners—should have the last word in this respect. One of the reasons for these above-mentioned and similar ideas, which their advocates like to stress, is that in this way it would be possible to achieve what they consider to be the necessary measure of avoiding provocation of the Soviet Union. Perhaps my way of thinking is too simple, but that I cannot understand, quite apart from the fact that I am not aware of any study of what

provocation against the West the Soviets are to remove. Either the Kremlin is determined *not* to attack, in which case it will not let itself be provoked into doing so, or it is determined to attack, in which case there is nothing that could provoke it. General Lemnitzer used to say, "You can't provoke the Soviets, even if you wish to," but it is fashionable to regard soldiers as *terribles simplificateurs.*

Somewhat different, of course, is the question of whether the tactical nuclear weapons that the United States has in Western Europe are suitable as bargaining counters. Given the condition that tactical nuclear weapons as such must not disappear as a link in the chain, changes that would also have political value may perhaps be possible. One of these, for example, is the replacement of nuclear-armed aircraft by highly mobile rockets whose range would not extend as far as Russia. Incidentally, that would also have other advantages. Another question to be examined would be a change in the present mix, in the direction of having fewer weapons with a greater yield and more with a very small yield. Also in this category is the transfer of certain targets, which up to now have been nuclear targets, to new, long-range, and very accurate conventional weapons. This applies to all targets in which a pinpoint and not an area effect is important—for example, large bridges. Such measures could facilitate a definition of which nuclear weapons are tactical and which strategic, which is still a disputed question between the United States and the Soviet Union.

However, these are all problems that are by no means ripe for negotiation and on which thorough consultation and clarification among the allies are necessary. In any case, there must be an adequate and effective arsenal of weapons for interdiction in the area between the eastern frontier of Germany and the western frontier of the Soviet Union, and this arsenal must not lack tactical nuclear weapons in adequate numbers and in the correct mix (so as to make a flexible response possible). Otherwise, what we call the *fliegenden Aufmarsch*, perhaps to be translated as the "deployment from the march"—that is, the bringing-up of reinforcements from base right into the battlefield, simultaneously with the attack itself, and the continual strengthening of an attack and its support from the hinterland—cannot be prevented.

3. In the conventional field the time required for bringing over the forces which are provided for in the plans for reinforcement in

Europe, but which are not dual-based, must be drastically reduced. At the moment it is much too long. The question is not so much one of mere transportation time as of the action necessary before the transportation begins and after arrival in Europe. I could enumerate a whole series of possible measures for improvement, but of course they must be wanted and they cost money.

In addition, and this remark is addressed to the West European countries, many reserve formations of a new "ready-to-fight" type must be set up, formations which can be mobilized in a few days—if possible not more than three—and whose armament and training must enable them to fight alongside regular formations, and, it should not be forgotten, to fight against Soviet troops. The creation of such reserve formations is very important; it requires the loosening of certain rigid patterns of thinking and above all a change in present systems regarding reserves and mobilization.

4. Finally, there is an urgent need to introduce in the conventional field a sufficient number of technologically advanced weapons such as precision guided weapons systems and area-covering antitank weapons. But saying this I must caution against the idea that we have with these new weapons the ultimate conventional panacea. Problems of command and control, tactics, doctrine, and logistics will set up in practice probably more efficiency limitations than we can perceive today. The inherent hope for saving men may be met only to a disappointingly small extent.

European-American Cooperation

André Beaufre

I. DEFINITION OF THE PROBLEM

This study is the product of purely personal reflection. It does not represent official opinion within the French government, for that is probably divided. French policy is in flux and, in the postelectoral period, subject to debate, to change, and to continuing uncertainty.

Cooperation between Europe and the United States is a vast and complex problem which is undergoing continuous change: in the areas of strategy and economic and monetary relations as well as in its impact on the diplomatic relations between Western Europe, the Soviet Union, and the Warsaw Pact powers. These areas are complementary and interdependent.

Centering specifically on the problems of security, this study is constrained by arbitrary limits. The conclusions drawn should be evaluated first in terms of the overall relations of Europe, the United States, and the Soviet Union, and again in light of the situation in Asia and the major problems posed by Vietnam, China, and Japan.

This study first will address certain aspects of European-American relations as they have actually operated within NATO, a subject which is not well understood in the United States. It will attempt to show the consequences of the American policy of direct agreements with the Soviet Union, and notably of SALT I. Then, setting political considerations aside, it will develop the outline of the new strategy that will be needed to assure Western Europe's military security. That new strategy implies a preferred organization and a new mode of European-American cooperation.

We shall use this theoretical structure, this "new strategy for European security," as a device for approaching the current and pending East-West negotiations and the current U.S.-European economic dialogue, in order to derive therefrom a set of feasible goals and to see how we might best work together to attain them.

II. CURRENT U.S.-EUROPEAN RELATIONS

Contemporary U.S.-European relations are determined by a number of factors:

- the process of implementation of the Nixon Doctrine;
- the prospects of Europe's ongoing evolution;
- the impact of Soviet pressure on Europe driven, in turn, by tensions originating in Asia.

The United States emerged from World War II as the winner who had suffered the least, and befuddled by its unexpected success. Strewing its forces throughout the globe, it found its economic strength eaten away by inflation. The Vietnam War and the dollar crisis imposed the necessity of a more rational policy. The Nixon Doctrine undertook to find a middle way between world-wide involvement and isolationist retreat. It sought new modes of cooperation with former allies in order to limit the degree of engagement in the world's problems while simultaneously safeguarding America's essential interests. At the same time a greater effort was made to restrain inflation, restore economic strength, and improve the American domestic situation.

During this same period, the Soviet Union has overcome the terrible destruction of revolution and invasion and is today at the

pinnacle of its military power. It is probably at least equal to the
United States in this area, as a result of consistent, steady effort.
This considerable success is partly offset by serious economic problems, as well as by the potential threat inherent in a collaboration
between China and Japan—a combination which would accelerate
the technical, economic, and military development of Communist
China. This is the source of the Soviet Union's desire to stabilize its
position in the West, in order to "stay ahead" of developments in
the East. If possible, it will extend its influence in Europe as the
United States withdraws; as a minimum effort it will maintain the
present division. Thus we have an orchestration of negotiating
initiatives and maneuvers aimed at exploiting internal divisions
within the European nations.

Western Europe recovered spectacularly from the devastation of
war, initially in part due to American aid and then through the vital
medium of the Common Market. It is now embarked on the
difficult task of elaborating the basis for a common policy. If it is
to succeed, this will eventually entail a set of strategic arrangements
which will replace the American military protectorate. That system,
crystallized in NATO today, is destined to disappear, or at least to
be gradually weakened. *For now, Western Europe is militarily weak
and politically disunited.*

Caught between the Soviet and American superpowers, Western
Europe can develop in three or four ways:

- It can remain disunited and in the American orbit, but only by
  virtue of a military and political commitment that is increasingly unpopular in the United States itself.

- It can remain disunited and break up further into Soviet and
  American spheres of influence. (In this case, the American
  "bridgeheads" [Spain? Britain? France?] will become increasingly difficult to maintain.)

- It can remain disunited and slide totally into the Soviet orbit,
  doubtless under a variety of pretexts and expedients.

- It can pull itself together in some way to create an entity
  balanced between the United States and the Soviet Union,
  probably closely tied to both.

The first three alternatives—especially the second—can be readily
achieved and they would be catastrophic both for the United States

and for Western Europe. But we must recognize that these are the most likely alternatives before we can achieve the joint effort that will be needed to stave them off. The fourth alternative is clearly the most desirable. It presupposes, however, the working out of a host of difficult problems. It also depends on assistance by the United States and acceptance by the Soviet Union. The incentive from the Soviets' point of view must be their preference for this as an alternative to the current American hegemony in Europe, and as an acceptable substitute for Soviet domination. Every effort must be bent toward the realization of this fourth possibility: of an independently powerful Europe, linked to the United States and the Soviet Union within a larger system of security. The economic problems of Euro-American competition must be relegated to a secondary level of concern, *because the politico-military stakes in Europe heavily outweigh any economic considerations. This ultimate goal must be understood and supported on both the American and the European side.*

In seeking greater unity, Europe will have to overcome the lack of confidence which has been part of the postwar heritage, as well as the dislocations of excessively rapid economic growth. Europe's present prosperity harbors the germs of disunity and disorder. Its future could be magnificent, but it could just as easily be thrown away. It must pull itself together, realize its latent strength, overcome narrow nationalism (including that of the United States), and suppress the extremes of competing doctrines. We cannot afford to fail in this crucial enterprise, and we shall need favorable circumstances, American understanding, and a great deal of enlightened good will.

It is in the light of this primary goal that we proceed to analyze the experience of the past: first the development of NATO and then the more recent changes and their strategic consequences.

III. THE UNITED STATES AND NATO'S EUROPEAN STRATEGY

When the Atlantic Alliance was signed, Europe appeared to be menaced by an immediate threat of Soviet expansion. Europe's military capabilities were almost nonexistent, its productive capacity in ruins. According to Western European Union (WEU) calculations, it could do very little for itself. Its salvation lay in American protection, and in America's embryonic nuclear capability.

The U.S. Government was quite ready to make commitments in Western Europe at the end of the war, for it well understood its vital importance. But it still had to overcome diehard isolationists in the House and Senate. For that reason, the treaty couched the American side of the commitment in very vague terms, stating a commitment in principle but, from the legal point of view, nothing more: "An armed attack . . . will be considered as an attack on all the parties." And, further on: "If such an attack occurs, each of them . . . will assist . . . by taking as soon as possible whatever action it judges necessary, to include the use of armed force."

To these legal precautions must be added the restrictions of the McMahon Act with respect to the security of atomic energy information. The Alliance possessed only conventional forces, and only those which each state (including the United States) "judged necessary" to provide. *Nuclear matters lay entirely outside the Alliance* and were exclusively subject to American control. But today nuclear capabilities, which were in their infancy in 1950, have become the backbone of allied strategy.

Confronted by this situation, the Europeans, with France in the lead, went out of their way to involve the Americans as deeply as possible in the organization of their command. In order that the Americans should be committed in practice even if they were not in law, they were given the lion's share in the commands and major headquarters. They were given every facility for stationing their forces in Europe, because it was on them that security actually depended. It was thus the wish of the Europeans that NATO should become a virtual American military protectorate.

This protectorate received further justification as NATO strategy, which had focused briefly on conventional defense, came to depend on the *indirect security* afforded by the threat of *nuclear retaliation* by the newly created Strategic Air Command (SAC). Local defense in Europe thereafter became nothing more than a "tripwire."

First Great Britain, then France acquired atomic weapons, and these capabilities too were outside NATO. General de Gaulle, when he came to power in 1958, felt it necessary to supplement the NATO agreement, which was purely conventional and therefore secondary, by a *nuclear treaty* among the three nuclear powers. These alone belonged to the "standing group" which theoretically—very theoretically—was supposed to be the strategic "brain" of the Alliance.

This proposal was unwelcome in the United States, whose policy
at the time entailed closer ties with the smaller countries of Europe
and with Great Britain, which desired to retain the "special relationship" developed during World War II. Therefore things stayed as
they were, and the American military protectorate remained total.

Thus it was that, with the advent of the Kennedy Administration
in 1961, American strategy could be completely changed without
the slightest consultation with the allies. The result for Europe was
the doctrine of "flexible response," which the allies were obliged to
endorse despite French objections. For its part France had supported the decisions of the Cuban missile crisis, even while noting
that they were entirely unilateral.

In spite of French reservations, based on the vagueness of the
American treaty commitment, it is well to recognize that the
strategic situation at the beginning of the sixties still justified an
American military protectorate. European security depended completely on the enormous superiority of America's strategic forces.
The expedients devised by the McNamara team in its anxiety over
the escalatory potential of tactical atomic weapons were of no real
consequence, because they ignored the great stability achieved at
the strategic level. The appeal to the Europeans to increase their
conventional capabilities went unanswered, because each listener
knew that it could make no difference.

Moreover, the Soviet threat receded due to both the military
outcome of the Cuban confrontation and expectations of an immi-
nent détente between the Soviet Union and the United States. It
was in this environment that France disengaged from NATO, while
remaining a part of the Atlantic Alliance. France did not want the
United States to be the only country free to "make a deal" with the
Soviet Union. The *defense* of Western Europe would, in such a case,
have become an issue overcome by events.

NATO strategy, the cumulative result of successive American
strategies, unquestionably lacked coherence. "Flexible response"
imposed an initial phase of conventional defense which compromised the "forward strategy" demanded by the Germans who
sought the deployment and early use of tactical nuclear weapons.
Soviet offensive planning could anticipate overrunning the ground
forces without difficulty and destroying the tactical air forces
concentrated on their advanced bases. The eventual initiation of
nuclear fires would come too late, if at all. The allies attempted to

debate this question of nuclear release, but the "Nuclear Planning Group" created for the purpose never achieved an effective, or clear, assignment of nuclear authority. However, this appeared to be of no great consequence—except to those who might be affected—*because European security still rested on American strategic deterrence.*

Once again, the direct military defense of Europe played the role of a political tranquilizer.

IV. SUBSEQUENT EVENTS AND THEIR CONSEQUENCES

The McNamara strategy did not last. Three factors dictated a rapid evolution.

First, the Soviet intervention in Czechoslovakia in 1968 demonstrated, over and above the political instability of Central Europe, the presence in the Soviet leadership of hardliners who did not recoil from the use of force. Hopes raised by "détente" were seriously tarnished. Moreover, the smoothness of the operation attested to the high state of readiness of the forces used.

During the same period all available intelligence confirmed the breadth of Soviet military programs. These ranged from the strategic area, where a growing ICBM force was accompanied by the deployment of the ABM, to the oceans, where conventional and nuclear submarines, surface combatants, and the merchant marine achieved an astonishing development. In both areas the Soviet Union was overtaking the United States.

Thus a new stage of the arms race was about to open, to the discomfort of a United States already committed to heavy expenditures by the war in Vietnam. The SALT negotiations were opened in order to curb the arms race and to explore the possibilities for real agreement with the Soviet Union. These negotiations led, after two years, to the initial agreement, SALT I.

The real agreement throws a clear light on the present strategic situation.

- The 200-ABM limit will operate to sustain a very high threat of destruction by strategic forces.
- Recognition of "parity"—despite numerical inequality—in ICBMs and SLBMs at the present level of technology assures a level of mutual destruction out of all proportion to conceivable political objectives. The obvious consequence of this

situation is that *strategic forces neutralize each other.* Their
only conceivable use will be in reaction to a direct attack on
their home territory by the adversary's missiles.

- In the context of SALT I, one can readily anticipate an
  acceleration of the technological race, bringing about the multiplication of MIRVs and probably of antisatellite weapons
  and of means to attack and defend missile-launching submarines.

For Europe it becomes obvious that the security derived from
the "extended deterrence" of American strategic forces tends to
disappear. At the least a margin of uncertainty begins to develop.
The "extended deterrence" which had been the foundation of
European strategy no longer constitutes an effective guarantee.
A new strategy thus becomes indispensable for Europe.

V. CONSEQUENCES FOR EUROPEAN STRATEGY

The strategic implications for Europe are simple and clear-cut:
Since protection by the American strategic deterrent has become, at
best, uncertain, *it is indispensable that European security be assured
by weapons stationed in Europe* and, sooner or later, essentially by
European weapons. No purely political arrangements can take the
place of a system of security which can restore to Europe a regional
balance with the present Soviet military power, unless it be a very
substantial reduction in Soviet strength, which is scarcely likely.

Under these conditions, Europe must:

- create a regional strategic deterrent capable of neutralizing the
  comparable Soviet systems (MRBMs and medium-range bombers),
- create a tactical deterrent sufficient to discourage conventional
  attack or any tactical nuclear strike.

Regional strategic deterrence could be absolutely assured by a
European nuclear force. However, there will be no such thing as a
sovereign European authority for many years, and in the interim
existing systems will have to be used: French and British strategic
nuclear forces, rounded out if possible, or eventually supplemented,
by American nuclear forces of the same type stationed in Europe.

The credibility—and hence the deterrent value—of such a force in
defense of Europe would be greater than that of weapons located in

the United States, contrary to the frequent contention that the opposite would be the case. France and Great Britain could not bring themselves to abandon Germany or Italy, to whom they are firmly committed, not to mention Denmark and Turkey, which guard vital straits.

On the other hand, it would be false to conclude that such a strategic force, no matter how large, could by itself protect Europe from invasion, especially from small-scale attack. The density of population alone *would prohibit the use of forces that could set off a devastating reaction.* These forces can be used only to "neutralize" comparable Soviet forces.

That is why there must also be a tactical deterrent.

Tactical deterrence has often been conceived of as resulting from the heavy reinforcement of the defense by conventional forces. This expectation rests on two serious misconceptions of the capabilities actually involved.

The first error resides in believing that today's conventional forces can be substantially reinforced. Such a belief ignores the high and rising costs of modern armament (tanks, aircraft, air defense, communications, missiles, etc.). A modern aircraft is worth its weight in gold, literally. It is no longer possible to maintain large numbers, because of rapid obsolescence. Modern conventional forces, even with substantial financial sacrifice (which will bring serious economic consequences, as in the Soviet Union), must be *extremely limited in size.*

Compared to the theater of operations, which must be defended in depth, these limited forces simply cannot achieve useful concentrations. It becomes necessary either to disperse forces along extensive fronts and thereby deprive them of any tactical effectiveness, or to concentrate them at a few locations separated by intervals which the enemy can rapidly penetrate with mechanized and airborne forces. Moreover, the defense is constrained to *react to* offensive initiatives which will be difficult to anticipate. In order to parry effectively the enemy's preplanned thrusts, the defense would have to have an "agility" far superior to that of the attacker (which is not the case for NATO forces facing the Warsaw Pact). Altogether, in contemporary conditions, the defense has lost the preeminence it has enjoyed for a century. Thus, where the accepted ratio has been a 3:1 advantage for the offense, today's conventional defense requires just the opposite, a 3:1 ratio in its favor. As the

Israelis have shown, today's battles can be won or lost in a day, just as in the time of Napoleon. Because of this, today's defensive systems are extremely fragile and unstable.

As a result, the only solution viable now is *to sharply augment the firepower of the defense*, by providing for the early employment of tactical nuclear weapons. Two results follow:

- The existence of this firepower prevents the offensive from concentrating. It must either lose strength by dispersing its forces or run an unacceptable risk if the nuclear strike reaction time is sufficiently short.

- The prospect of a two-sided exchange of nuclear fires—unprecedented in warfare—subjects the calculations of the enemy to total uncertainty as to the outcome of the attack.

Altogether the threat of prompt tactical nuclear strikes constitutes a *highly effective deterrent* to conventional attack, whether or not it is supported by nuclear means of its own. This form of deterrence becomes virtually absolute as soon as its existence is perceived by the enemy. It carries with it none of the risks with which tactical nuclear weapons are usually reproached:

- It does not invite destruction either of the battlefield or of population *because it will not have to be used* (same reasoning as for strategic deterrence).

- The ground that would have to be given up to facilitate the employment of nuclear fires will never be abandoned to the enemy because, having been deterred, *he will not attack.*

On the other hand, conventional defense invites attack and affords the aggressor the opportunity to mingle with defending forces so as to make nuclear strikes impossible, or at the very least so delayed that there would be further risk of

- the destruction of people and property,

- surrender pure and simple in the event of a decision to forgo the use of nuclear weapons.

One must conclude, despite all prejudices to the contrary, *that the prompt employment of tactical nuclear weapons is the only answer to the defensive problem*, and the one with the least risk.

In the longer range, a more stable defense can be realized with a significant gain in forces by resorting to the idea of a territorial militia, equipped at limited cost and supported by regular forces with the latest equipment and high mobility. The great power of such a system would rest on new weapons, antitank and antiair, as well as new air transport vehicles. The threshold for the introduction of tactical atomic weapons would probably, in this way, be raised. However, organizing these militias and achieving the psychological preparation of the populace will require considerable time and effort.

These implications for strategy represent the *only coherent military approach*. They conform to the capacities of a Western Europe that is richer, more populous, and more highly industrialized than the Soviet Union. They fit less well into the present state of European public opinion, still scarred by an inferiority complex arising out of World War II and kept in ignorance of strategic problems. Fifteen years of the American military protectorate have had their effect, as has the general disinclination to confront the problems of defense, reinforced by an often innocent propaganda that says war is no longer possible because no one wants it and because atomic weapons make it impossible. Public understanding of strategic problems differs greatly from country to country. Thus achievement of the full solution will be difficult and probably slow, if it ever takes place.

During the interval, political changes may occur; one might hope they would. But until they do, the presence and the assistance of the United States will be indispensable to European security as long as Europe lacks independent strength.

VI. IMPLICATIONS FOR THE ORGANIZATION
   OF COOPERATION

Even though American and European interests are linked together at the strategic level, they are, at least in large measure, geographically separable. *Therefore, there should be two separate components of the Alliance:* on the one side, the United States and Canada, and on the other Western Europe (which might eventually break down into regional groupings—Scandinavia, the Continent, the Balkans, and Asia Minor). This would have the effect of decoupling the United States from NATO and giving Europe over to a European command. U.S. forces in Europe would be associated with this command in the same way that French forces are now associated with NATO. This would lead to combined operations, particularly in the Atlantic, of both American and European forces.

This solution represents a long- or medium-term goal.

For the short term, we have NATO with the French association. This organization must adjust its strategy to the new situation.

The first essential is to reduce to the minimum or to eliminate completely the conventional defense phase of "flexible response," and to provide for early employment of American tactical atomic weapons. This can provide an excellent tactical deterrent without major force changes.

Europe also possesses the French and British strategic nuclear forces which already provide a tangible level of deterrence. Their ultimate coordination, along with that of the American "forward-based systems" (FBS) in Europe, furnishes a starting point, consisting for the moment of independent national forces, but which could be linked in emergencies by the coordinating capabilities of *a permanent tripartite organ.*

Finally, the European Economic Community, central framework of a future political community, will be called on to organize a European Defense Community. This could have been accomplished earlier by developing within the Western European Union, for example, a European permanent commission, a combined civil and military body to develop concepts and strategies for future application to the security of Europe. These would include, for example, a "common market" in arms as the only feasible way to secure that standardization which is absolutely vital.

At some future stage this commission would transform itself into an international supreme command, responsible for coordinating the actions of national forces, in preparation for relieving SHAPE of its responsibilities.

Such an organization of European-American relations would have further consequences.

A revision of defensive strategy would take place at the Atlantic Alliance level (and not at NATO), as the result of a new series of strategic studies in which, I would hope, France would take part. Decisions there would be reached jointly, to include the determination of overall policy for the use of nuclear weapons. These decisions would then be approved by the Council of Ministers of the Atlantic Alliance.

Coordination of European and American strategic forces would be organized on the basis of bilateral, then trilateral, agreements worked out by a three-sided body similar to that espoused by General de Gaulle. Four contingencies would have to be addressed: unilateral action by each of the national forces, combined Franco-British operations, U.S.-British operations, and coordinated U.S.-Franco-British operations. The requisite channels of communication would have to be established.

The organization for European security would be entirely independent of the United States, which would contribute only a liaison function. Strategy developed would be coordinated with the Americans through the Council of Ministers of the Atlantic Alliance, perhaps making use of a permanent staff along the lines of the former "standing group."

VII. IMPLICATIONS FOR THE CONDUCT OF NEGOTIATIONS WITH THE SOVIET UNION

The ideas presented above represent an optimum strategic concept which is probably, at least in part, beyond the current limits of the politically possible. They can nonetheless serve to give direction to the negotiations in progress, or those about to open, as a means of avoiding counterproductive expedients and of identifying promising policy options. Three things have to be accomplished more or less simultaneously:

- intra-European consultation leading to a common line of action for the future development and security of Europe;

- European-American consultations to coordinate policies vis-à-vis the East, cooperate in security, and avoid economic conflict;

- negotiations with the East in order to strengthen the détente and bring about improved East-West cooperation as well as a more stable strategic equilibrium, both in Europe and world-wide.

This is asking a great deal.

In accomplishing this, certain pitfalls are to be avoided.

The first is that of giving the Soviet Union the idea that Western Europe is hostile to it and represents a potential threat. This pitfall can be avoided only by subscribing to a set of treaties that reinforce the relaxation achieved: nonaggression, nonemployment of force, noninterference in the internal affairs of others, and collective security pacts among the European states, linking the Soviet Union, the United States, and a future Western Europe. There should be set up in Europe (in Vienna, for example) a permanent institution responsible for maintaining measures to anticipate and control crises and for developing useful means of arms control. This list, although it may seem too much, constitutes the very least we should propose on our own initiative.

The second danger is that the Soviet Union might succeed in neutralizing West Germany by offering it a special military ("nuclear-free") status and dangling before it prospects of reunification. This would be the end of Western Europe's hopes, for it would eventually shift the Iron Curtain to the banks of the Rhine. This risk can be avoided only by refusing any form of special treatment to Germany and by advancing, from the start, the full series of agreements outlined in the previous paragraph. Intra-European agreements should be expedited at the same time.

The third pitfall is that of excluding France, condemning it to strategic isolation by insisting on integrated military solutions either at the Atlantic or at the European level. France is indispensable to any European security organization, but it will not participate in any discussions which do not guarantee from the start its full freedom of action.

More serious than all of these problems is the risk of pushing Western Europe, in whole or in part, into the Soviet orbit. This could be the end result of a combination of excessive economic pressure on the Common Market and against a European monetary union (as is being produced by current U.S. policy) and the effective elimination of American strategic deterrence for Europe. The policy of direct negotiation between the United States and the Soviet Union, and the conduct of the Vietnam War, could not help but reinforce these tendencies. In reality, the United States has a vital interest in Western Europe's remaining independent and becoming stronger. The United States must, therefore, help Western Europe and must know how to get along with it.

These various considerations permit the development of an order of priority.

The first priority is to convince the Europeans that the United States is willing to help them become independent, unified, and even economically competitive, as well as to undertake genuine cooperation free of any hint of "domination." This is why the word "cooperation" has been chosen (in French) to render the word "partnership," to emphasize that an entirely new relationship must be established. This does not require a new multilateral treaty—which already exists in the Atlantic Alliance—but it does require a new relationship, based on mutual consultation seeking compromise in advance of any decision of international significance.

The second priority is the elaboration of a common strategy that will permit at the same time:

- progress toward European unity, including the economic area,
- the strengthening of European security by revision of NATO's defensive strategy,
- détente with the East by virtue of the negotiation of agreements that will establish a climate of confidence between Eastern and Western Europe.

The third priority is the deploying and strengthening of indigenous strategic and tactical nuclear capabilities in Europe and their overall coordination with American forces.

Fourth priority belongs to the effort, which should begin here and now, to create a European organization that will conceive and ultimately carry out a unified West European strategy, in order to guarantee the eventual supersession of SHAPE. This European initiative should be supported by the United States.

VIII. CONCLUSIONS

This study provides an objective analysis and a systematic approach, leading (perhaps with excessive detail) to the definition of an "optimum scenario." Achieving these goals in reality presumes a great number of favorable developments.

This strategy depends first on agreement among the European nations, and we are now far from such agreement. This is why it is so important to create a center for strategic planning, even if it should be private. Second, this strategy depends on Soviet acquiescence in a European structure, as a "lesser evil." *This is the reason why the political negotiations with the East are so important.*

None of this will be achieved without better diplomatic, strategic, and economic coordination with the United States. There is now commencing an economic and monetary conflict that runs directly counter to the goals of the Nixon Doctrine. The Americans cannot afford to overlook this inadvertent support to the Soviet policy of fragmenting Europe.

The real prize is Europe—more highly populated, richer, more industrialized than the Soviet Union and whose loss would make the Soviet Union the greatest power in the world. In order to win, the United States and Western Europe will have to decide to work together for their ultimate benefits, subordinating or suppressing the less important or self-defeating temptations that will arise along the way.

Appendix A

Participants

Dr. Achille Albonetti
Director for International Affairs and Economic Studies of the Italian National Committee for Nuclear Energy
Rome, Italy

Dr. Frank R. Barnett
President
National Strategy Information Center
New York, New York

General André Beaufre (Retired)
Director
Institut Francais d'Etudes Strategiques
Paris, France

General Charles H. Bonesteel III, USA (Retired)
Senior Advisory Consultant
Strategic Studies Center
Stanford Research Institute
Arlington, Virginia

Dr. Alvin J. Cottrell
Director of Research

Center for Strategic and International Studies
Georgetown University
Washington, D. C.

Dr. N. R. Danielian
President
International Economic Policy Association
Washington, D. C.

Mr. Pieter Dankert
Member of Parliament
Zaandam, The Netherlands

Mr. M. Mark Earle, Jr.
Assistant Director and Senior Economist
Strategic Studies Center
Stanford Research Institute
Arlington, Virginia

Professor John Erickson
University of Edinburgh
Scotland, U. K.

General Duilio Sergio Fanali (Retired)

241

Honorary President of the Institute for Defense and Strategic Studies
Rome, Italy

Mr. Richard B. Foster
Director
Strategic Studies Center
Stanford Research Institute
Arlington, Virginia

Colonel Michel Garder (Retired)
Member, Institut Francais d'Etudes Strategiques
Paris, France

Dr. Curt Gasteyger
Deputy Director-General
Institut Atlantique
Paris, France

Mr. Marc E. Geneste
Member, Institut Francais d'Etudes Strategiques
Poitiers, France

Dr. Gunther Gillessen
Foreign Editor
Frankfurter Allgemeine Zeitung
Frankfurt, Federal Republic of Germany

Mr. Walter F. Hahn
Associate Director for Research
Foreign Policy Research Institute
Philadelphia, Pennsylvania

Mr. Jerome L. Heldring
Director
Nederlandsch Genootschap Voor Internationale Zaken
The Hague, The Netherlands

Dr. Johan J. Holst
Director of Research

Norwegian Institute of International Affairs
Oslo, Norway

Mr. Charles Douglas-Home
Features Editor
The Times
London, England

Dr. Wynfred Joshua
Assistant Director and Senior Political Scientist
Strategic Studies Center
Stanford Research Institute
Arlington, Virginia

Dr. Werner Kaltefleiter
Director
Social Science Research Institute
Konrad Adenauer Foundation
Bonn, Federal Republic of Germany

General J. A. Graf Kielmansegg (Retired)
Chairman of the Council of the Research Institute for Defense and International Affairs
Munich, Federal Republic of Germany

Dr. William R. Kintner
Director
Foreign Policy Research Institute
Philadelphia, Pennsylvania

Professor Leopold Labedz
Editor
Survey
London, England

Mr. Walter Laqueur
Director

Institute of Contemporary History and Wiener Library
London, England

General Ulrich de Maiziere (Retired)
Former Chief of Staff of the German Armed Forces
Bonn, Federal Republic of Germany

General Baron Antoine del Marmol (Retired)
Vice President of the Belgian Atlantic Association
Brussels, Belgium

Mr. Roger Massip
Foreign Affairs Editor
Le Figaro
Paris, France

Air Vice-Marshal S.W.B. Menaul (Retired)
Director-General
Royal United Services Institute for Defence Studies
London, England

Mr. Jean-Paul Pigasse
Entreprise
Paris, France

Dr. Richard Pipes
Director

The Russian Research Center
Harvard University
Cambridge, Massachusetts

Mr. Sheldon T. Rabin
Conference Co-ordinator and Research Analyst
Strategic Studies Center
Stanford Research Institute
Arlington, Virginia

Professor Klaus Ritter
Director
Stiftung Wissenschaft und Politik
Ebenhausen/ISAR
Federal Republic of Germany

Dr. Lothar Ruehl
Deputy Chief Editor
Die Welt
Hamburg, Federal Republic of Germany

General Berton E. Spivy, Jr., USA (Retired)
Senior Advisory Consultant
Strategic Studies Center
Stanford Research Institute
Arlington, Virginia

Mr. Paul W. Thompson
Chappaqua, New York

Observers

Dr. Horst Blomeyer-Bartenstein
Minister
Embassy of the Federal Republic of Germany
Paris, France

Brigadier General Jurgen Brandt
Deputy Assistant Chief of Staff
Politico-Military Affairs and Operations
Ministry of Defense
Bonn, Federal Republic of Germany

Mr. Donald R. Cotter
Central Intelligence Agency
Washington, D. C.

Ambassador Roberto Ducci
Director-General for Political Affairs
Ministry of Foreign Affairs
Rome, Italy

Colonel Olivier de Gabory
Office of the Chief of Staff of the
  Armies
Ministry of Defense
Paris, France

Major General Edward B. Giller,
  USAF (Retired)
Assistant General Manager for
  National Security
U.S. Atomic Energy Commission
Washington, D. C.

Dr. S. J. Lukasik
Director
Advanced Research Projects Agency
Department of Defense
Arlington, Virginia

Mr. Pierre Morel
Ministry of Foreign Affairs
Paris, France

Mr. John H. Morse
Deputy Assistant Secretary of De-
  fense for European and NATO
  Affairs
International Security Affairs
Department of Defense
Washington, D. C.

Mr. James G. Poor
Director
Division of International Security
  Affairs
U.S. Atomic Energy Commission
Washington, D. C.

Colonel Juan M. Sancho Sopranis
Spanish Institute for Strategic
  Studies
Madrid, Spain

Mr. David Walder, M.P.
House of Commons
London, England

Dr. N. F. Wikner
Department of Defense
Washington, D. C.

Mr. John Wilkinson, M.P.
House of Commons
London, England

Appendix B

1. Western European research institutes should use the momentum generated by this conference and take the initiative in defense research collaboration.

2. The European research institutes should engage in research aimed at improving the present strategy and doctrine and at defining the role and the relationship of the strategic nuclear forces, the tactical nuclear forces and the conventional forces.

3. In order to keep the momentum of this conference going, the following steps are planned:

a. General Beaufre recommends the convening of an October 1973 meeting in France of the European research institutes to define areas of agreement and cooperation for European defense research. However, the projected October meeting should not preclude the convening of smaller meetings between individual institutes in the interim.

b. At the October meeting, these West European research institutes will explore the problems of the current East-West negotiations (SALT II, MBFR and CSCE).

4. West European research institutes should consult with each other in order to establish, as soon as possible, a European Defense Research Institute. The plans for the European Defense Research Institute should be discussed at the October meeting. General Beaufre requested that those who have studied the possibility of establishing such an institute to send him their suggestions at their earliest possible convenience.

5. To assist the European research institutes in addressing the problems discussed at the conference, the U.S. Government should make available, through appropriate channels, additional information regarding new developments in weapons technology, notably in the area of precision guided weapons systems.

Appendix C

THE ECONOMIC CONTROVERSY: A EUROPEAN VIEWPOINT

General André Beaufre

I am not an economist nor a financial expert, but I hope that you will allow me to tell you how many Europeans see the economic controversy with the United States. I have read with a great deal of attention the 1973 Economic Report of the President and Dr. Danielian's very interesting paper. These are my remarks based both on knowledge of the European situation and on common sense applied with the same candor as in strategy:

1. *Let us start from the Bretton Woods Agreement.* After World War II, the dollar replaced gold as the world currency. Because of its presumed stability, long term international contracts were concluded in dollars. In 1969, the International Monetary Fund created Special Drawing Rights (SDRs), which were denominated in dollars. This move was taken to increase global liquidity and to help nations in balance of payments deficits.

The requisite condition for the functioning of the post-war international monetary system was that the dollar remain stable. This stability, in turn, depended upon U.S. fiscal and monetary policies; the international currency was entirely dependent upon a national policy, that of the United States.

2. *Let us examine the changes of recent years.* Because of a number of American domestic policies, the Vietnam war and other American overseas commitments, the U.S. balance of payments has long been in deficit. Inflation in the United States became an international danger, because of the international role of the dollar. The U.S. balance of payments deficits were financed by passing off this inflation to America's trading partners. The result was the creation of some $80 billion held abroad, mostly in Europe. For years, the Europeans, and especially France with General de Gaulle, under-

lined the danger of this situation and the need for austerity measures. This was interpreted in the United States as an unfriendly attitude, when in fact it was only a common interest warning.

The Johnson Administration tried to resolve the monetary crisis of 1968, caused partly by feverish speculation in gold, by creating a two-tiered market for gold. Most Europeans felt that the opportunity should have been taken to introduce domestic austerity measures, but this advice was ignored. As a result, the dollar situation continued to deteriorate. A new policy was clearly necessary.

3. *Let us look at this new policy, as it was stated in the 1973 Economic Report of the President.* The guiding concept is entirely different from a policy of austerity and self-discipline. It relies completely on so-called liberal economic policy. This calls, among other things, for floating currencies. The dollar, the former world currency, would also float, and it was hoped that the resulting devaluation would help correct the payments deficits. This is a purely American policy, not a world policy.

The Economic Report also urges that trade imbalances be remedied by Special Drawing Rights—that is, by creating new dollars, as long as another world currency does not emerge. The Administration demands that international trade be liberalized and that regional barriers be lowered in an effort to increase world trade. American agricultural production, which is very cheap, should have free access to all foreign markets. Gold, of course, should have no role in that "wishful-thinking" economy.

4. *Let me tell you my own reaction to such a policy.*

First. As the dollar floats, it can no longer play its former international role. Since business needs a fixed yardstick for long-term contracts, it is necessary to create a new currency: a return to gold may be one solution, while another may be an artificial currency of a new definition which would be used for the Special Drawing Rights.

Second. Dr. Danielian said the economic benefits of the devaluation of the dollar may be nullified by the devaluation of other currencies. We may enter into an economic war of very grave consequences. Floating may be a gimmick but not a lasting solution.

Third. As I have already stated, Special Drawing Rights should be produced by a new world monetary organization, and not written in dollars.

Fourth. The liberalization of world trade is not a panacea, because in fact cheap labor and high efficiency give the advantage to Japanese, Formosan, and Hongkong production, and tomorrow possibly to Chinese production. Some kind of national controls remain necessary.

Fifth. U.S. agricultural production has an enormous market in those countries which are not self-sufficient: the USSR, China, and many countries of the Third World. The United States should certainly not attempt to preempt present agricultural activity in the self-sufficient countries, such as Western Europe. Dr. Danielian's presentation on that point forgets all the political, social, and even security factors which prevent the Europeans from abandoning their Common Agricultural Policy and relying instead upon cheaper U.S. products. Great Britain started to do so in the 19th century and as a result nearly collapsed during the Second World War. This is not a realistic option.

To sum up, I will dare say that the new American economic policy is based on many inconsistencies and even contradictions. Any free discussion on that subject cannot but underline these contradictions.

5. *Let us now enlarge the subject to the European-American economic relationship,* and there I will refer more directly to Dr. Danielian's excellent presentation of the American point of view. Three main points deserve mention: floating currencies, the American trade and balance of payments deficits, and the relative military expenses of the European countries and the United States.

Floating currencies. Dr. Danielian says that the Europeans have violated the GATT agreement. That may be true, but I will say that the devaluation and floating of the dollar have been flagrant and one-sided violations of the Bretton Woods agreement. Moreover, the consequences are very grave: *it is working against European unity,* because the European currencies are not of equal strength. By forcing the European currencies to float, EEC farm prices and the whole Common Agricultural Policy are jeopardized. In this situation, U.S. policy acts for the benefit of Soviet policy, which seeks to prevent European unity. The only answer to the floating currencies is to adopt a common European currency which would have fixed rates of exchange inside the EEC, and which would float for outside exchanges against the dollar.

U.S. trade and balance of payments deficits. Agricultural trade, which has received much publicity lately, is really of secondary importance. Dr. Danielian's figure is that the European Community's variable levy causes a decrease of $290 million in the American sales to Europe. The balance of payments deficit is $10 billion. Of the $10 billion only $1 billion and perhaps now $1.6 billion (because of devaluation) is the deficit of military expenses in Europe. The bulk of the deficit is due to merchandise trade—especially oil imports—tourism, and world commitments. This is the real cause of the deficits and not the Europeans' policy or the military commitments in Europe.

The U.S. military expenses in Europe. Most Americans have exaggerated notions of what these expenses really are. The American forces in Europe consist of five divisions and the corresponding air force, while the whole of the European forces in NATO is more than 60 divisions. According to the International Institute for Strategic Studies, the American military expenditure in Europe was $4.7 billion, while the European expenditure was $25.2 billion. Therefore, the Americans provide 1/10 of the forces and spend 1/6 of the European military expenditures. Is it a fair share? I do not know. But it is certainly not a very disproportionate share.

6. *Now that I have made my criticisms, I would like to conclude in a more constructive way.*

I entirely agree with Dr. Danielian on the necessity of determination and common sense. But it should not be a one-sided exercise.

It is true that America has some real economic headaches and that the prospect of an energy crisis calls for solutions worthy of statesmanship and not hard bargaining competition. We have to build up common policies towards the petrol sheikhs, the communist countries and the Third World. Such an effort is both feasible and necessary. However, the Americans must be mindful not to divide the Europeans at a time when Europe is weak and not strongly united; be careful not to try to open the European market to your agricultural goods when your role in that market is to export advanced technologies. Let us build together a world economic system with a world currency worthy of that role. Let us build together a security system in Europe less expensive and more efficient than the bulky NATO apparatus. If we do that then the American forces might be reduced to the figure of three divisions put forward by Dr. Danielian.

But first, let us agree together on a policy towards the East in Europe, a policy of detente and of safeguards, of military deterrence and economic cooperation. If we can, let us associate with Japan, but certain factors, such as the Sino-Soviet confrontation, may make cooperation here more difficult.

To sum up, *let us agree before we act*, contrary to what has been done up to now, and let us use common sense to understand both sides of the Atlantic and avoid selfish and self-defeating policies.

Index